S0-AIL-785

GOSHEN COLLEGE
LIBRARY

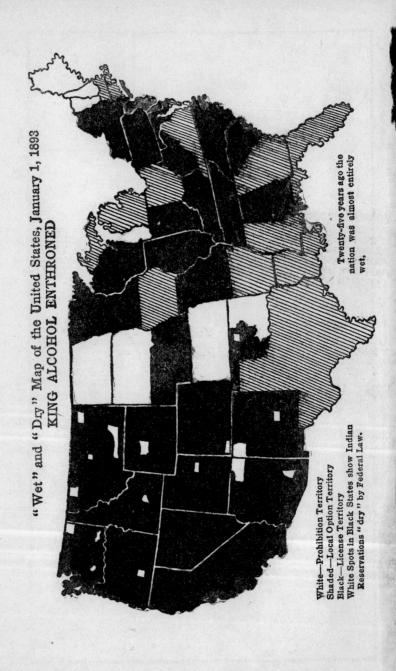

"Wet" and "Dry" Map of the United States, January 1, 1893
KING ALCOHOL ENTHRONED

Twenty-five years ago the nation was almost entirely wet,

White—Prohibition Territory
Shaded—Local Option Territory
Black—License Territory
White Spots in Black States show Indian Reservations "dry" by Federal Law.

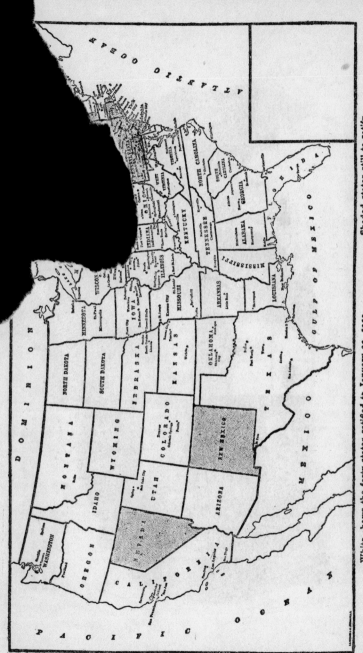

White shows the forty states ratified to January 22, 1919.   Shaded states still to ratify.

KING ALCOHOL
DETHRONED

BY

FERDINAND COWLE IGLEHART, D.D.,

Author " The Speaking Oak "

Lecturer on Sociology and Temperance,
Syracuse University.

THE AMERICAN ISSUE PUBLISHING COMPANY
WESTERVILLE, OHIO

HV
5089
I3

COPYRIGHT, 1917
BY THE CHRISTIAN HERALD

COPYRIGHT, 1919
BY FERDINAND COWLE IGLEHART

10315

PREFACE

THE dethronement of King Alcohol which is being accomplished in our time is perhaps the most important moral event in the history of mankind. Alcohol is the most ancient king in the world. An Arabian story tells of his presence as far back as the beginning of the race, as the conqueror of Satan who mastered our first parents. This is the story: Satan with the help of sin and death made a bridge from hell to earth. On his first trip across it he visited the Garden of Eden. Among other things he found growing a grape vine bearing luscious innocent fruit. He immediately began its cultivation to see if he could get a product from it that would hurt and destroy the race just started. He first poured the blood of a peacock down on the roots; when the leaves came out, he watered the vine with the blood of an ape, then he soaked the roots with the blood of a lion. He drank to his fill of the fruit of this innocent plant thus brutalized, and lay down among its leaves like a hog. The Arab imagination thus made King Alcohol the conqueror of Satan in the very garden where he himself was the master.

Moses only begins to write the Pentateuch when he thus mentions the mastery of the head of the new race by King Alcohol: "And Noah began to be a husbandman, and he planted a vineyard; and he drank of the wine and was drunken." As the ancient nations grew King Alcohol's empire extended over them, destroying some of them, notably Babylon.

In classical antiquity this demon king is named Bacchus, the god of wine. He was the unlawful son of Jupiter brought into the world by the anger of Juno in a fierce thunderstorm to incarnate every evil, and inflict every earthly suffering. Seated in his chariot drawn by panthers he drove from nation to nation promising it joy and prosperity but bringing to it misery and ruin.

When the Anglo-Saxon race became the dominant one of the earth, King Alcohol conquered it, loading ships that had Bibles and missionaries for the heathen with barrels of liquor and giving the most Christian and civilized nations of the world the distinction of being the most drunken. This present revolution that is shaking Bacchus from his throne is the revolt of the Anglo-Saxon conscience against his baleful rule, which was weakening and destroying the race. From its birth alcohol ruled our nation. Ten years ago there were only three dry States, now there are twenty-six, seven within the past twelve months, and two-thirds of the area and sixty per cent of the population is under Prohibition. The Rum King is dethroned in the United States.

This book records in detail the agencies employed in deposing this rum despot from his authority, including those of science, big business, politics, the ballot, the home, womanhood and the church.

Facts, facts, facts are killing the liquor traffic, and hence I have packed this book as full of them as I knew how. I have taken a few facts from the books but almost all of them from living men in our own land, and taken them first off from their lips or pens. I have not hesitated to go hundreds of miles to find a man who had a fact that I needed for record here. The facts revealed by these pages contradict things the liquor people say are facts and claim as such in their literature. For instance, they say that beer is liquid bread; the facts we have show conclusively that it and the other intoxicants are not liquid food but liquid poison to kill the body and mind.

Much space has been given to proving the fact that Prohibition prohibits. The last ditch into which the liquor forces have retired is the argument that Prohibition does not prohibit. Deserting the old argument of personal liberty and opposition to sumptuary laws, driven from the field of high license, they have made this last stand on the claim that prohibition is a failure. And the claim is made with such shrewdness that many of our best people are deceived by it. This book contains the positive testimony of the Governors and

United States Senators of a majority of the dry States that Prohibition does prohibit, and that that is the reason why no dry State is thinking for a moment of going back to license and why other States follow their example.   If time and space had been allowed other Governors and Senators of Prohibition States would have given their testimony.

We regret that there was only space enough to make a record of the fight on alcohol in the States made dry. The temperance workers in the near-dry States and wettest ones have been as able, consecrated and successful in proportion as the heroic ones in the Prohibition States.

This book is radical from start to finish.   In questions of policy there are two sides.   In a question of principle there is but one side, and that is the right side.   This we believe is a question of principle and that the right thing to do is to exterminate the saloon.   This book is radical but it does not contain one harsh word against the individual liquor dealer; it is only his business that is condemned.   If I had been born in the country and under the circumstances that surrounded him I would likely have shared his views and maybe have followed his business.   I have made clear that I consider the people who license the business as responsible as the dealers themselves for its miseries and crimes.

The book is a militant one.   Those who are in

the campaign, the preachers, editors of secular and religious papers, speakers, workers in the temperance and church organizations, in Young Men's Christian Associations, Sunday Schools and reform service of all kinds, and the millions of voters who have now entered into this war on alcohol, will find ammunition and inspiration for the conflict.

It is the intention that this book should emphasize the moral and spiritual instrumentalities in the dethronement of Alcohol, should regard religion as the dominant element in overthrowing this evil, recognizing God as a personal factor in leading the Church against this vice for its destruction, and thus become a real Gospel message. The Galilean peasant who rode into the city over the palm branches is the real King today. With truth, righteousness, love and life, he is not only dethroning but destroying King Alcohol.

This book goes out with the hope that it may reclaim some drunkard; draw away from danger some moderate drinker who can drink or leave it alone, as he pleases, who can quit any time, but never does; keep some young man or woman from the first glass that has all the rest of evil in it; may inspire the old temperance workers to renewed diligence; may give encouragement to the millions of voters in the churches to a double quick drive that shall overthrow the demon King, and wake up the cowardly and sleepy ones in and out of the Church who have let God and good people destroy the greatest evil of the centuries in their time and under their very eyes, and they have no part in the contest; and that some soul may be saved for time and eternity.

The book goes out with a prayer that God, who is destroying the liquor traffic, may take it and use it to honor Him, promote His Kingdom, and bless our fellowmen.

F. C. I.

CONTENTS

KING ALCOHOL DETHRONED

CHAPTER I

ALCOHOL AND PSYCHOLOGY

THE drink problem is primarily a psychological one, having its basis in the deepest instincts of the human soul.

To get at the bottom of the liquor question we have to go down into the center of the human heart. There we find two thirsts, one for drink, one for gold. The thirst of the man for intoxicants who consumes, and the thirst for money that prompts the man to manufacture and sell to him, are the two halves or the all of the liquor problem.

The appetite for intoxicants is a soul thirst. If it were a body thirst it could be satisfied, and there would be no liquor question to disturb or settle. All the forms of intemperance are only the floggings the poor body gets because it can not drink enough to satisfy the thirst of the soul. The lower animals will not get drunk; they are too wise to take stimulants even in moderation. The reason why they will not touch intoxicants is that they have no soul. It is only because man has this immortal nature that he can have a thirst for strong drink, reel with rum or fill a drunkard's grave.

The thirst of the soul which alcohol pretends to satisfy is that for stimulation, illumination and inspiration. This is a God-given appetite which He intended should be satisfied by truth, righteousness, love, by himself, the embodiment of these attributes. He gives himself: all truth, all holiness, all love, to be the soul's satisfaction, food, growth, life and destiny. To satisfy this appetite the father of lies, in the person of King Alcohol, offers himself as a substitute instead of God as the inspiration, the life, the joy of the soul. What a failure, what a fraud, what a tragedy is the substitute, and how long-continued and widespread has been his diabolical deception! God made fruits and grains and vegetables as food for the body, but the evil one set his ingenuity to work to produce something to touch the immortal soul, and has seized upon these products and compelled them to yield some "spirits" that will pander to it, and by his baleful alchemy has turned grapes and other fruits, wheat, barley, corn and other cereals, potatoes and other vegetables into wine, whiskey, brandy, beer and other intoxicants. He killed the vitality of the fruit and grain by fermentation and distillation, and transmuted the food into a poison to destroy soul and body, which product is death as a substitute for life, a demon in the place of God as a food for the soul. This demon alcohol science calls a "spirit"; Shakespeare names this spirit a "devil." In "Othello" he says: "O thou invisible spirit of wine! If thou hast no name to be known by, let us call thee devil!"

The craving for strong drink, then, is a divine appetite which is perverted by the devil alcohol. One of the most distinguished English authors, in a poem, "The Drinking Pot," tells the story of John and Jane, brother and sister, who had a pewter mug which served as a mutual drinking-cup for both. In the bottom of the mug there was an angel's face etched by some rude carver on the metal. John would pass over the frothing mug to Jane, who, to his intense astonishment, drained it to the bottom. Thereafter he would quench his own thirst first, but still Jane would drain what was left. John stoutly expostulated, but, as the poet tells,

"She loved to see the angel there,
And so she drained the pot."

John resolved to stop her drinking, so he took the tankard to the pewterer, who hammered the angel's face inside and etched that of a devil instead. To John's disgust Jane's thirst was as insatiable as before.

The intoxicating cup has etched in it the face of an angel to which the drinker looks for exhilaration, happiness and peace; but the angel's face is hammered out and that of the devil takes its place.

The soul thirst of the drinker is one-half, the soul hunger for money in the dealer is the second half of the liquor problem. The thirst for gold, like that for stimulation, is perverted into the vice of avarice. The desire for accumulation is proper when it does not become supreme, and when it renders an equivalent. Earth witnesses no more greedy avarice than that of the liquor traffic. It so loves money for the money's sake that it will not only not render an equivalent, but will inflict damage on those who buy its wares. It is this insatiable greed for money that has built every brewery and distillery, and opened every drinking place in the land, and keeps it going. It is this hunger for money that puts up the fight in every village, city, State, and at Washington against all measures to restrict or abolish the iniquitous traffic. If it were not for this base greed for ill-gotten gain the manufacture and sale of intoxicants as a beverage would instantly cease, and the liquor problem would be solved. King Alcohol, having all the beastly vices, is impelled by this polite vice of avarice, and by it he has become fabulously rich and proud. He holds a golden scepter and sits upon a throne of solid gold. Shakespeare, who knew the human heart so well and seeing alcohol there called it "devil," saw also there the devil avarice, in whose description in "Macbeth" he gives us this life-sized portrait of Alcohol, the bloated money king:

> "With this there grows,
> In my most ill-composed affection, such
> A staunchless avarice, that were I a king,
> I should cut off the nobles for their lands,
> Desire his jewels, and this other's house,
> And my more-having would be as a sauce
> To make me hunger more, that I should forge
> Quarrels unjust against the good and loyal,
> Destroying them for wealth."

Moloch of old, whose brazen form held out its hand for the money of the people, and whose fires consumed the sons offered as victims, was merciful compared to the Moloch of rum, whose hands demand a billion dollars of the people's money and every year one hundred thousand of their best sons.

INJURY TO THE BRAIN

God put brains in a cup at the top of a man's head to give him his place in the scale of being, and to dominate himself and the world. Alcohol attacks the brain and disturbs its mental processes, reduces man in the scale of being to that of bestiality, makes him the slave of every circumstance and of every evil habit. There are certain fat-like substances called lipoids, which are a part of every body cell and are found in largest proportion in the brain and other parts of the nervous system. When either chloroform or similar drugs are used to produce unconsciousness they do so by combining with these lipoids. Alcohol, a narcotic drug, with an especial affinity for them, goes straight for these substances, injuring them, and, if allowed to do its finished work, destroying the tissue and rational mental processes proceeding from it.

Doctor Henry Smith Williams, the noted psychologist, in speaking of the influence of alcohol on the brain cells, says: "It is a fact familiar to every student of evolution that, generally speaking, the most unstable tissues of an organism are the ones most recently evolved, that is to say, the most highly developed and complex tissues. The most delicate and unstable of all organic tissues are the complex central nerve cells of the gray cortex of the brain—the cells directly associated with the exhibition of mental processes. These are the most delicately poised, the most easily disturbed in function, of all organic tissues. It follows that these are the tissues that come earliest and most persistently under the influence of the alcoholic poison. A given individual may have a highly susceptible liver or kidney or heart, through hereditary influences, or through some peculiarity of his environment; but in general the brain, the organ of the mind, is the organ whose tissues are the most susceptible. So when the dissecting-

knife reveals, post mortem, a hobnailed liver, or
an alcohol kidney, stomach or heart, it will almost
invariably reveal also a shrunken and watery
alcohol brain."

Doctor Adolph Meyer, psychiatrist-in-chief of
the Johns Hopkins Hospital in Baltimore, Maryland, whose knowledge and experience make him
an authority on the subject, dictated to his stenographer for me a statement from which I quote
the following:

The nervous system is remarkably resistive to most
narcotics and capable of far-reaching recoverability from
the effects of the majority of acute intoxications. Profound intoxication, and especially repeated occurrence of
profound intoxication, does, however, give evidence of
deterioration of certain types of nerve cells and nerve
fibers (the commissure fibers in the cerebellum and in the
corpus callosum), and especially the peripheral nerves,
which are apt to be affected in the form of multiple
neuritis. Of greater importance is the change in the circulation, as shown in the tendency to "wet brain" and
the thickening and water-logged condition of the mem-
branes, involving the general circulation of the brain.

As in all intoxications, the functional disorders in alcoholic intoxication are seen before the tissue changes.
Excessive relaxation of inhibition and animation along un-
critical lines constitute the supposed gain from alcoholic
stimulation. The reduction of fears or doubts, of nervous-
ness, might appear as a beneficial result, but the effect is
temporary and apt to leave the person paralyzed for all
efforts of a more lasting character. The "desire for more,"

which is the necessary consequence of this sham help, and the great tolerance of the stomach for these beverages constitute the most serious points in the vicious circle produced by alcohol consumption.

CONFUSION OF MENTAL PROCESSES

There is ample testimony to the ill effects of alcohol on mental processes. Hermann von Helmholtz, who won a world fame in the realm of science in his professorship of Physics at Koenigsburg, Bonn, Heidelberg and Berlin, successively declared that the very smallest quantity of alcohol served effectively, while its influence lasted, to banish from his mind all possibility of creative effort, all capacity to solve an abstruse problem. Professor James said, "The reason for craving alcohol is that it is an anæsthetic even in moderate quantities. It obliterates a part of the field of consciousness and abolishes collateral trains of thought."

At a time when about everybody drank and it was universally believed that spirituous liquors braced the body and brightened the intellect, Goethe, that splendid specimen of physical and mental manhood in youth and old age, whose writings have influenced for good every civilized nation, and whose influence increases with the years, sounded the note of alarm at the damage of drink to the intellect. In his conversation with Eckermann of January 18, 1827, he says: "Schiller never drank much; he was very temperate. But at such moments of physical weakness he sought to increase his strength by taking some brandy or other spirituous liquor. This preyed upon his health, and was also detrimental to the productions themselves. For what judicious critics find fault with in his writings, I refer to this source. All those passages which they say are not quite right, I should like to call pathological passages, since he wrote them on days when he had not strength to find the proper and true motives." In his conversation with Eckermann of March 11, 1828, Goethe said, "Should he (the dramatic poet) then try to force this productivity that he lacks by means of spirituous liquors, and to supplement what is insufficient, this would probably be feasible, but all the scenes that he had forced, as it were, in this way would show it to their great disadvantage." Schiller himself came to that conclusion and said, "Wine invents nothing, it only blabs it out."

Doctor John Jacob Abel, professor of pharmacology, Johns Hopkins Medical College, and editor of the Journal of Pharmacology and Experimental Therapeutics, has written: "One-half to one bottle of wine, or two to four glasses of beer a day, not only counteract the beneficial effects of 'practice' in any given occupation, but also depress every form of intellectual activity; therefore every man who, according to his own notions, is only a moderate drinker, places himself by this indulgence on a lower intellectual level and opposes the full and complete utilization of his intellectual powers."

Professor Emil Kraepelin, formerly of Heidelberg, now director of the clinic of psychiatry at the University of Munich, in an address to the students said: "From the recommendation of a wine-dealer I learn that wine enlivens the imagination, facilitates thought-connection, quickens the memory, is favorable to the clear and rapid reception of impressions and to the formation of judgments. *Every word a lie!* Careful investigation, continued for decades and conducted with the finest apparatus, to determine the physical effects of alcohol, has shown beyond a doubt that exactly the opposite of all those assertions is actually the case. Alcohol paralyzes the imagination, renders the connection of ideas more difficult, weakens and falsifies the memory, and produces a very marked derangement of the power of apprehension and of judgment."

Science has learned to measure the damage of alcohol to the mind. Fürer, Rudin, Kraepelin, Smith and others took individuals and groups and after administering to them moderate doses of beer or wine tested their ability to memorize, add figures, read paragraphs or associate ideas, and it was found that there was marked deterioration in the ability to remember, to cast up figures or to do any serious kind of thinking, and that the deterioration in the test was marked by the sounding of gongs, the lifting of the fingers from electrical keys, and by closing the periods every half-hour or so and minutely recording the hits and misses. It was also found that this reduced capacity for the exercise of the mental functions persisted one or two days or even more after the alcohol had been taken. In other tests alcohol was given on one day or group of days and none allowed for the next period of similar duration. A test was made with a squad of quick-firing soldiers who on days when they drank nothing could hit the target twenty times in thirty shots, and when they had taken from three to four pints of beer could only hit it three times.

Aschaffenburg, a former pupil of Kraepelin, made a test in a printing office. The experiment extended over four days. The first and third days were abstinence days; on the second and fourth the men were allowed to have a little less than a tumblerful of Greek wine. The printed copy was identical. The result of the experiment was that on the drinking days, and those of most moderate drinking, too, the men set up ten per cent less type than on the days they took no liquor.

Wundt, the father of physiological experimental psychology, measured the discharge of single reactions from a single stimulus. Kraepelin introduced the chronometer for measuring prolonged mental work, and Dr. A. Smith of Schloss Marback made still further experiments and discoveries in the important field of measuring the deteriorating influence of drink on mental processes.

These discoveries of the ill effects of alcohol on the mind were a great surprise to science. For from time immemorial alcohol in moderation was considered not only beneficial but indispensable to the highest mental and physical effort. This opinion was held because subjective psychology declared it to be true. Through all the centuries men had declared that use of alcohol had made them feel better and enabled them to do more work, and science accepted that verdict as admitting of no debate. And when the scientists who have discovered the damage of drink to the intellect began their investigation only comparatively recently they did so with the full belief that alcohol was a blessing and started in to measure the beneficial effect on intellectual processes. Lo and behold, to their astonishment, they found that the opposite was true, that alcohol was a positive injury to the mind; and they measured that injury so accurately and conclusively that science has been compelled to change its mind and reverse its verdict of the ages; and psychology, which has been one of the strongest friends and supporters of alcohol, has become one of its most irreconcilable enemies.

Professor Emil Kraepelin, than whom there is no greater authority on this subject, in an address to the students of the University of Munich, confesses that he began the measurement of mental processes with the firm belief that alcohol was a benefit to the mind, but that positive scientific facts under his own eye had compelled a change in his opinion. These are his words:

I myself have been greatly surprised at the results of accurate experiments, for I was looking for such favorable effects of alcohol upon our mental life as should compensate for the mischief wrought thereby. But now we see clearly what is the nature of the condition into which we put ourselves by the use of alcohol; a paralyzing of the power of apprehension and the highest mental functions, which finally leads to the well-defined clouding of consciousness, and an excitation in the realm of the impulses, which lets the control of our wills slip away from us more and more. And this is the condition that we light-heartedly make the center of our good times, for the sake of which we fondly form those drinking-customs which devastate our nation. Even if alcoholic intoxication produced all those desired effects upon our mental life which are ascribed to it by liquor-dealers and drinkers in their enthusiasm, we should have to turn from it in horror as soon as we beheld its terrible footprints on our national life.

The friendliness of science to alcohol and its championship of it is mentioned in an address by Professor Smith of Schloss Marbach in a lecture before the Munich section of the German Society for Ethical Culture, in which he says:

It was to be expected that with the animosity prevailing among all classes toward all experiments that discredit the use of alcohol, strictly scientific circles being no exception, voices would be raised charging the experiments with at least an auto-suggestive influence, if not directly accusing them of intentional misrepresentation. The necessity for forestalling such objection was so impressed upon me from the start that I had a second person repeat some of my experiments and obtained in a friendly way for this purpose a schoolmaster who lived near me, whom I knew to be a thoroughly reliable man, but who on the other hand, I must admit, would have been glad to have his tests produce results opposite from mine, for he was of the opinion that alcohol in moderate doses was practically indispensable for promoting physical and mental work. This man practiced total abstinence for four days before beginning the experiment. Then for eight successive days he worked without alcohol, then for six days under the influence of eighty-gram doses of alcohol so arranged that the work was done twenty hours after the alcohol was taken. Then there were six days without alcohol and then again two days with it at the close. His working ability for both memorizing and adding fell for the first time directly, after the first alcohol was taken; then it arose again as suddenly in the following non-alcoholic periods, and with the second alcoholic period it again suddenly dropped.

Aschaffenburg makes this record of a test show-

ing the mental effect of beer- and wine-drinking
on the school children of Vienna:

Observations were made by Bayer, who investigated the
habits of 591 children in a public school in Vienna.   These
pupils were ranked by their teachers into three groups, de-
noting progress as "good," "fair" or "poor" respectively.
Bayer found on investigation that 134 of these pupils
took no alcoholic drink; that 164 drank alcoholics very
seldom; but that 219 drank beer or wine once a day;
71 drank it twice daily, and 3 drank it with every meal.
Of the total abstainers 42 per cent. ranked in the school
as "good," 49 per cent. as "fair," and 9 per cent. as "poor."
Of the occasional drinkers 34 per cent. ranked as "good,"
57 per cent. as "fair," and 9 per cent. as "poor."   Of the
daily drinkers 28 per cent. ranked as "good," 58 per cent.
as "fair" and 14 per cent. as "poor."   Those who drank
twice daily ranked 25 per cent. "good," 58 per cent.
"fair" and 18 per cent. "poor."   Of the three who drank
thrice daily, one ranked as "fair," the other two as
"poor."

The present Department of Health of New
York City issued a bulletin on the deleterious effect of alcohol on the brain and thought growing
out of it.   The following quotations from it are
peculiarly appropriate here:

The chief difference between man and the lower animals is the brain development.   The brain is man's dearest possession, and nature's best gift.   Now, because of the
fact that the brain is such a wonderful piece of machinery,
and such a complicated machine, it is the most delicate

and most sensitive part of the body. Moreover, the parts of the brain that distinguish it most are its most sensitive parts. These parts are the ones that have to do with thinking, judging and controlling our actions. A thing that is very sensitive is a thing that is very easily bruised, hurt and damaged. Alcohol is a poison to all parts of the body, but it is easy to understand that the part which alcohol can damage most quickly and to the greatest extent is the delicate and sensitive brain. And that is a fact. The first effect of taking alcohol into the system is felt by the brain; the worst damage is done to the most delicate parts of the brain; and so it follows that when a man takes a couple of drinks of strong liquor it promptly muddles his thinking, weakens his judgment, and loosens his control over his actions. In other words, it quickly steals from him what is best in him; it reduces the force of highest brain control which nature has given him, which he has developed through ages, and which marks him out as different from brute animals. Civilized man equals brute animal plus high brain development. Alcohol blots out the "high brain development" and leaves behind the brute animal.

Now, of course, we don't mean to say that when a person takes a drink of anything containing alcohol he is reduced at once to a brute animal; but very few will dispute that a drunken person is not much better than a brute animal. And the reason he has been reduced to such a state by the alcohol is that before he can take enough of it to kill his body he has had enough to paralyze his brain, especially the highest parts of his brain. It has paralyzed his power to think, it has paralyzed his power to judge, it has paralyzed his power to control his actions. The amount of alcohol which makes a person drunken varies with different people. Some can stand very little, others a great deal. However, even a very little, though it does not show itself in drunkenness, has a damaging effect on the brain. This is what we want to point out particularly. Too many people think that if they drink alcohol in moderation, such, for example, as three or four glasses of beer a day, or one or two drinks of whiskey a day, they are not doing themselves any harm at all. Very many think that they may safely drink as long as they stop before getting drunk. These are very dangerous and mistaken ideas to have. Drinking, even in moderation, has dangers for the brains and nerves, and steady drinking is vary bad.

Women and young persons sooner become victims to the brain-weakening effects of alcohol than men and older persons. That is because women and young persons have more sensitive nervous systems and brains. So it is clear that women and young persons should be particularly careful to steer clear of liquor.

The effect of moderate drinking on the powers of the brain were carefully studied. For example, a number of bookkeepers who have to deal with figures, which is the kind of work which requires a clear brain and also the kind whose quality can be easily compared from time to time, were given alcohol daily for two weeks in amounts that would equal what is contained in about four glasses of beer. At the end of two weeks their ability to add simple figures was reduced by 15 per cent.

There are psychologists of great ability and re-nown who hold to the old opinion of science that

alcohol does not harm, but helps the mental processes. The late Doctor Hugo Münsterberg, for
twenty-five years the head of the psychological
department of Harvard University, the highest
authority in America on German ideas and ideals,
in McClure's Magazine for August, 1908, makes
the most specious plea for that side of the question we have seen. That plea the editor of the
magazine in the same issue declines to be responsible for. But the same article has confessions
that largely counteract the effect of the professor's
scientific contentions. Here is one of them:

Of course, alcohol before serious intellectual work disturbs me. I live most comfortably in a pleasant temperance town which will, I hope, vote no-license year
by year as long as freshmen stroll over the old Harvard
yard.

The pleasant temperance town to which Doctor
Münsterberg refers is the city of Cambridge,
Massachusetts, the seat of Harvard University,
small as compared with Boston, of which it is a
suburb, but itself a city of ever 100,000 inhabitants; and it is likely that this brilliant scientific
champion of alcohol and other distinguished
members of the faculty at Harvard voted no-
license in the wet and dry campaigns carried on in
that college town for the past twenty years.

Professor Münsterberg then continues his admissions:

The problem of Prohibition does not affect my thirst, but it greatly interests my scientific conscience; not as a German, but as a psychologist, I feel impelled to add a word to the discussion which is suddenly reverberating over the whole country. But is it really a discussion which we hear? Is it not rather a one-sided denunciation of alcohol, repeated a million times with louder and louder voice, an outcry ever swelling in its vehemence? On the other side there may be the protests of the distillers and brewers and wine-growers and bottle-makers and saloonkeepers and perhaps some timid declarations of thirsty societies, but such protests do not count, since they have all the ear-marks of selfishness; they are ruled out and no one listens, just as no one would consult the thieves if a new statute against pickpockets was planned. So far as the disinterested public is concerned, the discussion is essentially one-sided.

The professor makes another confession in the article which might be used to advantage as a leaflet by the Prohibitionists in wet and dry campaigns anywhere. It is this:

Exaggerated denunciation of the Prohibition movement is, of course, ineffective. Whoever simply takes sides with the saloonkeeper and his clientele—yes, whoever is blind to the colossal harm which alcohol has brought and is now bringing to the whole country—is unfit to be heard by those who have the healthy and sound development of the nation at heart. The evils which are connected with the drinking habit are gigantic; thousands of lives and many more thousands of households are the victims every year;

disease and poverty and crime grow up where alcohol
drenches the soul. To deny it means to ignore the teach-
ings of medicine and economics and criminology.

In the Ladies' Home Journal Professor Münsterberg wrote.

There is nothing more degrading and no more atro-
cious insult to civilized life than the American saloon. It
has poisoned the social atmosphere for the masses; in
it the workingman squanders his savings, and the healthy
man devastates his energies and becomes a wreck. Political corruption radiates from the saloon into the whole
public life, and a thousand ways lead from the saloon to
the penitentiary. It is a blessed movement which now
turns with overwhelming energy against the horrors of
this evil and unites the clean minds of the whole nation
in an untiring fight against this source of infection. There
may be disagreements as to the best ways and means, disagreement whether strict Prohibition or education toward
temperance is the more reliable method; but there is no
disagreement as to the fact that the saloon has to be wiped
out; and the day seems near indeed when—thanks to
women—the fight against the saloon will be taken up
in almost every state.

While the laboratory of the chemist, the experiments of the psychologist, the accurate measure-
ments of the specialist reveal the damage of drink
to the brain cells and mental processes, the school
of practical life is teaching the same truth in the
every-day illustrations. It is seen in communities

where intoxicating liquors are allowed in the giggle and gabble of the girl in the street car, who, usually reserved, inflamed with wine, makes a fool of herself; in the man who, not usually bold, without voice or invitation, befuddled with rum, insists on singing a solo in a crowded railway car; or in the man stupefied with beer who has sunk down in a stupor in the corner of the seat and has to be shaken by the conductor till his teeth rattle to be made to understand that it is his ticket that is wanted; in the poor fellow who walks out of the corner groggery and incoherently undertakes to enter into conversation with every stranger he meets to tell him how much he loves him; in the smartest boy in the school who learned the way to the saloon, and as a man walks the streets a driveling idiot; in the cool, level-headed, honest, industrious man who was made crazy with rum, and as a maniac slew his best friend.

A SOURCE OF INSANITY

Rum is a demon dominating the mind, knowing that, having that, it possesses all the rest there is in man. It dulls the perceptions, beclouds the memory, unsteadies the judgment, crazes the imagination, unbalances the reason, freezes the affections, sears the conscience, and paralyzes the will.

Alcohol not only deteriorates the brain cells, befuddles the intellect, and furnishes the tottering drunkard and wretch with the delirium tremens, but it becomes the devil incarnate in its assassination of the intellect, making the victim unwittingly a mental suicide, and society, by its license, his torturer and mental murderer.

Doctor Frederick Peterson in New York City is an acknowledged authority on mental diseases; for twenty years he has been connected with Columbia University, the past fourteen years as clinic professor of psychiatry. I called upon Dr. Peterson to ask him to give me some facts as to the ill effects of alcohol on the brain, nervous system and mental processes. His knowledge and experience in this field of medical science make his opinion of untold value to the cause of truth. He said, "I have read a paper before the New York State Conference of Charities and Correction, which is printed in the New York Medical Journal, which I think contains what you want." It was exactly what I wanted. Among other things in the paper Doctor Peterson said:

Insanity and epilepsy are among the diseases that taint our progeny. Alcohol is the chief poison that has this baneful power. As an example of what one individual may do I might cite the oft-quoted Jukes family in the State of New York. One hard drinker was the originator of this family which, over a generation ago, when Dugdale wrote his book, had become already 1,200 in number. In his summary of the study of the Jukes family of degenerates the author says: "Over a million and a quarter dollars of loss in seventy-five years, caused by a single family, 1,200 strong, without reckoning the cash paid for whisky or taking into account the entailment of pauperism and crime on the survivors in succeeding generations, and the incurable disease, idiocy, and insanity growing out of this debauchery, and reaching further than we can calculate." This is one family.

In the State of New York there are now some 30,000 insane in the public and private hospitals, and it is estimated that twenty per cent. of these, or 6,000 patients, owe their insanity to alcohol. In all the asylums of the United States there are 150,000 insane, and assuming the same percentage there are 30,000 individuals in this country in whom alcohol has brought about insanity. Doctor MacDonald calculates that one insane person is an approximate loss to the State of $400 a year. Hence the actual loss in money to the State of New York through alcoholic insanity is $2,400,000, and to the United States $12,000,000 every year. There is not time here to take up the subject of the relation of alcohol to pauperism and crime. But what I want to point out is that the asylums for the insane, the institutions for epileptics, idiots and feeble-minded, the prisons and the county poorhouses, are representative, as far as their alcoholic population is concerned, of the extremes of alcoholic indulgence and debauchery. Here alcohol has done its worst to the living individual. Below this topmost wave of ruin and desolation are innumerable gradations of alcoholism down to the moderate drinkers and the temperate or occasional drinkers.

The race is reasonably safe from further contamination

of those victims of alcohol who are locked away in the
retreats that our charitable world provides for them.
It is otherwise with the vaster number of excessive
drinkers, who are free to work any havoc in the social
organism and who are direct and indirect feeders of the
institutions named. What these may do to themselves,
their wives and their children and their children's children we have come to learn, and it is because of this
awakening to a common danger to the human race that
the nations of the earth are combined in a common
campaign. It is not a single Jukes family that society has
ranged itself against, but against the legions of Jukes
families that menace the human stock. My views on this
subject briefly expressed are printed on my own prescription blanks as follows:

Alcohol is a poison. It is claimed by some that alcohol
is a food. If so it is a poisoned food. The daily regular
use of alcohol, even in moderation, often leads to chronic
alcoholism.

One is poisoned less rapidly by the use of beer than by
drinking wines, gin, whisky and brandy.

Alcohol is one of the most common causes of insanity,
epilepsy, paralysis, diseases of the liver and stomach, dropsy
and tuberculosis.

A father or mother who drinks poisons the children
born to them, so that many die in infancy, while others
grow up as idiots and epileptics.

Mr. Filmore Condit, a merchant of New York,
a modest potential factor of moral reform, gave
me a copy of his pamphlet on "Alcohol and Insanity," quotations from which follow:

"August Arrivey, thirty years old, a printer by trade, is under arrest here, the confessed murderer of his mother, Mrs. Mary Arrivey, fifty-eight years old. 'The man in the airship told me to do it,' Arrivey continually mutters as the only reason for his crime. Because of his actions the police believe him insane. Liquor is believed, however, to be at the root of the man's crime, as he had for the last few years obtained one position after another, only to lose them in rapid succession on account of sprees. Mrs. Arrivey was found lying in a pool of blood in the kitchen, with her skull crushed and her face gashed as if from blows from a hatchet. Search of the premises disclosed the son, muttering like a child, hiding behind some bushes in the yard. Confronted with the dead body of his mother, he confessed his crime." This paragraph, which appeared in a Stockton, California, paper, a few days ago, is one which shocks us for a moment as we read it, and is then forgotten as a commonplace incident of life.

The causes of insanity in our nation are so interwoven with the warp and woof of violated moral law that no single explanation is sufficient, but from hospitals and authorities upon the subject comes abundant and conclusive evidence that alcoholism overshadows all other causes in the destruction of human minds. It produces insanity in three ways: First, directly, to drinkers as a result of their overindulgence in intoxicants; second, indirectly, through heredity, drinkers transmit to their descendants a predisposition to insanity and neurotic weakness; third, indirectly, as a cause of family, social and business trouble, it often is a contributory cause of insanity.

Doctor T. S. Clouston, of Edinburgh, who is

one of the highest living authorities upon unsoundness of mind, says: "Alcohol is by far the most common and the most characteristic of the poisons introduced from without, that have a markedly hurtful influence on the brain cells. If Socrates or Marcus Aurelius or Job had continuously poisoned their brains with London gin they would inevitably have become unsound in mind."

Recent annual reports from forty hospitals in Pennsylvania, New Jersey, California, Delaware, Wisconsin, Minnesota, Indiana, Massachusetts, Ohio, Washington, Wyoming, Nevada, Colorado, Maryland, Iowa and Connecticut show that in 15,363 cases of insanity where the causes were known, in 3,383, or 22 per cent., alcohol was stated as the single direct cause.

Albert Warren Ferris, M.D., Sheldon T. Viele and William T. Parkhurst, Lunacy Commissioners of New York, having charge of thirteen great hospitals containing over thirty thousand insane people, stated that 27.5 per cent. of admissions from cities, and 14.2 per cent. from rural districts are due to alcohol, and that it is an etiological factor in almost 40 per cent. of all admissions.

The leading authorities of the entire world are in close accord in tracing insanity to alcoholism. Berkeley, Spitzka and others say: "Of all the varied causes of mental infirmities, heredity and alcohol are the most important." Kraepelin says: "We are fully acquainted with some im-

portant and widespread causes of insanity. Among
these stands first and foremost the abuse of alcohol."

Mr. Condit, by a comparison of wet and dry
States, and groups of States, shows that the heavy
drinking States furnish by far the largest percentage of insanity. "From January 1, 1910, to July,
1914, the insanity of New York, Pennsylvania,
New Jersey and Massachusetts increased from
64,000 to over 88,000, or an annual increase of
6.12 per cent., while that of Kansas and Maine
increased from 4,170 to 4,583, or an annual increase of 1.52 per cent. New York had 31,000
insane in 1910 and over 40,000 July 1, 1916,
while the sixteen States which were without
saloons in July, 1916, had only 32,000, or eight
thousand fewer insane people than the State of
New York alone. In tracing to alcohol the destruction of the intellect we remember that New
York State has 31,000 dealers in intoxicating
liquors, more than all the fifteen States of the
South and Southwest. Not only have New York
and New Jersey heavy burdens for their own
taxpayers, but their alcoholic insane and neurotics
are taxing the people of other commonwealths.
Thus the latest report of the Ohio hospitals for
the insane showed that in 1914 they contained
874 patients who were natives of New York, 193
of New Jersey, 321 of Massachusetts, and only
32 of Maine and 28 of Kansas."

THE SEWER GANG

I here call to the witness stand a young man plucked as a brand from the burning.

At the close of a meeting of the Men and Forward Religious Movement, held in Carnegie Music Hall in New York, I was coming down the steps of the speakers' platform when a tall, handsome young man standing near me asked: "Were you ever at Bloomington, Illinois?"

"Yes," I replied, "I was pastor of the First Methodist Church of that city thirty years ago."

"I remember you," he said. "I am Jim Goodheart, Jr."

"Jim Goodheart, Jr.! God bless you, my boy!" I cried, "I could hug you for the love I have for your father, the simple, modest man, and yet the great and good heart his name indicates, veteran of the Union Army, Sheriff of McLean County, Illinois, my trusted class leader and strong help in our revival."

"I remember that revival well," he said. "It lasted two months and resulted in five hundred conversions. I was a member of the 'Sewer Gang,' the 'Dirty Dozen,' which often attended the meetings in a body to criticize, make fun, and scoff. Some of us felt a strange divine influence, but the pull of the devil on us through the saloon was too much for us, and we were kept away from God and the good. Did you ever hear of the tragical fate of that gang?"

I replied, "I never heard till just now that there was such a gang."

"The story of their fate is almost too horrible to tell or believe," he said. "Every one of the twelve went to the dogs through strong drink, I among them. I came back. I was picked up drunk out of the gutter and saved, and am now the superintendent of the Sunshine Rescue Mission of Denver, Colorado, and a delegate to this laymen's convention. The rest never reformed, and all the eleven came to a bad end."

By this time the surging crowd had pushed us to the door. Having an immediate appointment elsewhere, I said, "Their tragical story shocks me. When you get back home write me briefly some of the particulars of that 'Sewer Gang' and the terrible fate of which you speak."

I got a letter from Jim Goodheart, Jr., written from the Sunshine Rescue Mission of Denver, from which I quote verbatim:

"The group of persons of whom I spoke to you was known in Bloomington as the 'Dirty Dozen' or 'Sewer Gang.' It had a president, vice-president and secretary, and was composed of boys from fourteen to nineteen years of age, desperate in character. Four of that gang of twelve are murderers, and are serving life sentences in various penitentiaries. One is in an insane asylum, a hopeless wreck. Five are dead, either having been killed in saloon brawls or in railroad accidents

while under the influence of liquor. The eleventh
is a confirmed drunkard in Bloomington, and I am
the twelfth. Ten of our 'Dirty Dozen' are in the
ground and behind bars."

Recently I was asked by the National Anti-
Saloon League to spend a week speaking in the
wet and dry campaign in Bloomington and vicin-
ity, and the wreck of the "Sewer Gang" aroused
my conscience and stirred my zeal in the fight
against the saloon. If Bloomington had been dry
thirty years ago, as it is today, it is likely there
would have been no "Sewer Gang," and that those
composing it would have been in the church, leading useful, honored and happy lives. The four
who were murderers and the five who were killed
had their minds bereft of reason and bodies
poisoned with alcohol. With the record of this
wreck, the statement of the liquor editors and orators that alcohol is not a poison but a food, that
it does not shorten life, that it does not pollute
character or damage the community, that it is not
the parent of lawlessness, seems an impertinence
and a mockery. The damage it does is destroying the saloon as much as anything else. The ruin
of precious boys' lives like those in Bloomington
is doing as much as the preachers or women or
professors or doctors or big business men or legislatures to dethrone King Alcohol.

The fate of the Bloomington boys calls to mind
the Greek fable of the twelve young men and

twelve young maidens who were eaten every year
by the serpent king.   The story is that a king in
his travels came on an island of surpassing beauty.
He lingered at a lake surrounded with flowers of
exquisite hue and delicious perfume.   Looking
out, he saw fierce lions ready to devour him.   The
lake spoke to him and told him that the king of
the island was a serpent with seven heads and that
he killed all that set foot on his shores.   The serpent came from his palace and told the visitor that
he would spare his life on the condition that he
would send twelve of the finest young men and
maidens each year to be eaten by him, threaten-
ing that if the toll of young life were not sent
he would take his beasts and destroy the whole
nation.   Twelve of the most beautiful young men
and women volunteered each year to save the
nation.   And in a ship painted black, with jet
black sails, amidst universal lamentation, went the
precious lives to their terrible fate.   The horse of
the prince told him the sacrifice made for so many
years was unnecessary and sent him to a woman in
a cave in the mountain, who told him how to kill
the serpent king.   And he muffled the alarm bells
of the bed chamber with cotton and took the
sword which hung above him, with which he killed
others, and with it cut off the seven serpent heads,
and the toll of precious life was ended.   Alcohol
is the seven-headed serpent king who demands a
toll for death of not only twelve young men and

maidens but of one hundred thousand each year. There is a deep conviction in the land that the toll is unnecessary and that the thing to do is to kill the serpent king. This is being done. The "Sewer Gangs," the "Dirty Dozens" of the nation are doing their part in dethroning and destroying King Alcohol. They have turned on the serpent to torture him. They are decapitating him with the same sword with which he slew others.

CHAPTER II

ALCOHOL AND PHYSIOLOGY

ALCOHOL breaks down the body as completely as it shatter the mind. Every organ of the body, the lungs, the heart, the liver, the stomach and kidneys, is affected by this drug. Science has discovered that alcohol is a poison. Over three hundred years ago a Swiss physician and chemist of ability and renown, who called himself Paracelsus, devoted much of his time in his laboratory searching for the elixir of life, that should turn the baser metals into gold and prolong human life. He loudly proclaimed to the world he had found it; it was our alcohol. He partook of it freely to demonstrate its immortal influence on the body and in the prime of life died drunk on the floor of a tavern, murdered by what he thought was the "elixir of life." Ever since then the world has been making the mistake of this alchemist and suffering the consequences.

Doctor Haven Emerson, Commissioner of Health of New York City, deserves the gratitude of the whole nation for his courage in proclaiming alcohol a poison which breaks down all the organs of the body, and calling upon the people of the city and nation to put their faces against it. The scientific and medical journals, and the secular press generally, have given wide publicity to his bulletins, especially those warning against the damage of intoxicating liquors. I take the privilege of making extensive quotations from those bulletins.

In one of the bulletins I found a slip about three inches long and an inch and a half wide, in black and yellow, with yellow letters at the top, "Health Book-Mark." In the center of the card is a bottle of whisky representing the body of a man on legs which is being broken. Underneath the picture and at the bottom of the book-mark there is printed:

"Whisky is poison. Save your body. Save your brain, whisky brings you death and pain."

Under this in small gilt letters is: "This is one of a series. Collect the rest. Department of Health of the City of New York."

In one of these bulletins Doctor Emerson says:

If a flagon of alcohol were offered to a student of pharmacology to test as a curiosity, and he applied the standard methods of physiological experiment to it, he could but come to the conclusion that he was dealing with a more dangerous chemical than any now available in the whole range of materia medica, not second to opium or its derivatives as a destroyer of character, a disturber of function and a degenerator of tissue; and he would be quite justified in advising the prohibition of its manufacture and use as a beverage.

Alcohol, a consistently depressing, habit-forming drug, causes characteristic, easily recognized diseases of the brain, nerves and special senses. Alcohol causes definite damage to the heart, kidneys, blood vessels and organs of digestion, especially the stomach and liver. When alcohol is used so moderately as to cause none of the special diseases due solely to its effects, it is known to damage the unborn babe, the nursing child and the grown man and woman in such ways as to render them peculiarly susceptible to the infectious and communicable diseases to which all people are exposed.

From the records of the Department of Health of the City of New York it appears that there are annually at least two thousand deaths admittedly due to the excessive use of alcohol. It is a matter of record that eight thousand cases of acute alcoholism are treated annually at Bellevue Hospital, New York. Anybody familiar with general medical practice or the service in the general medical wards in any hospital in the large cities of this country, where the use of alcohol is common, will be willing to testify to the very considerable, if not determining rôle that alcoholic habit plays in the course and termination of a large proportion of the diseases which come under observation.

Is this not sufficient to justify the use of such powers as the Board of Health has to prevent the use of alcohol in the community?

Almost all lung specialists of any ability or note record the manifest damage alcohol does to the lungs.   Doctor Emerson's bulletin, "T. B. and His Friend, Mr. Alcohol," shows how intimate the relationship is between tuberculosis and strong drink.   The bulletin follows:

MR. T. B. AND HIS FRIEND, MR. ALCOHOL

Two of the worst enemies you and I have are tuberculosis and alcohol.   We have become pretty well acquainted with Mr. T. B., and are fighting him tooth and nail; but many of us seem not to realize that Mr. Alcohol is an even worse enemy than tuberculosis.   So we go on drinking alcoholic beverages, and because we don't die of what the doctor calls alcohol poisoning, we think they have done us no harm.

The trouble is that most of us need to have a skull and crossbones staring us in the face before we think that there is any danger.   Tuberculosis is an honest enemy who lets us know when he has arrived.   We hear a dry, hard cough and see a thin, tired-looking person with some flush on his cheeks.   At once we turn away in horror and say "Look out! that's T. B."   But with alcohol it is different. Disguised by the good taste of beer or by the bracing feeling which whisky gives, Mr. Alcohol easily makes friends, and in our ignorance we believe that he is a jolly good sport who will never do us any harm.

But this foxy old poison, alcohol, is a friend of Mr. Tuberculosis, a sort of scout who goes about getting things ready for the germs to settle. He works slowly, doing a little damage here and there, and then when the victim catches a cold, in walks Mr. Tuberculosis and settles down to do his deadly work, and nobody ever thinks of blaming Mr. Alcohol, who is really behind all the trouble.

This is the way it works: Jim drinks a little beer, not much, say four glasses in the course of the day. That's a quart of beer. In the quart of beer are two ounces of alcohol. Jim's body can stand it for a few days, but after a while his blood begins to wear out, the blood vessels in the skin and in the lungs become weak, and the tiny cells that make up the body get less nourishment because the circulation of the blood is sluggish. When this happens and any disease germs come along, there is less power to resist them, and Mr. Tuberculosis, or some other disease germ, gets in his work.

At the Otisville tuberculosis sanatorium, conducted by the New York City Health Department, the doctors found that the patients who use alcohol have much less chance of getting well. Almost all of those who do not drink improve greatly in health, but only about a quarter of those who drink improve. Twice as many drinkers die as those who leave Mr. Alcohol alone. This shows how close friends Mr. Alcohol and Mr. Tuberculosis are; they are hard enough to beat one at a time, but when they get together they are a deadly pair.

You can not be absolutely sure of escaping Mr. Tuberculosis, no matter how hard you try, but you can make his chance of getting you very slim by leaving all alcohol alone.

Doctor Emerson, at a meeting at the Hotel Savoy in New York a few months ago, said: "The death rate during an epidemic is always higher among alcoholics than among temperate men. The user of alcohol cannot fight off an infectious disease because his power of resistance has been broken down by the alcohol. This is especially true of pneumonia. What a man did for himself before he got pneumonia is vastly more important than what the doctor does for him after he gets it. If he has been a steady user of liquor his system cannot withstand pneumonia. Years ago it was the custom to give pneumonia patients two ounces of alcohol every two hours; many of them died under this treatment who would have been saved today. Today no alcohol is used, and the percentage of deaths has decreased greatly."

This close relationship between alcohol and pneumonia was made the cause of a bulletin of warning issued by the United States Public Health Service on March 5, 1917: "The United States Public Health Service brands strong drink as the most efficient ally of pneumonia. The liberal and continuous user of alcoholic drinks will do well to heed this warning, especially at this season. Indulgence in alcoholic liquors lowers the individual vitality, and the man who drinks is peculiarly susceptible to pneumonia." The United States Public Health Service is a conservative body. It does not engage in alarmist propaganda, and it insists that this warning is a fact that will bear endless repetition.

Strong drink leaves a patient in poor condition for an attack of typhoid fever, Bright's or any other disease. In reference to the intimacy between alcohol and Bright's disease, Doctor Emerson makes this reflection: "You don't need alcohol for health; you don't need it for strength; you don't need it for food; you don't need it for drink; it never does you any good. Then why drink?"

ALCOHOL AND THE MEDICAL PROFESSION

Scarcely anything has been more marked than the change of attitude toward alcohol on the part of the medical profession. Not very many years back almost all doctors prescribed liquors of one kind or another for nearly every ailment that flesh is heir to. But now, since science has proven alcohol, even in small quantities, to be a poison, very many physicians will not prescribe it at all, and almost all of them do so with extreme caution.

Some time ago, at a convention in London, at which 10,000 physicians gathered from all nations of the world, alcohol as a medicine was condemned, and the president of the convention made a most powerful address, calling upon the physicians of the world to take a place in the forefront of the battle against intoxicants, the deadly enemy of body and mind.

The complete revolution of the medical profession of the United States on the use of alcohol as a beverage or medicine is seen at the annual meeting of the American Medical Association recently held in New York City. Doctor Frank Billings of Chicago, the chairman of the Council on Health and Public Instruction, introduced a resolution, unanimously passed by the Council, in which was expressed the opinion that alcohol had no drug value, either as a tonic or a stimulant; that it had no value in the treatment of disease, and that its only legitimate use in medicine was as a preservative and in the preparation of certain pharmaceutical products.

Dr. Charles H. Mayo of Rochester, Minnesota, the world-famous surgeon, in his address on taking the chair as the president of the American Medical Association strongly advocated Prohibition for the nation, not only for the war, but for peace as well. The 1,500 delegates to the National Convention of the Association in the Waldorf-Astoria ballroom cheered their approval of his demand that the doctors form a fighting phalanx for Prohibition. Doctor Mayo urged that the doctor's prescription of intoxicating liquor be thrown into the wastebasket. Medicine, he said, no longer needed alcohol, for it had something better.

If alcohol is the poison that science says it is and the medical profession believes it is, then we have a perfect right to expect the shortening of life on the part of those who use intoxicating drink. In searching for information upon the subject, I visited the actuaries of several of the leading life insurance companies of America, and while they differed somewhat in their figures as to the number of years less that the drinker has, all agreed that his life is shortened.

Dr. Arthur Hunter, the Actuary of the New York Life Insurance Company, himself the best authority in the nation on the subject of the relation of drink to mortality, communicated with forty-three other life insurance companies, on the subject, and asserts that seven American companies have proved that abstainers have from 10 to 30 per cent. lower mortality than non-abstainers.

ALCOHOL POISONS LIFE AT ITS FOUNTAIN

One of the most tragical features of rum's ravages is its deadly attack on the origins of life. It hunts life at its very foundation and kills the babe before it opens its eyes on this world or so disables it physically and mentally as to leave it a poor weakling, with pain, disappointment, failure and early death as the result.

It is only within the last few years that science has discovered this most enormously important fact which gives falsehood to the statement that alcohol is a food and proves it to be a poison of the most insidious and deadly form.

DR. STOCKARD'S EXPERIMENTS

Experiments with the lower animals have proven conclusively that alcohol is transmitted as a virulent poison to their offspring. Perhaps no one in the two hemispheres is higher authority on the poisonous effect of alcohol upon animal offspring than Professor C. R. Stockard of Cornell University Medical College, in New York City. He has been studying for a number of years the effects of alcohol on the growth and development of different animals, as well as the influence of alcohol on the descendants, that is, the children, grandchildren, etc., of alcoholized animals. The results of Doctor Stockard's experiments have been published in different medical and scientific journals of this country and Europe, and I shall give here the main result as gathered from these various scientific articles.

His first work showed that when the eggs of a fish were developing normally in salt water, a little alcohol added to the water would cause the young fish to be deformed and usually unable to live. When chicken eggs were put in a dish filled with alcoholic fumes the vapors would soak through the shell, and the chickens that developed in these eggs were often deformed or died in the shell before hatching. Thus, the effect of alcohol on the early developing body poisoned it in such a way as to spoil its regular development.

The most important studies by Doctor Stockard have shown the effect of alcohol on the children and grandchildren of animals that were given regular doses of alcohol for long periods of time.

Guinea pigs are used in this experiment, and have taken enough alcohol to make them almost drunk six days a week during several years. Inhaling alcoholic fumes until intoxicated does not seem to injure the body of the guinea pig. The animals remain in good health and live long, yet if the same alcohol is given the guinea pig in its stomach, the results are very injurious, and the animal does not survive the treatment very long. Unfortunately, man takes his alcohol through the stomach, and gets more injurious effects on digestion than the guinea pigs get by inhaling alcoholic fumes. But even inhaling the fumes does injure the guinea pigs, as may be seen by studying the records of the young born from alcoholic parents.

After studying these animals for six years, Doctor Stockard has published facts to warrant the following conclusions from the records of six hundred and eighty-two offspring produced by five hundred and seventy-one matings:

One hundred and sixty-four matings of alcoholized mammals, in which either the father, mother or both were alcoholic, gave 64, or almost 40 per cent., negative results or early abortions, while only 25 per cent. of the control matings failed to give full-term litters. Of the 100 full-term litters from alcoholic parents 18 per cent. contained stillborn young, and only 50 per cent. of all the matings resulted in living litters. Forty-six per cent. of the individuals in the litters of living young died very soon after birth. In contrast to this record 73 per cent. of the 90 control matings gave living litters, and 84 per cent. of the young in these litters survived as normal, healthy animals.

The mating records of the descendants of the alcoholized guinea pigs, although they themselves were not treated with alcohol, compare in some respects even more unfavorably with the control records than the above figures from the directly alcoholized animals.

Of 194 matings of the children from alcoholics in various combinations 55 have resulted in negative results or early abortions; 18 stillborn litters of 41 young occurred, and 17 per cent. of these stillborn young were deformed. One hundred and twenty-one living litters contained 199 young, but 94 of these died within a few days, and almost 15 per cent. of them were deformed, while 105 survived and 7 of these showed eye deformities. Among 126 full-term control young of the same stock not one has been deformed.

The records of the matings of the grandchildren of alcoholic grandparents are still worse, higher mortality and more pronounced deformities, while even the few great-grandchildren which have survived are generally weak and in many instances appear to be quite sterile, even though paired with vigorous, prolific, normal mates.

The structural defects shown by the descendants of alcoholized animals seem to be confined chiefly to the central nervous system and special sense organs. Many of the young animals show tremors or paralysis in the hind legs, fore legs or both legs of one side. Eye defects are very common; some have only one good eye, and finally several cases of complete absence of eyes have occurred, the entire eyeballs and optic nerves being absent.

Inbreeding tends to emphasize the alcoholic effects. This is probably due to related animals responding to the treatment in closely similar ways on account of the similarity of their constitutions. Inbreeding, as such, may be harmful. But inbreeding added to the alcohol effects produces a much worse condition in the offspring than either inbreeding or alcoholism alone could do.

Dr. Stockard showed me his collection of 400 guinea pigs, and when I asked to see the defectives he said, "Oh, we cannot keep them, they all die."

These experiments of Doctor Stockard certainly prove beyond doubt that alcohol taken by the parents causes a poor quality of offspring, and that the injury is handed on even to the third and fourth generation, in guinea pigs at least. There are many things in the history of human families which give one some justification in believing that the horrible effects which Professor Stockard has

GOSHEN COLLEGE LIBRARY

shown experimentally on guinea pigs may also follow in families of drunkards—either man or woman. In fact, the reliable men of science have discovered positively that the children of alcoholized parents are fewer than those who do not touch drink, and those few children are liable to be weak and defective in body and in mind.

A pamphlet printed by the Scientific Temperance Federation, edited by E. L. Transeau and C. F. Stoddard, says among other things: " 'Every ten seconds a baby dies' is an estimate for the whole world. In the United States alone not far from 250,000 babies die each year. Among the causes of this enormous loss of child life is the use of alcohol by parents who do not know or realize the possible results to their little children, as it is only within a few years that the facts of drink have been so carefully studied."

Dr. Sullivan found that 120 drinking mothers of 600 children lost more than half of them before the children were two years of age (55.8 per cent.). When he compared 21 drinking mothers with 28 mothers who were their relatives but were sober and had sober husbands, he found that the sober woman lost less than a quarter of their children.

Dr. Laitinen, in Finland, made inquiries about the deaths of children in 3,611 families which had had 17,394 children. Where the parents were abstainers only 13 per cent. of their children had died.   The parents who were "moderate" drinkers lost 23 per cent., and the heavy drinkers lost 32 per cent.

Aside from the blight of child life by alcohol through heredity, there is an additional peril to babies born into the drinker's home. The parents that drink, often do not have enough money left over after their drink bill has been paid to buy sufficient food to nourish the children properly, or to provide the clothing they need; and the mother who has to go to work to support the family the drunken father neglects, or who stays at home and drinks, does not give the children the proper nursing and adds to the slaughter of the innocents. When parents realize this tremendous fact which science has demonstrated, that if they drink even in moderation their children are liable to be weaklings in body or mind with a shortened life expectancy, they will cut out champagne from the sideboard of wealth and the beer mug from the poor man's cottage. Many are already recognizing this fact and are giving up the personal use of intoxicants in behalf of the generations that are to follow them. Babies have a right to come into this world without such a handicap, and to have a fair chance for life after they have entered it.

Since science has proven the damage drink does to the brain and mental processes, since it has shown what a poison it is to the body, we should expect to find inefficiency in the drinker. This is precisely the fact. In all departments of human endeavor, the one who uses intoxicants even in so-called moderate quantities is reduced in his efficiency and is discounted in his service. The athlete has recognized this damage to the body.

ABSTINENCE IN THE SPORTS

In the realm of sport, where men play games with each other, abstinence is required for efficiency and success. The beer-mug or wine-glass befuddle the mind of the athlete so that he cannot see keenly or act quickly or strongly. American baseball is about as clean a game as there is in the world. The whole nation is deeply interested in it. From Maine to San Francisco the people gather at the bulletin boards and join the fun of the game as each play is recorded over the wire. I know a farmer boy who gets up very early, not to hoe the patch before breakfast, nor even to get his breakfast, but to get the morning paper with the report of the ball game the evening before. I know a missionary in Japan who takes a New York City paper and reads with enthusiasm the baseball news each day, and though nearly a month has elapsed since the time the season has closed and the championship declared, he finishes his perusal of the account with as deep interest as the fans on their benches. One reason why the game is so clean is that it is free from alcohol. The leading baseball clubs of the country are about as good temperance societies as can be found. The greatest baseball players in America in the past as well as the present have been total abstainers from drink. They have been eloquent advocates of temperance by precept as well as by example.

Ty Cobb does not need to be introduced to the American public. He is known by the professor in the college and by the cowboy in the ranch, by the governors of States and by the newsboys and bootblacks on the street corner. Known to them not because he plays ball, but because he is the champion ball player of the country, if not of the world. It was for this reason that I sought an interview with him to get first-off facts with reference to the rule of abstinence from drink in baseball.

TY COBB ON ABSTINENCE

Mr. Cobb had just come in from a long railroad ride and was taking breakfast in his hotel room. The table had plenty of good food upon it, but no bottle.

I said, "Mr. Cobb, your reputation as the champion baseball player in America is not much better known than is your attitude on the drink question. Why do you cut intoxicants out of your bill of fare?"

"Because they do not go at all with baseball," said Ty Cobb. "No man who expects to succeed at the game should ever think of taking strong drink. We are all interested in the question, for if one man lets down in his efficiency we all suffer a handicap. It is a rule among baseball men to let drink alone. I don't believe one in fifty baseball players of any clubs of importance in the country attempts to mix drink with his ball-playing."

"Does your club have a rule on this subject?" I asked.

"No," he said. "The only rule is one of efficiency. The minute a man loses his efficiency even in a small degree, he commences to drop out, and it has been learned unerringly that those who drink do lose their efficiency, drop out of the game, either of their own accord, or are bounced by the management."

Ty Cobb is the peerless batter. When the pitcher throws him the ball, eight of the nine persons of the opposing club set their whole attention upon stopping that ball. More than any other player in the world, Cobb has managed to send that ball into the field where his enemy did not want it and where it would with greatest difficulty be stopped. It would be impossible for him, with a drink of beer in him, to discriminate thus keenly, and secure the marks to his credit as a batter. Cobb is the champion base-stealer.

10315

The deep, downright cunning, with the almost perfect agility and sustaining physical force that gives him his success in the running of bases, would be impossible if he used liquor even in a moderate degree. The hand of sport, that of Ty Cobb and his crowd of baseball players, and that of other athletes is inflicting an incalculable damage upon the liquor traffic.

JESS WILLARD, COLD WATER CHAMPION

Even prize-fighters find that they are stronger and can fight better when they leave liquor alone. I called on Jess Willard, the champion heavy-weight prize-fighter of the world. He looked least like a pugilist. To be sure, he was very tall and very strong in appearance, but he had a fine and you might say a handsome face, which had no finger-marks of the calling in which he was engaged.

"Mr. Willard," I said, "you are known throughout America as a temperance man by your open and avowed statements that drink is an injury to the pugilist and that intoxicants are entirely cut out of your personal program. I noticed in the paper that you said, after your fight with Jack Johnson, that he damaged his chance very greatly in the contest because he used so much liquor, and that you attributed much of your success in it to the fact that liquor did not dull your brain nor weaken your muscle. I consider you a first-class witness as to the damage of alcohol to physical efficiency."

"What you say about my habits and statement is true," Mr. Willard replied, "but I refer you on the subject to my partner, Tom Jones, who will give you for me whatever information you want."

Tom Jones said: "If Jess Willard had his way, there would not be a drop of liquor made or sold in America. He says it does no good to any one and least of all to the pugilist. He does not condemn or even criticise people who use liquor or sell it, but he is particular himself in his own personal habits. He cares nothing at all for any of the temptations of the Great White Way. You will not find him drinking in carousing places at night. He keeps splendid hours. After the fight next week he will not take a glass of drink nor join in any convivial celebration of any kind with friends, but will simply take the train the very same night and go home to his wife and family in Chicago. He is an ideal family man, as he is an example of temperance."

Willard paid this tribute to cold water: "The old aqua has a great booster in me, for it has more reviving power, as far as I can figure, than all the other beverages put together. Water inside and water outside is a combination that stands without an equal."

James J. Corbett, a pugilist himself, in a minute description of Willard after one of his fights, names his abstinence from drink as one of his strongest points.

It is claimed that Jess Willard has laid away between four and five hundred thousand dollars in cold cash in the last few years. Does anyone imagine that if he had used liquor, as some pugilists have done, he would have four or five hundred cents left over now, even if he could have secured the championship?

Herbert Kaufman has thus described a pugilistic champion who, having mastered others in the ring, was conquered by rum: "He lurched into Jack's at midnight, stumbled along the lane of crowded tables and sprawled into a seat—a sodden, glassy-eyed, pulpy parody of the superb creature whose clean fists once held a championship. Then he was without a peer—invincible. Man after man, the shrewdest pugilists of America vainly contested with him for the title. The pride of England's rings and the best talent of Australia fell before his incomparable science. His was the keen vital strength that surges from uncontaminated sources. In a day of brawling brutes he stood apart, a class unto himself. Then suddenly he rotted at the core. In old John Barleycorn he met his master. What no arena ever saw, the pot-house and the sample room soon beheld—'the best of 'em all' reeling and rocking in defeat.   It's a sure bet when the battler meets the bottler."

Boxing within limits is a manly sport. I never saw a prize fight. I never failed to condemn it as demoralizing, and yet I could not ask any stronger testimony to the value of abstinence to bodily strength than that of Willard, the pugilist. Jess Willard has knocked John Barleycorn down in the ring and has thrown him over the ropes.

In the basal realm of temporal support, in callings to make a living, liquor is such a disturbance and hindrance and damage that the business world protests against it.

CHAPTER III

ALCOHOL AND LITERATURE

FROM the earliest times the literature of all nations has been full of praises of the joy and blessing of wine. The student of ancient classics finds constant references to them in the plays written, the songs sung and the amusements enjoyed. The bacchanalian revels were counted only as an abuse of a custom mentally valuable, and they were often apologized for rather than condemned.

OLIVER GOLDSMITH

English literature took for granted as true the mistaken verdict of science that alcohol is not only friendly, but necessary, to the highest mental exercise. This thought is thus expressed by Oliver Goldsmith in "She Stoops to Conquer":

> "Let schoolmasters puzzle their brains
> With grammar and nonsense and learning,
> Good liquor, I stoutly maintain,
> Gives genius a better discerning."

Certainly that is the idea he had when, as the son of a poor Irish preacher, he entered Trinity

55

College in Dublin at seventeen. His genius won him a prize of six dollars, and to "give it a better discerning" he spent it in buying some "good liquor" and giving a supper and dance in his college room and causing such a hilarious time that his tutor rushed into the room, gave him a good thrashing and kicked his guests out of doors. Disgraced, the student resolved to leave college and had to sell his books and some clothes for money to get out of town. He loafed around Dublin with convivial companions till all of his money was gone except enough to take him to Cork. He managed to get back into college again and gained his degree of Bachelor of Arts a year or so after the regular time. Oliver, the young graduate of twenty-one, the son of an Irish minister and brother of a curate, decided to enter the ministry. He began his two years of probation. He read everything else but theology and made himself conspicuous among the drinking revelers at the "little inn of Ballymahon." When he came up for ordination he was rejected, the good liquor having failed to give his genius the kind of discernment required.

He tutored a year in a private family and saved one hundred and fifty dollars and a horse on which he rode to Cork. There he sold his horse and booked a passage for America. He squandered his money in his debauches, and while he was in a carousal with gay companions at a country inn, the ship on which he had engaged to sail went off without him. With the thirteen dollars he had left he bought a little pony and rode to the home of his mother, where he was welcomed as a returned prodigal. His uncle, who had great faith in his ability, and who loved him, set him on his feet again with a gift of two hundred and fifty dollars and started him off to London to study law. He got as far as Dublin, when drink tempted him to stop off there and have one last farewell "rounder" with his old companions. They drank up every penny of his money and left him stranded again. Some friends put up money and sent him to the Medical Department of the Edinburgh University, where he studied two years, still clinging to his convivial habits and companions. He went to Paris to perfect his medical studies and was reduced to such a financial strait that he drifted out on the road, a traveling minstrel, with his flute and songs among the peasantry for a support. He found himself in London little better than a tramp, glad at times to lodge among the "beggars of Ax Lane," as he says, "without friends, recommendations, money or influence." And he was now twenty-eight years of age.

He drifted into the field of literature, for which his genius had so eminently fitted him. He wrote for the magazines. His first important production, "An Inquiry into the State of Polite Literature," caught the eye of Samuel Johnson, the king among men of letters. Goldsmith continued his drinking habits, and was in dire distress of poverty. Knowing Johnson's estimate of him, he wrote a note to him, frankly stating his condition and begging him to hasten to his rescue. Johnson sent him a guinea, and followed it soon with a visit to his cheap quarters. He found Goldsmith quarreling with his landlady because she had had him arrested for the non-payment of rent. He had not given the woman a penny of the guinea sent, but he had spent a part of it for wine, a bottle of which was standing on the table. Johnson calmed the woman, told her she would get her money, and talked very plainly to the young author. Goldsmith came to himself, determined to abandon his convivial habits, and get down seriously to the work of life. Johnson's splendid character, strong will and sympathy (for he himself had a hard scuffle with poverty in his early history) were prevailing influences to better things in the young poet's history. He wrote the "Vicar of Wakefield," for which he got three hundred dollars, with which he cleaned up his debts. Afterwards he wrote "The Traveler," whose serene beauty, easy grace, sound good sense, magic numbers and occasional elevation captivated critics and publishers and secured for him a place in the permanent literature of the world, for which manuscript he received the pitiful sum of one hundred dollars. He wrote other splendid books, died at the early age of forty-six, and a monument was placed for him in Westminster Abbey.

Goldsmith gave up his convivial habits when he came to responsibility and fame, but he, like the rest in those days, the best of them, continued what would be called the moderate but constant use of intoxicants.

What did alcohol do for Goldsmith? It did not destroy him, but it grievously injured him. To be sure, he was of a wandering disposition, and was shiftless in his habits. But what else would a young man be but wandering and thriftless who did little else but drink liquor to excess up to the time he was a man thirty years of age? It was a miracle he came to himself, instead of going to the graveyard, whither he was tending. If he had let drink alone he might have come to himself at twenty-one, splendidly equipped, and taken his rightful place as a prince in the world of letters, instead of staggering from teaching to theology, to law, to medicine, as a drunken man, a mockery to his genius and a parody on a human life, and he would have sung songs as sweet or sweeter, and would probably have sung them twenty or thirty years longer, holding the lyre at sixty or seventy instead of laying it down at forty-six. For the many years of hard drinking had left their scars on the vital organs of the body as distinctly as the marks the smallpox left in his face when he was a boy, and cut short a life of glory and usefulness just fairly begun.

These words are not intended as a harsh criticism of Goldsmith's weakness; they are written with the highest appreciation of the admirable qualities he possessed as a man and poet, and of our gratitude to him for the sweet songs that have delighted and benefited our better mental life. They are written as a protest against the universal belief of his time that drink was an aid to the highest mental exercise, an inspiration to genius, and especially to the poet. We do not apologize for Goldsmith. The times were as much to blame as he. They were thoroughly alcoholized, and the literary era to which he belonged was saturated with wine. These words are meant as a flat denial to the claims of the brewers and distillers in the pamphlets sown broadcast among our people, our young men, that the great thinkers of the world have been so because they have used intoxicants, and that the Anglo-Saxon race is the most brilliant because it consumes the largest amount of alcohol. These great men, these Anglo-Saxons have been and are great in mental ability in spite of alcohol, not on account of it; and the most brilliant men mentally among all civilized nations today are coming to this conclusion and are not only letting drink alone themselves but doing what they can to expel it from their communities and countries.

In the light of modern science that reveals the damage of alcohol to the brain cells, in the light of modern psychology which demonstrates the injury of drink to mental processes, in the presence of a life so harmed by alcohol, how pitiful do the words of Goldsmith sound:

> "Good liquor, I stoutly maintain,
> Gives genius a better discerning."

ROBERT BURNS

Burns is another poet to whom the apologists for drink point as an example of the advantage of intoxicating stimulants to genius, of the wings that wine gives to the imagination. They quote words of Burns in their favor, among them these:

> "John Barleycorn was a hero bold,
> Of noble enterprise,
> For if you do but taste his blood,
> 'Twill make your courage rise.
> 'Twill make a man forget his woe,
> 'Twill heighten all his joy."

The liquor dealers of today seem to take pride in holding up Burns as the champion of their cause, as an example of the brilliancy of intellectual genius inspired by their wares. But Burns's history refutes their contention and furnishes one of the most powerful arguments against their claim. The study of that history, written by the most friendly biographers, furnishes the

most positive testimony to the damage drink did
to the poet at the beginning of his career, and of
the complete wreckage it caused at its close. His
nation was one of the most intellectual in the
world, not on account of alcohol, as the liquor
men maintain, but in spite of it. At the time
Burns came to his majority everything, from the
pastor's study to the disgraceful hovel, smelled of
Scotch whisky or some other stimulant, and young
Robert drank, of course, as they all did. And
when he felt the symptoms of his poetic genius
arising in his soul he continued to drink, as all
poets were expected to do, to inspire his imagination, warm his affections, and add charms to his
conversation in the highest circles of society. One
of his earliest poems was written while he was
drunk. He did not publish it in the first edition
of his poems, but he did in the second. He was
so brutally frank with himself and with others,
and the times were so whisky-soaked, that he made
no concealment of the fact that he composed
"Death and Doctor Hornbook" while drunk, and
the true story at the bottom of it was verified by
his companions at the time. The genius of the
man was so great that the poem he wrote while
drunk is better than the verses most sober men
can make. This is the occasion of the poem:
John Wilson, a school teacher at Tarbolton, not
far from the farm on which Burns lived with his
father, had a smattering knowledge of medicine,

got an office, a few bottles and drugs, and entered upon the practice of medicine. He was a member of a literary club to which Burns belonged. One night Doctor Wilson and the young poet got into a spirited debate over a question of medicine, in which Burns became offended. From the club Burns went to the Freemason's lodge which he loved so dearly, and which was so proud of him, and after the meeting was over he started late to his home in the country. He says in the poem he was "not full," but that he "had a plenty," and that on his way home he took more than a plenty, and was only able to get as far as the bridge. Seating himself on the stone abutment with a good support for his back, he dosed in a drunken stupor. On his way to the bridge he had seen a man lying in the road dead drunk, but he was so near that condition himself that he could not help the man. Seated on the stones of the bridge, overcome by booze, the sight of the drunken man in the road reminded him of death, and the deep insult of the evening reminded him of Doctor Wilson, whom he called Hornbook, and so he composed a poem of a number of stanzas on "Death and Doctor Hornbook." He fell fast asleep and did not know anything till the clang of the church bell awoke him, and he found the early morning sun shining on his face. He remembered the stanzas he had composed in his drunken delirium and wrote them down as we have them today.

Death complained bitterly that Doctor Hornbook was encroaching on his territory; that while he had a scythe and dart and slew many, the doctor killed more with his medicine; and he gave as instances the case of the weaver's wife who had "ill bred nerves" and called in Doctor Hornbook to quiet her. He did. He gave her something to put her to sleep and she never awoke. And also the case of the innkeeper's daughter who got tipsy on beer and called in the doctor to hide her disgrace, which he did by sending her to her long home, etc. Of the poem Wordsworth says:

"When Burns wrote his story of 'Death and Doctor Hornbook' he had very rarely been intoxicated, or perhaps much exilarated by liquor. Yet how happily does he lead his reader into that track of sensations, and with what lively humor does he describe the disorder of his senses and the confusion of his understanding, put to the test by his deliberate attempt to count the horns of the moon:

> " 'But whether she had three or four
> He couldna tell.'

"Behold a sudden apparition which disperses this disorder, and in a moment chills him into the possession of himself. Coming upon no more important mission than the grisly phantom was charged with, what mode of introduction could have been more efficient or appropriate?"

An evidence of the public sentiment of the times on the subject of the drinking habit can be seen in the fact that so serious, so deeply a religious man as Wordsworth has no word of criticism of the conviviality of the young genius, only words of commendation at the cleverness with which he performed the intellectual feat when drunk. Though Burns advertised his indiscretion unduly in the poem in the beginning of his literary career, Wordsworth was right in the statement that this drunk at the bridge was an exception, and that he was usually a man of temperate habits.

The very year he produced "Death and Doctor Hornbook" he wrote "The Epistle to Davie," "The Twa Herds," "The Jolly Beggars," "Hallow E'en," "The Cotter's Saturday Night," "Holy Willie's Prayer," "The Holy Fair" and "The Address to a Mouse." This year's work, if he had never written another line, would have given him immortality. The next year produced a harvest for his pen. All his poems were printed in a volume in 1786, which gave the author instant and universal fame in Scotland and throughout the world. The finest drawing-rooms of Edinburgh and other cities were opened wide to this brilliant plowboy poet. He got one hundred dollars out of his first book, but he republished it the next year and realized twenty-five hundred dollars from it. The next year appeared in Scott's

Musical Museum, published by Johnson, one hundred and forty of the shortest and best things Burns wrote. They were bewitchingly beautiful and tender songs, many of them adapted to old Scotch airs, nothing in any language sweeter than they.

But the heart of the singer grew suddenly sick and his songs became few and feeble. Drink had done its cruel work with him in four short years and dealt him the fatal stab. In four years from the time that he, as a young man of twenty-six, surprised the world with his first stanzas and became the acknowledged chief of Scottish poets, he stood, a poor wreck, broken in spirit and health, with no money and few friends, measuring casks of liquor at a few hundred dollars a year.

Of his position in the excise department he was not proud, and generally referred to it with an apology, and often with bitterness. Of it he writes: "I am a miserable buried devil, and for private reasons am forced, like Milton's Satan, 'To do what yet, though damned, I would abhor.'" To Mrs. Riddell he says, "Sunday closes a period of our curst revenue business, and may probably keep me employed with my pen till noon —fine employment for a poet's pen! There is a species of the human genus that I call the gin-horse class: what amiable dogs they are! round and round and round they go. Mundell's ox that turns his cotton mill is their exact prototype—

without an idea or wish beyond their circle, fat, sleek, stupid, patient, quiet and contented; while here I sit, altogether Novemberish, a mélange of fretfulness and melancholy, not enough of the one to rouse me to passion, nor of the other to repose me in torpor; my soul floundering and fluttering round her tenement like a wild finch caught amid the horrors of winter and newly thrust into a cage. Well, I am persuaded it was of me the Hebrew sage prophesied when he foretold: 'And behold, on whatsoever this man doth set his heart, it shall not prosper.' "

While gauger he tried hard to get the position of a supervisor, so that he might be eligible to the office of collector of revenue at a good salary and abundant leisure for literary work, and made an earnest plea to Patrick Heron, whom he had aided in the election campaign with his pen, but failed in his ambition. To think that the man who only five years before had been the most talked of and best-beloved man in Scotland, with all the help of influential friends he could summon, could not get the supervisorship of the town of Dumfries! Was there ever so great a fall in so short a space of time? The Scotch drink to whose laudation he devotes a whole poem, is directly responsible for his fall. Was Bacchus ever so delighted as when he took the most brilliant intellect of Scotland and set him as his slave to the task of poking a measurer into a cask to find out how much liquor it contained, and held him to it at a starvation wage and would not let him up?

The drinking habit and the social irregularities that so often go with it and grow out of it put Burns into the gauger's office as the last ditch. His drinking while in the excise department was so excessive that some of his best friends remonstrated with him, among them Mrs. Dunlop. The reply of the poet was "occasional hard drinking is the devil to me. Against this I have again and again bent my resolution, and have greatly succeeded. Taverns I have totally abandoned. It is the private parties in the family way, among the hard-drinking gentlemen of this country, that do me the mischief, but even this I have more than half given over."

Burns makes this apology to Mrs. Riddell after a social bout at a dinner she gave at her house. "I write you from the regions of hell, amid the horrors of the damned. Here am I laid on a bed of pitiless furze, while an infernal tormentor, wrinkled and cruel, called 'Recollection,' with a whip of scorpions, forbids peace or rest to approach me, and keeps anguish eternally awake. I wish I could be reinstated in the good opinion of the fair circle whom my conduct last night so much offended. To the men of the company I will make no apology. Your husband, who insisted on my drinking more than I chose, has no right to blame me, and the other gentlemen were partakers of my guilt."

To his gentlemen friends who undertook to admonish him on the rapidity with which he was wrecking himself by his convivial habits, the poet was not so polite or patient as he was to the women who had spoken to him. When William Nichol undertook to give him advice as to the damage that drink was doing him, Burns answered him with one of the most cutting satires in any language, showing up the weakness of his accuser. And when John Syme was entertaining him one afternoon at his home at Ryedale, and the wine flowed freely and the poet got singularly gracious and confidential, the host criticised the conduct of his guest. The criticism was resented instantly. Syme said: "I might have spoken daggers, but I did not mean them. Burns shook to the inmost fibre of his frame, and drew his sword cane, when I exclaimed, 'What, wilt thou thus, and in mine own house?' The poor fellow was so stung with remorse that he dashed himself down on the floor."

Sir Walter Scott, in referring to this incident, says, "It is a dreadful truth that when racked and tortured by the well-meant and warm expostulations of an intimate friend Burns started up, in a paroxysm of frenzy, and drawing a sword cane which he usually wore, made an attempt to plunge it into the body of his adviser;—the next instant he was with difficulty withheld from suicide."

Burns went to a shop and bought a pair of revolvers to avenge some imagined injury done to him, remarking that they were unlike some men whom he knew in that they "reflected the honor of their maker." Thus, perhaps the most brilliant intellectual genius of the world at the time, in those spells of intoxication, was made a madman, a demon, through rum.

Without money in his pocket and with little food in the house Burns wrote to Thompson: "After all my boasted independence, curst necessity compels me to implore you for five pounds. A cruel haberdasher, to whom I owe an account, taking it into his head that I am dying, has commenced a process and will infallibly put me in jail. Do, for God's sake, send me that sum, and that by return of post. Forgive me this earnestness, but the horrors of a jail have made me half distracted."

"Poor Bobbie," not more to be blamed than the alcoholized times that made him a victim; not more than the science that taught falsely, the literature that was mistaken, and the social customs which were counted proper, yet were so demoralizing! The lords that wined and dined him, and the ladies that offered him the social glass to sharpen his wit or promote good fellowship, had much to do with his downfall. And after they had thrown him down, many of them closed their drawingrooms and their friendship to him. Alcohol poisoned him, mind and body, depressed his spirit and racked his body with pain, and allowed him only four years of melody with his lyre when he should have had ten times as long a period for his song. Alcohol disintegrated his brain cells, dulled his imagination, corrupted his affections, weakened his will, tore down his body and sent him to the grave in poverty and distress at thirty-seven, when, with a temperate life, free from rum and the social irregularities that so often go with it and grow out of it, he might have lived to be seventy and blessed the world thirty-three years longer with his immortal songs.

I have dwelt upon the dark, the drink side of Burns's life with deep pain, for I have the highest appreciation of and warmest affection for his poems. I have wanted to cry rather than blame all the while, seeing how cruelly wine had deceived and mocked and slain him. My mother sang the songs of Burns to me when I was a little boy in our home on the farm. How sweet! oh, how sweet they sounded to me then! Sweet, oh, how sweet is their echo in my soul today! I can not get them out of my heart, nor would I for the world. To me his was one of the sweetest lyres ever swept by human fingers. His voice, his song, came by wireless across the sea to charm me when a boy, and to bless me now a man.

This poor Scotch gardener, with scanty wages, living in a poor man's house, struggling against all kinds of misfortune and weakness, with genius enough to be the poet laureate of the realm, but hired by the government to a menial task at a few pounds a year, was the one who discovered the richest truth in the most unlikely places, the purest gold in the roughest rocks, the costliest pearls in the homeliest shells. He found the splendors of a palace under the roof of straw, the beauties of Paradise amidst the humblest earthly scenes, the divinest instincts in the breast of the lowliest and most forgotten. He had a heart of sympathy for everything God has made, even the little mice in the nest upturned by the plow, and poured the wealth of his affection without stint upon the hearts of his fellow men. What a pity that this sweet singer, this prince of poets, should have had a will so weak and appetites so strong, and that his rising sun which promised such a glorious day should have gone down at noon! Some of his acts and verses we condemn. The hand of charity scatters leaves of poppy over them that they may sleep in the grave of oblivion where they belong; but many of his poems are so embalmed with sweet sentiments and principles that they will live as long as the English language is spoken. At times his imperial spirit would soar to the loftiest heights of truth and love and life, as in these lines from his "Cotter's Saturday Night":

"Then kneeling down, to Heaven's Eternal King
The saint, the father, and the husband prays;
Hope springs exulting on triumphant wing,
That thus they all shall meet in future days;
There ever bask in uncreated rays,
No more to sigh, or shed the bitter tear,
Together hymning their Creator's praise
In such society, yet still more dear,
While circling time moves round in an eternal sphere."

THE AMERICAN POETS

With the rarest exception, American literature
has been free from alcohol. Its fumes have not
appeared in the lines written or in the personal
life of their authors. In the literary history of
nations men of genius have often been so reckless
in their morals that the world half looked for
social weakness where the poetic instinct was discovered. The singers who have made American
poetry what it is have shown that temperance,
social purity and religious vigor are most becoming to the poet.

We have had great poets in this country, of
whom we are justly proud, but it seems to us that
no one great enough has yet appeared to fittingly
express the greatness of our marvelously great
nation. In America, where the blood is the best
because it is the best blood of the world mixed
here; where genius flames out into discoveries of
science and practical art such as the world has

never known, where the desert as by magic has been made to blossom as the rose; where gigantic enterprises have been promoted and wealth accumulated the like of which has never been seen since the world began; where the schools and colleges are prospering on so large a scale; where mighty moral reforms have been effected and the church has been so triumphant, it would be thought that some poet would appear large enough to incarnate and fittingly sing of these majestic things. But no poet has appeared high as our Rockies, broad as our prairies, fertile as our fields, rich as our mines, colossal as our industrial enterprise, rugged as our reforms, sweet as the nation's home life, beautiful as its spirit life.

About all the American poetry worth considering has been produced in the past hundred years. It was two hundred years after the landing at Plymouth before a single American poet worthy of the name appeared. In this New World, with its beautiful gardens and fruitful fields, its magnificent mountains, sequestered vales, and widespreading prairies, its majestic rivers and mighty seas, with its sweet home life, the divinest ideal of liberty, and the firm faith in the Everlasting, there was not a son born with enough genius fittingly to sing of its beauty and glory. There were statesmen and generals and orators, and one or two prose writers, whose fame belongs to the centuries, but there was not a single poet. Then there came upon the stage a group of men almost simultaneously who created and immortalized American poetry. Among them were Bryant, Emerson, Longfellow, Whittier, Holmes and Lowell. These men were all singularly clean in their social habits and free from alcohol.

Longfellow thus voices the anti-alcohol sentiment of American poetry:

"Now to rivulets from the mountains
  Point the rods of fortune-tellers:
Youth perpetual dwells in fountains,
  Not in flasks and casks and cellars."

These bards did not reflect the sentiment of their times, which was almost universally in favor of the use of liquor. The sideboard with its decanter and glasses was considered a necessary article of furniture in the home of luxury or even of respectability, and the little brown jug could be found nearly everywhere in the home of the artisan as a promoter of happiness and industrial efficiency; political life and drinking were associated with each other as a matter of course. Some of the greatest statesmen and orators of the nation drank heavily, sometimes to drunkenness, and little was thought of it except maybe to laugh at the silly things such wise men would say or do, or pity them that they should use to excess a thing which in moderation was so good for them. The capital of the nation itself was a colossal bar, where the representatives of the people could the more conveniently drink and get happy and even drunk in their revels, a disgrace to them and to their constituencies. Drink was sold at many of the stores with as little hesitation or compunction as flour, sugar, coffee, or any other article of food. And yet at this time, when about every department of American life was saturated with alcohol, our poetry, which in the opinion of the centuries should be allowed the largest liberty in the use of stimulants, and would be expected to furnish exhibitions of the most excessive revelries, was sober. There were no spells of clownishness, no breaking of social law as the privilege of the highest genius, no sprees nor wreckages of body or mind, with financial bankruptcy and untimely death. The founders of American poetry mentioned were prudent, dignified, honored by the whole nation. They were good men, with lovely families, great men, professors at universities, examples to young men, men of sterling character, loyal to God and their fellows; and with cleanliness and supreme self-mastery that all lived to be old men, to sing during the many beautiful years their sweetest songs to charm, and wholesome sentiments to bless the hearts of their fellows for a long generation or more. Whittier particularly, who exerted a larger temperance influence upon our national life than any other poet, was a total abstainer from strong drink. He never tasted liquor in his life, and in his robust style by precept as well as by example he maintained and promoted the principle of abstinence. This principle is notably expressed in his poem on the celebration of St. Crispin's Day, in which he has the courage to propose the health of the shoemakers in a glass of water instead of wine:

> "Then let the toast be freely quaffed
> In water cool and brimming."

EDGAR ALLAN POE

We omitted one name from the group which founded and immortalized American poetry, that of Edgar Allan Poe, who was contemporary with the poets mentioned. He was in a class by himself in temperament, life and song. He was, perhaps, the greatest native poetic genius of all the group, and one of the greatest any nation ever had. The imagination, the creative faculty, the one that pictures and rhymes and sings, he possessed in so large a degree that there was no limit to the heights to which he soared when he felt most free. In keen, clear, intense lyrical quality his best songs have seldom been surpassed. His two volumes of short tales were up to the highest literary standard, and have furnished and have been taken as models for the story-writers of France for the past sixty years.

Poe was the only one of the great American

poets who toyed with intoxicants and was ruined by them. The smoke of the distillery and brewery settled down as a cloud upon him, and many of the things he wrote in poetry and prose were darkened with misery and hopeless gloom, prophecies of the tragedy to follow. Did not his habit steadily, almost insensibly at first, but surely, build about him a cage against which he wounded the wings of his great soul, and against the bars of which he threshed out his precious life?

One of the best literary authorities has this to say of the effect of Poe's drinking habits upon his professional career. "His brilliant and well-known ability readily procured him employment, and his frantic habits of dissipation, with the regularity of a natural law, insured his early and ignominious dismissal."

In 1835 Poe was made editor of the Literary Messenger, in Richmond, with the promise of a good income and opportunity to redeem his name from the youthful follies and sins that had disgraced it, but his habit was so strong and will so weak that he went on frequent sprees, for which the owner of the paper discharged him. He wrote a letter with a pitiful plea for reinstatement, and the publisher sent back this reply: "That you are sincere in all your promises I firmly believe, but when once again you tread these streets, I have my fears that your resolution will fail and that you will drink again till your senses are lost.

If you rely on your own strength, you are gone. Unless you look to your Maker for help you will not be safe. How much I regretted parting from you is known to Him only and to myself. I had become attached to you. I am still. I would willingly say return, did not a knowledge of your past life make me dread a speedy renewal of our separation. You have fine talents, Edgar, and you ought to have them respected as well as yourself. Separate yourself from the bottle and from bottle companions forever."

But he did not take the advice of this good man, did not give up the bottle nor bottle companions; he did not lean on God for help, but floundered, the mighty genius that he was, in the mire, a slave of evil habit. A biographer says he became so besotted that he sold the memoir of his beautiful wife whom he loved devotedly to get money to buy rum to drown his sorrow.

In 1859, realizing what a fearful wreck he was, and knowing that he would soon fill a drunkard's grave if he did not reform, he did what he had so often done before, resolved to quit drinking; and to help his resolution he joined a temperance society and took a pledge of total abstinence, which he kept for six months, to the joy of his friends and himself. Sobered up as he was, with a new start for life, he became engaged to marry a wealthy widow of Richmond, Virginia, whom he had loved in his youth. He went to Baltimore to make some preparations for his wedding, and there met some of his old convivial friends, who carried him away on a carousal which left him dead drunk in the gutter, from which he was carried to the Marine Hospital of that city. Awakening out of his drunken stupor, he opened his eyes widely and said, "Where am I?" The physician replied, "You are cared for by your best friends." With a look of insufferable weariness and inexpressible agony he answered, "My best friend would be the man who would blow out my brains." In four days after, on Sunday, October 7, 1859, he died.

Edgar Allan Poe died at forty years of age, with a life only fairly begun! What a sad commentary on the alcoholized times that were as much to blame as he for his ruin! If the trend of his environment could have been toward temperance and piety, and his will could have had better help to withstand the temptations of appetite, it is possible he would have lived to threescore years and ten, as all of his contemporary poets did, and sung sweet and marvelous songs all that time to bless his fellows in our own land and throughout the world.

What a glorious group of veterans his contemporaries were! Lowell lived to be seventy-three; Longfellow to be seventy-five; Bryant to be eighty-four; Whittier and Holmes each to be eighty-five.

It is mere speculation, and yet it is possible that Poe was made by nature to be the great American ideal poet, matching and expressing the magnificences everywhere else, and that the drink habit hindered and dwarfed him, cut his life short. If with his creative genius he could have had the abstinence of a Whittier and the religion of a Longfellow, whom he so mercilessly lashed in his criticisms, he might have measured up to the demands of so mighty a nation and been crowned as its poet laureate. Since Poe, under his fearful handicaps of drink and brief life of misery, could secure such a permanent place in literature, to what an eminence might he have been elevated, on what a throne of power might he have been seated, and what a scepter of authority might he have wielded, had he been free from those handicaps, free to soar and sing through a generation and generations to come?

The poet for whom the great America has looked has not appeared. God will send him in his own good time. In poetic genius, righteousness, truth, love and faith a giant like those of classic story, whose feet were on the earth and whose head was among the stars, and yet a charming minstrel, whose lyre will be sweet enough and strong enough to be heard by the millions of all nations and by the centuries to come.

CHAPTER IV

ALCOHOL AND CAPITAL

A THING so bad for the individual as rum is bad for society. Individuals injured by drink make a damaged community. And the people who do not use intoxicants are greatly pestered and distressed by those who do. Hence it is natural that society should resist and fight this enemy.

Society is putting up a fierce fight against booze on account of the inefficiency that it causes in every department of industry.

Nearly all the biggest forms of industry in this country discourage, if they do not forbid, the use of intoxicants by their employees.

The railroads of the United States forbid their men to take liquor. Many years ago a rule was made in reference to their men drinking or entering a saloon, which has been well kept by most of the railway lines, and has become more and more strict each year. It seems that the men themselves do not consider this prohibition a hardship, but as a rule recognize that it is for the mutual good of the men and of the roads. They recognize that the perils even to sober men are very great, and know that those perils are largely increased when liquor is in evidence.

RAILROAD RULE "G"

I called on Mr. Hardin, first vice-president of the New York Central Railroad, for details as to the rule forbidding drink among the men. He handed me a pamphlet and said: "Here it is, Rule G, which is that the use of intoxicants by employees while on duty is prohibited. Their use or the frequenting of places where they are sold is sufficient cause for dismissal."

I asked Mr. Hardin whether this is a contract with the men or a rule of the road. He said:

It was a rule agreed upon by the railroads of the country many years ago, at the time when railroad men were rougher than they are now, and at a time when most people drank. The rule is kept, and the most hopeful thing is that the men themselves do much to enforce it. About all of the men holding positions of responsibility keep this rule. The various labor organizations also help to enforce it. If, for instance, an engineer should be found taking a drink, a representative of the organization would come to him and say: 'You must stop; this will not do. If you have liquor in you, you may run into my train and kill me and kill yourself.' Scarcely a man holding any responsible position of importance on any of the great railroads of the country can be coaxed to take a drink of intoxicants. The railroad men are a fine set of men. When you come down to the man on the track with his shovel and pick, we cannot enforce our rule so strictly, though we wish to discourage drink in the home of the humblest laborer. With reference to abstinence of men charged with responsibility I know whereof I speak. I have 400 secret service men, many of them unknown to the other men themselves, to report to me in detail the habits of the men. If a man were found drinking anywhere on our lines, we would hear about it within a week. There was a trial of a railroad case the other day, involving the carelessness or fault of an engineer, and the lawyer of one side slurred the railroad men as being tough and addicted to drink. The opposing lawyer with feeling denied the charge, and defied any one to show an engineer on the whole line of the road who used intoxicants at all, and that if one could be found drinking he would be instantly discharged. This trial was with reference to a road other than our own, but it illustrates the fact as to the total abstinence of men charged with the gravest responsibility in the railroad industry.

I had interviews with a number of leading locomotive engineers, firemen, conductors and trainmen on the subject and found not only unanimity of opinion on the subject, but real enthusiasm in their friendliness to Rule G, calling for prohibition. They said that when they took the lives of the people in their hands they felt the gravity of the responsibility—that it would be a crime, even the highest crime of murder, to take intoxicants that would dull their senses or their intellectual faculties and cause fatal accidents. One of them called my attention to the fact that on a leading railroad which stood well up toward the head of the column in the few accidents that had occurred annually, a man running an engine called at a saloon before daylight on his way to his cab and became stupid with drink. After the train left the station he let his engine run wild and crashed into the train in front of him, killing fifty people and occasioning a large number of damage suits. This is an illustration of the terrible crime of a railroad man who is charged with great responsibility having anything whatever to do with drink.

Mr. Stone, the president of the Locomotive Railroad Engineers of the country, has said and written some of the sanest and soundest things on the damage of drink to the railroad man and to the working man in any department of industry that we have seen in American temperance literature.

Leaving Mr. Hardin's office, I found a bar down stairs. That costly, magnificent building had become prostituted to the low task of housing a saloon. I thought that Rule G, forbidding any of the men to drink and a saloon in the station, tempting the men to intoxicants and debauching the public, were contradictions. I felt that the lowest down Bowery joint was as respectable in the eyes of a good conscience and of God as this bar in the Grand Central Station.

The directors who are responsible for the installation of this iniquitous place are saloon-keepers and hypocrites. No matter what important pews they may occupy on the Sabbath in the sanctuary, or how conspicuous they may be in their leadership of the church, no matter how prominent they may be on the boards of educational or benevolent institutions; no matter how conspicuous as leaders they may be in business or the social world, no matter how much they may cry out against the "low groggery" and demand national Prohibition, they are saloonkeepers themselves.

Standing in the bar-room of the Grand Central Station, in imagination, I strapped the white apron of a bartender on each one of these millionaire directors and put the black stamp of "hypocrite" on his forehead. I do not forget that these same directors founded one of the finest Railroad Young Men's Christian Associations in America, a few blocks up the avenue. I have personally enjoyed its hospitality, and feel that the public owes a debt of gratitude to these officers that it can never repay. And yet that magnificent Y. M. C. A. to save the young men does not justify the saloon in the station in destroying them, but makes it more improper and hypocritical. It was the love for the damnable dollar that opened the bar in the Grand Central Station, the same vice that built every brewery and distillery, and opened every saloon in the country.

There are other railroads besides the New York Central which have bars in their stations, and they are included in these words of condemnation.

Deep as the hypocrisy of the station saloon is that of the dining-car where intoxicating liquors are sold. Such a dining-car is a saloon on wheels, and gives the lie to Rule G. The engineer, the fireman, the conductor, the brakeman, the baggageman, the peanut-vender, are all forbidden to touch a drop of liquor, and yet a saloon car is put on the train and the dining-car conductor, in the service of beer, whisky, and wine, is the officially authorized barkeeper. And the charge is made that some diners serve drinks going through dry States and districts in defiance of the law, and in so doing become bootleggers of the lowest and most contemptible sort. The negro in the dry village down in the canebrake, with the razor, and with bottles of illicit liquor in his bootlegs, is just as honorable as those responsible for the blind-tiger dining-car. Fortunately the conscience and decency of the directors of many of the railroads have taken the drinks off the dining-car bill of fare, and our words of criticism of course do not refer to them.

There is no more reason why there should be a Rule G for the employees than for the officers of the road, from the directors and president down. The same sagacity, wisdom, level-headed-ness, freedom from alcohol and strength is required of the officers who plan, as is demanded of the men who execute those plans. Fortunately, a large proportion of the officers of the roads are strict temperance men, many of them total abstainers, who keep the rule they require of the men.

STEEL MANUFACTURERS

The steel manufacturers are dealing the liquor business a staggering blow in their opposition to drink among their men. It is a cold question of economy. It used to be thought by both manufacturers and men that drink was necessary to those who were among the furnaces. At the close of each heat, the men laid off a little time to go to the nearest saloon for refreshment. This false notion has been reversed by both the proprietors and workmen.

This placard is posted all over the works of the Illinois Steel Company at Joliet: "To the employees of the Joliet Works, Illinois Steel Company: For the promotion of safety and welfare it is hoped that all employees will avoid the use of intoxicating liquors. Under the rules of the Joliet Works, any employee who uses intoxicating liquor while on duty will be discharged. In making promotions in any department of the plant, superintendents of departments and foremen will select for promotion only those who do not use intoxicating liquors."

Any one entering the great works of the United States Steel Corporation at Gary, Indiana, at night, will see huge electric lights blazing out these questions: "Did booze ever do you any good?" "Did booze ever get you a better job?" "Did booze ever contribute anything to the happiness of your family?"

In regard to abstinence at the mill at Coatesville, Pennsylvania, Mr. Charles L. Huston sent me the following:

When I first took hold as superintendent of the works some twenty-five years ago, I decided after careful consideration that I could not be satisfied to give any countenance to drinking on the part of the men. So I began to deal with them in a kindly, forceful way when I found out they were in the habit of indulging even when away from their work, and, of course, could not permit anything like drinking or evidence of intoxication while at work. I was a little fearful lest it might result in a shortage of capable men, but found just the reverse, as we never had to hunt for men or advertise for them. We have always found a sufficient number of applicants, good, respectable men, who were glad to work in a place where there was decent behavior and a freedom from things which make it obnoxious or painful for Christian men to work with satisfaction.

The problem was a comparatively simple one until we began to get foreign-speaking men to do the unskilled labor—American men not relishing this work when they could get anything else to do. We housed the foreign workmen in comfortable quarters built upon our own property, where we could control their actions. When the beer wagons started to deliver we warned them to keep off, and when they persisted we arrested them and forced them either to plead guilty or to suffer conviction, on the charge of selling liquor in an illegal manner, the restriction of this kind of traffic being quite stringent and effective, if one will take the time and trouble to look it up and handle it vigorously. In addition to this, all of our foreign-speaking men, who are the principal offenders in this line, are required to sign in their rental contract that they will not bring liquor nor allow it to be brought into their houses, and the men themselves recognize the manifest benefit that has come to them by this restriction.

We find in our work that the very best men are the men who never have touched intoxicants; Christian men who work at every opportunity and who are dependable at all times and can stand the physical strain of the hot work of the furnaces better than drinking men can; retain their abillity to work through a longer period of years, and give a totally different degree of satisfaction in the manning of all our different departments. I most firmly believe, from all standpoints, that drink is an absolute evil, ruining a man physically, morally and spiritually, and that the only right course is for every man to let it absolutely alone. I believe a great deal of our economic unrest would be remedied if the liquor business were put out of our land, as it destroys the efficiency of such an enormous army of men and wastes such enormous sums of their hard earnings for that which is not bread. Our concern has been established for a long time, having grown from a modest-sized establishment to one employing about two thousand men, paying out, when running full, about $100,000 a month in wages.

Mr. James Brown, president of the Gulf States Steel Company, has sent me the following communication, dated July 23, 1917:

As president of the Gulf States Steel Company, I can state that it is our inflexible rule not to promote to a position of any importance men who to our knowledge are addicted to the drinking of intoxicating liquor, either on or off duty. To the best of my knowledge, every holder of a position of trust either indoors or outdoors in our various departments is an abstainer. I myself became one forty years ago as an example to the workmen employed under me. We find the percentage of accidents is materially reduced in our steel works, as compared with some others where the management is not so pronounced in keeping away intoxicating liquor. With us it is ground for immediate discharge if any man is found bringing liquor into the works.

As vice-president of the Bessemer Coal, Iron and Land Company, which sells homes on the long instalment plan, I can state that that company in 1907 had several hundreds of sale contracts running with ore and coal miners of the Bessemer district, near Birmingham. At that time the county voted out liquor, and the change was quite surprising. The vote took place the same day in October as the big panic in New York, with the suspension of the Knickerbocker Trust Company. Nearly half of the blast furnaces, coal mines, and ore mines in the district closed down in the supervening panic, and the others went on short time; but we found that, owing to the prevalence of total abstinence, the money was paid to us on home purchase instalments that might otherwise have gone for whisky. Collectors of rents and dealers in furniture told me the same thing, and that the condition of the negro miners was better under panic-abstinence conditions than it was before the crash under prosperity-whisky conditions. I am personally a determined foe to whisky. I realize that our men work very hard, and I want to see them save their money and buy homes and furniture, and be well fed and clothed.

During the past week it has been decided in this city to pull down the south side jail, and build a negro school-house on the site. The commissioner in charge of street improvements has complained to the city commission that he has not enough prisoners to keep the streets clean, and must hire free men for the purpose. This is the result of Alabama going dry, which has so greatly reduced the number of crimes and prisoners that one jail now in the city will take the place of two under whisky.

Almost all the forms of big business are radically opposed to drink among their men in the interest of greater efficiency.

In 1914, the National Safety Council, in a convention of seven hundred members, representing a very large element of the employees of labor, unanimously adopted a resolution declaring that "the drinking of alcoholic stimulants is productive of a heavy percentage of accidents and of disease affecting the safety and efficiency of workmen."

In going through the large manufacturing establishments of the country, one's eye is greeted, whichever way one may turn, with the following placard:

"We want only clear-thinking men in our employ. You cannot think clearly and act safely if you are a boozer. Booze poisons the brain. It stimulates for a short time only—then deadens the senses. When men's minds are dull, accidents are bound to occur. It takes alertness—quick thinking and acting—to avoid danger. If you must booze, then don't report for work. We don't want boozers on our premises. They are dangerous, not only to themselves, but to all others who come in contact with them. Booze will never get you a job nor help you to hold one. Booze will never help you pay your debts, nor increase your earning power. Booze and work won't mix. Sooner or later one must be sacrificed for the other. Sidetrack booze before booze sidetracks you."

In a letter dated Portsmouth, Ohio, July 17, 1917, Mr. George D. Selby, president of a shoe manufacturing company, says:

We have given careful attention to your request for information on the question of "Alcohol and Efficiency." We have been earnestly and carefully trying to eliminate the use of intoxicating liquors by our employees for the past twenty-five years, but have not wholly succeeded, on account of the ease with which intoxicantss can be obtained in our "wet" town.

Notwithstanding all the care we have given this question, we have been compelled to discharge a number of our employees recently, on account of the drink habit. Will say that after all we can do in "wet" territory it is a handicap of perhaps from three to five per cent. of our payroll, the aggregate of which is over $1,000,000 per annum, considering the inefficiency of the drinker himself and the loss of wages to others on account of the delayed and inefficient work.

We have always done and will continue to do everything we can to eliminate the intoxicating liquor traffic for beverage purposes, and we think we have a good pros pect of our State going "dry" in November.

I heard ex-Governor Foss of Massachusetts make a powerful address on the reason why the business world is fighting rum, and how certain it is that it will never cease that warfare until the traffic in liquors is destroyed. I asked him to prepare in succinct form his views on the subject to be used as a paragraph in this chapter on Business Against Booze, and he gave me this, which hits the nail on the head:

In my practical experience as an employer of labor (5,000 men) I have found that drink causes more trouble than almost any other one factor. It is at the bottom of irregularity in work, lost time, and many other dislocations and irritations. It causes a very large proportion of accidents. This is serious for the employed.

It is also serious for the employer, who is liable for the results of accident.

Drink is distinctly injurious to production. It takes the fine edge off mental tools; it slows down efficiency. Brewing and distilling are destructive industries. They lower the purchasing power of the masses for legitimate products to a very serious degree. This means that great quantities of clothing, shoes, food, furniture, and manufactured articles remain unbought. The result is stoppage in industrial production until the stocks on hand are lowered. In this way drink plays an important part in producing periods of depression and industrial crisis.

Drink, by diverting money to socially unproductive industries which otherwise would be deposited in banks, lessens the amount of capital available for new productive enterprises, and in this way shuts off thousands of possible openings for employment. It is a well-known fact that capital invested in alcohol manufacture has a low employing power.

Mr. J. Ogden Armour of Chicago, whose meat-packing company does an annual cash business of $500,000,000, and which has an army of 40,000 on its pay-roll, has assured me that he is personally an advocate of temperance and sobriety, and that the organization of Armour & Company puts a premium on men who abstain from the use of liquor and, in accord with the trend of the times, the drinkers are gradually being weeded out and replaced by more efficient men who do not drink.

One of the strong reasons why the big business of the country is fighting drink so vigorously and driving it so swiftly out of their communities, is the Workmen's Liability Law which has been passed in so many States, which makes the proprietor responsible for the accidents of the workmen. Drink is the fruitful cause of accidents in the establishment, and hence the fierce warfare against intoxicants.

At the Raritan Cooper Works in Perth Amboy, New Jersey, they studied their accidents and found that the time of greatest peril is the first hour of the day shift on Monday and on the days following holidays. They have a General Safety Committee which gets the facts and publishes them in a bulletin called the Ingot. Here is the Ingot's comment on the accident figures:

To any man who can think in a straight line these statistics mean just one thing. It is a plain fact, and we will state it plainly. Too much drinking at night means foggy eyes and unsteady nerves next morning. Then the accidents pile up. Now, let's get right down to brass tacks. This is no grape-juice journal; we hold no brief for Prohibition. What we are working for is safety. Cut down the booze, and as surely as day follows night you will cut down the accidents.

CHAPTER V

ALCOHOL AND LABOR

THE workmen are greatly pleased with the prohibition that industry has required. At first they thought it was an infringement of their rights, which they were inclined to resent; but on a trial they found that they were so much stronger and better able for their work, that they lost fewer days, that their families were so much better provided for, and so much happier, that they not only acquiesced in the rule, but have been among the most vigorous instrumentalities for enforcing it and driving rum out of their communities.

Terence Powderly, the old grand master of the Knights of Labor, said:

Had I ten million tongues, and a throat for each tongue, I would say to every man, woman and child here to-night, throw strong drink aside as you would an ounce of liquid hell. It sears the conscience; it destroys everything it touches. It reaches into the family circle and takes the wife you have sworn to protect and drags her down from her purity into that house from which no decent woman ever goes alive. It induces the father to take the furniture from the home, exchange it for money at the pawnshop, and spend the proceeds for rum. It damns everything it touches. I have seen it in every city east of the Mississippi River, and I know that the most damning curse to the laborer is that which gurgles from the neck of the bottle. I would rather be at the head of an organization having one hundred thousand temperate, honest, earnest men, than at the head of an organization of twelve million drinkers, whether moderate or any other kind.

John Mitchell, a famous leader in the labor world, said: "I have no sympathy with the statement, so often made, that the manufacture and sale of liquor has contributed to the industrial development of the nation. On the contrary, I believe that liquor has contributed more to the moral, intellectual and material deterioration of the people, and has brought more misery to defenseless women and children, than has any other agency in the history of mankind.

Hon. William E. Borah, United States Senator from Idaho, in his speech on the Food Bill in the Senate, July 6, 1917, thus powerfully portrays the disastrous effects of alcohol upon the laboring man:

"A few years ago in a Western State, during some labor troubles, it became necessary to invoke martial law. Martial law was invoked and extended over a very large portion of the State, a portion of the State in which thousands of men were in the employ of mine operators and of other owners of industries. It was a very extraordinary situation, one in which riot and crime for a time held almost complete sway. Before those who had charge of the situation could even begin to restore order and law it became necessary to close the saloons and drinking places in that district, and, under the authority of martial law, every saloon and every place where intoxicating liquors were sold or could be had were closed. They remained closed, and the prohibition of the sale and of the drinking of liquor remained in force for many months.

"I had an opportunity to observe personally the effect of that upon that entire district, upon the workingmen in the district, upon the industries, and upon the efficiency which it brought to labor. The homes underwent a change which it would be very difficult for language to portray. When night came the laboring man did not remain at the saloon or upon the streets, but he went to his home. When Saturday night came he did not spend the evening in the saloon, but he returned to his home and took his week's pay with him. When he left his home on Monday morning it was an entirely different home to what he had been in the habit of leaving while the saloons were open.

"The experience which we had there in the few months while those saloons were closed was one of the most potent factors in the cause of absolute prohibition in that State. I had not myself prior to that time been what you would call a radical advocate of the prohibition cause, but I became so by reason of my opportunity of witnessing with my own eyes the effect upon the labor world of taking liquor out of the laborers' lives. It was not by reason of any theory, but by reason of example, as to the effect of which and the importance of which and the significance of which there could be no doubt."

The liquor men have claimed to be the champions of labor. They have counted upon workingmen as their friends, their unfailing allies. For a time, they had untold influence over labor organizations, arranging that the meetings of many of the large units should be held in the rooms back of or over saloons.

The disappointment of the barroom is bitter at the manner in which the working people of the nation have thrown off the yoke of allegiance and have marched up to the ballot boxes and voted against the saloon. That is why the saloon is going so fast—because the common people, the working people, are against it. They know better than any one that the wife and children and job are their friends, and that the saloon is their bitterest enemy.

The plea of money losses to the laboring man in the destruction of the liquor traffic by Prohibition is answered conclusively by Rev. Chas.

Stelzle, an authority on the subject, in the following communication which he furnished me:

According to the defenders of the saloon, 1,000,000 workingmen would permanently be thrown into the labor market following the introduction of national Prohibition. This argument is based entirely upon the absurd proposition that if the liquor dealers fail to get the money now spent for beer and whisky nobody else will get it. It is assumed that if a man does not spend a dollar for booze he will throw that dollar into the sewer or into some kind of a bottomless pit, instead of using it to purchase some other commodity which will do good instead of harm, which will have a permanent value, and which will give the workingmen of the country more work, more wages, and greater prosperity every way than if the same amount of money were spent for beer and whisky.

For every $1,000,000 invested in the average industry, practically four times as much raw material is required, four times as much wages are paid, and four times as many workers are employed as is the case in the liquor industry.

The figures given by the liquor interests as to the number of men who would be affected by the abolition of the liquor traffic are greatly exaggerated. The Census Report of 1910 tells us that in all manufacturing industries there were then employed 6,616,046 persons. The liquor industry employed 62,920, or just about one per cent. of the total. But of this number only about 15,000 were brewers and maltsters, distillers and rectifiers. The remainder of the 62,920 were employed as engineers, carpenters, machinists, teamsters, bottlers, etc.—occupations which are not at all peculiar to the liquor business. There were more teamsters employed than there were brewers and maltsters, distillers and rectifiers.

There are about 100,000 bartenders in the United States. What will become of these when the saloon is abolished? What is it that makes a successful bartender? It is his ability as a salesman, and a man who is a good bartender will make a good clerk or salesman in practically any other kind of business. Furthermore, it requires many more people to sell $2,000,000,000 worth of bread and clothing, for example, than it does to sell liquor of the same value. And it is more likely that at least as many salaried employees, such as traveling salesmen, bookkeepers, and stenographers, will be employed.

But what about the 15,000 or so brewers and maltsters, distillers and rectifiers? They will, of necessity, be compelled to adjust themselves to changed conditions. But this does not mean that they will either go adrift or cause a labor panic. The constantly changing situation in the industrial world in this country often compels men to transfer from one occupation to another, many of them being required to learn entirely new trades. Take, for illustration, the situation when the Mergenthaler typesetting machine was introduced. The printers thought that their trade was destroyed. However, they immediately learned how to run typesetting machines, with the result that today there are more printers employed than ever before, and they are receiving higher wages than at any time in their history. As a matter of fact, however, more workingmen lose their jobs because saloons are open than would be the case were the saloons to be closed.

As somebody put it, "When liquor puts a man out of a job it unfits him for another job. When no-license puts a bartender out of a job, it makes him a wealth-producing workingman instead of a wealth-destroying workingman. It is better that the bartender should lose his job and get a better one than that dozens of his patrons should lose their jobs and be unfitted for any job."

Big business has no more right to demand abstinence of the workingman than the working-man has a right to demand abstinence on the part of the employers in the interest of the same efficiency. A management befuddled with alcohol is as bad a business proposition as one where the growler is constantly rushed in the mill. The rich man does unjustly and unwisely when he takes beer away from his workmen and has champagne on his own table. It is a blessing to take the beer from the workman. It will be as great a blessing for the proprietor to cut out his champagne in the interest of business efficiency, if for no higher motive. Fortunately, a large majority of the cap-tains of industry are abstainers from strong drink.

This fact is verified by the economical reasons which Mr. Edward Bok, Editor of the *Ladies' Home Journal*, gives for being a total abstainer. He says:

As I looked around and came to know more of people and things, I found the always unanswerable argument in favor of a young man's abstinence; that is, that the most successful men in America today are those who never lift a wine-glass to their lips. Becoming interested in this fact, I had the curiosity to inquire personally into it. I found that of twenty-eight of the leading men in the country, whose names I selected at random, twenty-two never touch a drop of wine. I made up my mind that there was some reason for this. If liquor brought safe pleasure, why did these men abstain from it? If, as some say, it is a stimulant to a busy man, why do not these men, directing the largest business interests in the country, resort to it? And when I saw that these were men whose opinions in great business matters were accepted by the leading concerns of the world, I concluded that their judgment in business matters could command the respect and attention of the leaders of trade on both sides of the sea, and their decision as to the use of liquor was not apt to be wrong.

CARNEGIE ADVISES ABSTINENCE

A little Scotch boy came over to this country. His widowed mother was poor and had to work hard to support him. When a mere lad he struck out to earn a few dollars a week to support his mother. And Andrew Carnegie went from the foot of the ladder of poverty and labor to the head of one of the greatest industrial institutions in the world. He is an excellent authority on the value of abstinence to both labor and capital, and to its efficiency in all the callings of life.

I had known the deep interest Mr. Andrew Carnegie had in the war on King Alcohol, but had not realized how intense was his hostility to rum, or his practical labors personally to prevent its sale or use, until I had a conversation with him at his Fifth Avenue home. He told me how dangerous he considered strong drink, how it reduced the physical, mental and moral efficiency of many, and how fatal it was to so many victims. He said it harmed everybody, but his greatest anxiety was for the young men who were most likely to be tempted by the iniquitous saloon, and who in many cases would be destroyed by it.

Mr. Carnegie has made a permanent record of his radical temperance views in an address he made in October, 1905, in Dundee, Scotland, at the formal opening of a gymnasium building in connection with the University of St. Andrews, of which he was Lord Rector. This address of dedication was made in the presence of many notable men in business and professional life, with leading representatives of the educational institutions of that country. In that address Mr. Carnegie said that the first and most serious habit was the use of alcoholics. A dangerous habit very likely to cause grievous results, all agreed; that it could cause no beneficial results all agreed. It was therefore the part of wisdom to abstain from the habit that might work evil and could do no good. That no ill effects were visible from indulgence during the vigorous period of youth rendered the danger of serious consequences in after life still greater than if the ill effects were visible from the beginning. They were playing with an insidious foe. Viewing them as young steeds training for the race of life, he knew of no one habit so likely to defeat them in the contest as the drinking of alcoholic liquors. That taken in excess, they destroyed the character of men and rendered them useless members of society, they all knew. The line between excess and sufficiency was so narrow that it was very seldom the drinker knew and observed it. Better be on the safe side. Why run into danger? As no possible good could result from indulgence, no risk should be incurred. In the stern game of life they had all to play, they could afford to throw no advantages away. He did not wish to preach to them. He put the case to them simply as a matter of policy. Drink was the greatest danger in front of them, against which they could protect themselves completely in the campaign of life by a firm resolution of abstinence. It was good sense for them to do so. Drunkenness was the great rock ahead in the career of every young man. It was far more important that he insure himself against it than against death. A drink policy was worth ten life policies in their case.   Abstain and avoid the danger.

In another address to young men Mr. Carnegie has said:

The first and most seductive peril, and the destroyer of most young men, is the drinking of liquor. I am no temperance lecturer in disguise, but a man who knows and tells you what observation has proved to him; and I say to you that you are more likely to fail in your career from acquiring the habit of drinking liquor than from all other temptations likely to assail you. You may yield to almost any other temptation and reform— may brace up and, if not recover lost ground, at least remain in the race, and secure and maintain a respectable position. But from the insane thirst for liquor escape is almost impossible. I have known but few exceptions to this rule.

Mr. Carnegie handed me a copy of his book, "Problems of To-day," saying, "On pages 10 and 11, in my chapter on 'Wealth,' you will find my views on the damage of drink to the working-man." This is the passage to which he refers:

The dire consequences resulting from the use of liquor would justify much higher taxation upon it in the interest of the workers themselves. The greatest single evil in Britain to-day is intemperance. Seven hundred and eighty-five million dollars yearly is the drink bill. How much of this is paid by the working classes is, we believe, unknown; but even if it be only one-half, here is three hundred and ninety-two and a half millions worse than wasted by them. The liquor interests have now received title to their drinking places, when before they had only licenses from year to year—a present made to them, as estimated by some, equal to fifteen hundred million dollars. When one asks himself what would most benefit the worker, there is no hesitation in the reply—to avoid liquor and gambling. The workingman who indulges in either is, to the extent he does so, the architect of his own poverty. Here is the issue of greatest moment to the workingmen. One cannot help those who do not help themselves. One man cannot push another up a ladder. The moment he releases his grasp the assisted one falls. It is only possible to really help those who co-operate with the helper. It is not the submerged but the swimming tenth that can be steadily and rapidly improved by the aid of their fellows. The former should be the special care of the State, and should be isolated.

As I bade Mr. Carnegie good-by, he said: "I will treat you as I do the rest of my visitors and give you my personal card." This was the card: Printed in large letters at the top, "Andrew Carnegie on the Curse of Drink"; and this was underneath, printed pretty nearly as large:

The curse of drink is the cause of more failures in life than anything else, and while it may be possible to surmount any other faulty habit, the man who is a confirmed drinker has not one chance in a million of success in life. Liquor will conquer you a million chances to one if you give it sway.

On thinking with gratitude and joy over the visit and what it revealed, I wondered whether his testimony to the damage of liquor would not be stronger than the testimony of the brewers and distillers and saloonkeepers who hold that drink is food, is good for the body and mind, and will not hinder but promote success in life.

Mr. John A. Poynton, Mr. Carnegie's competent and courteous private secretary, confirmed a rumor I had heard that Mr. Carnegie has a rule that the men on his large estate of Skibo, Scotland, who abstain from liquor during the year receive a bonus of ten per cent. on their salary. I asked what number of the men employed on the estate were included in the proposition, and the answer was, "Every mother's son of them." Mr. Poynton continued: "In all industrial enterprises he never ceased to hammer home the total abstinence policy to his workmen and heads of departments, in every way possible. He has rarely made an address or written a pamphlet or book without frequent references to the desirability of leaving liquor alone."

Besides Mr. Carnegie's keen individual interest in this subject, he takes a wide view of the subject and contributes generously to the cause. He told me once that he not only contributed money to fight the saloon in this country, but that he also gave cheerfully to the cause in other lands in the hope that there would be a speedy and complete elimination of the liquor traffic in this country and throughout the world, that peace, sobriety, prosperity, happiness and usefulness might universally prevail.

THE FARMERS FOR PROHIBITION

The farmers are pretty nearly solid against the saloon. They fight it because it damages farm labor, and also because it corrupts public morals. The farmers used to befriend drink. Within the memory of some men the whisky-barrel was in every country store, and the "little brown jug" in every country home. Especially did they use liquor in harvest time, to prevent sunstroke, they said. An old man told me that he cut and hewed the logs for his new home in the West and sawed the joints to fit, and set the day for the neighbors to come in to help with the log-raising. He said he was one of the few in that rural neighborhood who was a total abstainer, and did not provide the whisky that was always in evidence on such occasions. The men refused to lift a log, and he had to send out and get a supply of grog before a hand was moved. They said he was mean and discourteous, and that as they donated their labor they thought the least he could do was to set up the refreshment. It was a common sight to see a splendid young man spend years of hard work to get a farm, and then drink it up at the crossroads grocery, and go to disgrace and the grave.

The annual meeting of the National Grange in Washington declared for Prohibition for the farmers and demanded the passage of the National Constitutional Prohibition measure and its ratification by the States. The farmers with their families number 20,000,000 of our hard-working people, and the action at Washington has considerable political as well as moral significance. The liquor men who have talked so flippantly about the green "country Jakes" being the only ones against them know that it is the ax of the farmer on election days that is doing so much to chop down their business.

ABSTINENCE FOR SOLDIERS

Colonel L. M. Maus, Assistant Surgeon General of the United States army, retired, delivered an address before the American Medical Society for the Study of Alcohol and Narcotics, from which I quote the following statements regarding abstinence in the army:

In order to attain success in war, as well as in other walks of professional life, the individual must preserve his general health, which is the keynote to efficiency and success; and from an experience of over forty years as an army medical officer, I know of no factor which contributes more to the general health and efficiency than total abstinence.

During one of General Wolseley's campaigns, he divided some of his men into squads for marching experiments. The first squad was given a daily ration of whisky, the second a ration of beer, and the third water. At first the whisky squad marched gaily ahead, but was soon overtaken by the beer squad, which in turn was passed by the water squad. The water squad followed an even gait, and after passing both whisky and beer squads, reached its destination long before its competitors.

Lord Kitchener allowed his men no spirits whatsoever during his campaign in the Soudan. Lord Roberts was equally firm in encouraging abstinence from alcohol. Dr. Wahlberg, surgeon-in-chief of the Finnish army during 1877-8, said non-drinkers endured better, and that the old drinkers were the first men to break down.

The Boers, whose endurance was generally commented upon favorably, used neither spirits nor beer. Sir Frederick Treves, who served at Ladysmith, says that the drinking men fell out and dropped as regularly as if they were labeled with the big letter "D" on their backs.

During the Swedish alcoholic investigation among soldiers, a number of picked non-commissioned officers and men were selected for rifle practice. The tests covered a number of days, part of which time the men were tried out with small quantities of alcohol, about 1½ ounces of brandy. When alcohol was taken during the quick fire, the hits were thirty per cent. less, though the men imagined they were firing quicker. During slow aiming, the difference was fifty per cent. in favor of abstaining days.

During the marching test, some of the men were allowed alcohol, while others were deprived of its use. The drinking men were found inferior in marching and enduring qualities; besides, all the sunstrokes and heat exhaustions occurred among the drinking classes. As a result of these series of experiments the Austrian soldier is not allowed to carry brandy on his person, as was previously the case.

The use of alcohol as a beverage among troops contributes more to camp diseases and detracts more from efficiency than even poor camp sanitation. This was true during the recent Spanish war and the Philippine insurrection. Especially was this true of diseases which stood for years at the top of camp diseases due to immorality in our army, and it became a subject of congressional discussion.

During 1898-1902 the Government permitted the unlimited introduction and distribution of all kinds of alcoholic beverages among the army of 70,000 regular and volunteer troops which were on duty in the islands during that period, as a result of which the admission rate to sick report ran up four or five times as high as the present rate in the United States.

While a large amount of the sickness was no doubt due to climatic influences and poor sanitation, at least fifty per cent. of the excess was due to the use of alcohol. Hundreds of the men were invalided home on account of intestinal and stomach troubles, insanity, neurasthenia and other forms of neurosis, due more or less to alcohol, ninety-five per cent. of whom recovered before they had reached San Francisco, during the month's voyage of return.

Besides sickness and loss of efficiency in the army as a result of alcohol, we know that practically all of the crimes and military offenses committed in military circles are due to the use of intoxicants. All of the murders, suicides, court-martials, and dismissals of officers, prison and guard-house desertions are usually confined to the drinking element.

From a careful study of the effects of alcohol on the human organism I find that:

1. As a beverage it lowers all the mental faculties, such as judgment, memory, perception, thought, comparison, caution, and quickness of action.

2. It lessens working capacity, marching endurance, accuracy and rapidity in rifle firing, ability to command troops or navigate ships, to act as members of military courts or boards, or to perform the higher administrative duties of official life.

3. It causes sickness, impairs health and usefulness, adds greatly to the non-efficiency of officers and men, increases the burden of the medical department in time of peace and war, deprives the government frequently of the services of those who drink, and increases unnecessarily the retired and pension lists of the army and navy.

4. It lowers the moral standard, lessens self-restraint, and is productive of unreliability, untruthfulness, dishonesty and crime.

The United States Government shares these opinions of Colonel Maus, and by legislative action shields our noble soldiers and sailors from the curse of drink.

ABSTINENCE FOR SAILORS

Admiral Dewey, a short time before he died, put himself unequivocally on record as to the value of abstinence to the officers and men of the United States Navy. The record was in an interview by George Creel for the New York *World*. The Admiral gave his opinion about the "wine mess" in answer to the question, "What about the famous drinking order?"

"A good thing!" His answer was instant. "There was some feeling about it at first, because the papers made fun of it, and there was also an attempt to make it appear that Secretary Daniels was charging officers with intemperance. I think that the feeling has disappeared completely. Every railroad, every great corporation, has long had an ironclad rule forbidding men to drink while on duty. Isn't a ship as important as a locomotive? Practically every European power has copied the order, by the way."

At this point Admiral Dewey handed to Mr. Creel an article by Hector Bywater, the famous naval expert, written for a British journal, after a careful study of the American navy. The Admiral had the following paragraph marked: "Those best qualified to speak assert that the last four years have witnessed a remarkable all-around improvement in the quality of the personnel. Thanks to the Secretary's drastic order shortly after he came into office, intemperance has disappeared from the navy, and although the drink prohibition excited ridicule and bitter opposition at the time, the majority of naval officers now agree that it has had a most beneficial effect on efficiency and discipline."

"Do you stand for that?" Mr. Creel asked, looking up after reading the paragraph aloud.

"I would be dishonest if I didn't," the Admiral answered.

The learned professions as well as the industrial world are fighting rum on the ground of efficiency as well as of principle.

DR. ELIOT BECOMES ABSTAINER

For a generation the liquor men have been quoting Doctor Charles W. Eliot, president emeritus of Harvard, as their friend and champion. Hence my surprise when I saw his name among those asking for Prohibition during the war as an economic measure. I wrote Doctor Eliot asking him if he would not write me his views on the liquor problem generally for my book. He at once sent me the specially prepared essay which I have set down bodily in this volume. It will astound and confound the liquor people as much as it will surprise and delight the friends of Prohibition. In the commnnication Doctor Eliot announces to the public that he reversed the views of a lifetime on the drink problem, after he was eighty years of age. This is his remarkable and powerful essay, which is a temperance library on one shelf, in a single book:

My opinion about war prohibition is that the law should prohibit the manufacture and sale of distilled spirits as a beverage; but that it should permit the manufacture of beer containing not more than two per cent. of alcohol. Such beer is not intoxicating, no matter in what quantity it is swallowed; and yet it tastes and smells like beer. It does not seem to me to be safe to permit the manufacture and sale of beers and wines in general; because they may easily be taken in quantities which diminish the self-control of the person who drinks them freely. Beers and wines of the ordinary strength in alcohol diminish the productiveness of workers in many, indeed most, of the national industries through the injurious effect of alcohol, even when taken in moderate quantities, on accuracy and speed in manual and clerical labors.

Until the United States went to war with Germany, I had never advocated a prohibitory law. The process by which I have arrived at that advocacy is correctly described as follows:

I have never been a total abstainer in any part of my life, until within two months. I drank beer or wine occasionally, but not habitually, and never perceived that it had any bad effect on me. Having lived about forty summers at Mount Desert in the State of Maine, I saw the very serious evils which have there accompanied an imperfect execution of a prohibitory law. The Maine law did good in communities in which a decided majority were opposed to any use of alcoholic drinks, but in the larger towns and summer resorts the law was either of no effect, or, when imperfectly or unfairly enforced, had a bad effect on the administration of justice and the people's respect for law in general. I have therefore advocated in Massachussetts and elsewhere a local option law, and have witnessed great community benefits from local Prohibition, in spite of the well-known difficulties created for no-license towns and cities by the contiguity of towns or cities whose voters were in favor of license.

During the past thirty years biological, chemical, and physiological science has made great advances in respect to knowledge of the effects of alcohol on the human body; and in recent years it has been to my mind demonstrated beyond a question that any man who wishes to do his best work with brains or hands, or both, is better off without alcoholic drinks, even the mildest forms, than with them. I have thence inferred that it was wiser to be a total abstainer than a moderate drinker. Accuracy and speed are reduced by even moderate doses of alcohol, not only in factory or group work, but also in individual or detached labor.

During my fifty-five years' service as teacher and educational administrator, I came into more or less close contact with thousands of young men in whose subsequent careers I took an interest. Among the personal and family tragedies which have come to my knowledge have been some which have occurred not from the habitual use of distilled spirits or of the strong wines and beers, but from the occasional use of the milder alcoholic drinks in quantity sufficient to diminish temporarily the drinker's self-control. While in that condition, young men of good character, whose conduct is habitually unexceptional, can contract disease with which years afterward they may infect innocent persons. Of course hard drinkers are liable to the same disasters; but their conduct and visible characteristics warn the innocent, so that the worst tragedies may be avoided.

For twenty years past I have paid much attention to the subject of social hygiene; and these studies have shown me that drinking alcohol and the male demand for prostitution are always intimately connected. I have learned, too, that when young men are herded together in camps and barracks, as they must be in all armies, commercialized vice is always rampant in their neighborhood, and requires a vigorous repression which is not to be expected from the professional soldiers of any nation. I am informed that effectual repression was not provided in many of the cantonments of the American troops on the Mexican border. When the United States went to war with Germany, and it appeared that our soldiers would soon be serving in large numbers in France, I thought it was high time to provide for our boys such protection as a national prohibitory law can give them in their training places and camps, both here and abroad.

Since I was eighty years old, I have had a suspicion that I could work better if I took no alcohol at all, so last May, having become an advocate of total abstinence for others, I became a total abstainer myself with much satisfaction.

I write thus, because when an old educator, who has always opposed prohibitory laws, changes his mind and advocates Prohibition, it is fair that people who pay any attention to his exhortations should know the grounds or reasons for his change of opinion and conduct.

JOSEPH H. CHOATE

In a delightful interview I had with Mr. Joseph H. Choate in his home, only a few weeks before his death, I asked him as the President of the Associated Charities of New York State, and as the acknowledged head of the American bar, what he considered to be the relation between the saloon and suffering and crime. He promptly replied that he had no hesitation in saying that much of the suffering, and most of the crime of the land, can be traced directly to the saloon; the most conservative possible estimate would be 50 per cent. of the suffering and 50 per cent. of the crime are the direct result of the saloon.

DR. LYMAN ABBOTT

In a conversation with Dr. Lyman Abbott, whom the liquor people have quoted so often as friendly to them, he showed me statistics to prove the success of Prohibition in Cornwall, his home town, and expressed his sympathy with the movement to drive the saloon out of the states and nation.

CHAPTER VI

THE ATTITUDE OF LINCOLN

FOR fifty years the liquor people have claimed Lincoln as their friend and champion, and have featured him as such in their advertisements in the papers and in their trade circulars. They have boldly claimed that Lincoln used intoxicating drinks and that he had been a saloonkeeper. From year to year, the face of dear "Old Abe," the homeliest to the eyes of clay but handsomest to the eye of the spirit, in all the commonwealth, has been put in the newspapers to advertise some brand of whisky or other liquors. The liquor dealers did so partly because they made much of the "personal liberty" argument in defence of their business, and featured the Emancipator as the chief exponent of freedom, and partly because with their befogged intellects and befuddled consciences they really thought that Lincoln had been one of their craft, and were boasting that a saloonkeeper had gotten to be President of the United States.

For half a century, I have seen that lovely face debauched by its foul setting in the liquor advertisements, and have been filled with anger and contempt at the sight. I have felt like spitting on the page that was debased by it, and have often taken my knife and cut out this picture advertisement and, tearing it into pieces, have thrown it into the waste basket. This advertisement does not appear as frequently as it used to; for the personal liberty argument for liquor has been pretty well abandoned, and the temperance sentiment of the nation has grown to be such that the people count it an impertinence, if not a sacrilige, to use the face of so great and good a man as Lincoln to represent so low and diabolical a business.

What are the historical facts which give the liquor dealers even the flimsiest excuse for claiming Lincoln as their friend and champion? Simply this: When Lincoln was twenty-four years of age, he concluded to try the mercantile business in New Salem, Illinois. He bought an interest in a country store and had as his partner a man by the name of Berry. Country stores in those times almost without exception kept dry goods, boots and shoes, hats and caps, sugar and coffee and other goods, and whisky. I myself remember when the decent, respectable country stores, almost all of them, kept whisky, which they sold with no more compunction of conscience than they did anything else they had in stock.

Lincoln never drank; disliked the whisky feature of the business; protested strongly to Berry against it, with a demand for its removal; and he himself declined to have anything practically to do with that part of the business or be charged with any of its responsibility. And he told Leonard Swett, one of the greatest lawyers of Chicago and America, and one of the most intimate friends he ever had, that he did not know the taste of one kind of liquor from another, and that the main reason for his quarrel with Berry which led to the dissolution of the partnership, was that Berry would not consent to cut the whisky feature out of the store. After the dissolution of the partnership Berry went off and established a low groggery, answering to the meanest saloon of to-day.

Judge Weldon, a warm personal friend of mine, said that he was in a hotel at Bloomington, Illinois, one day when Lincoln called on Judge Douglas in a personal, courteous visit. Judge Douglas took out his flask, as was his custom and the custom of almost everybody, and offered Mr. Lincoln a drink, who thanked him but declined, stating, "Judge, I do not drink at all."

We will here record historical facts which prove conclusively that Lincoln was a total abstainer all his life from boyhood, and that he was one of the most consistent, persistent, and powerful enemies the liquor traffic in America ever had.

MAJOR JAMES B. MERWIN

I called on Major James B. Merwin at his residence, 1732 Grove street, Brooklyn. I found him an invalid, seated in an easy chair, and past eighty-four years of age. Major Merwin had been very close to Lincoln, especially during the period of the Civil War, working in harmony with him in one of the most tragical periods of the world's history. Whoever was really close to Lincoln at that time was in the business of empire-building, and Major Merwin was one of the makers of history in the second place, because he was one of those "crank" pioneer Prohibitionists who started the greatest moral revolution in the temperance line in six thousand years.

"I have come to see you," I said, "especially about your relation to Lincoln in the war against alcohol, and for your testimony as to what you know personally about Lincoln's temperance habits and the immensely efficient service he rendered in fighting strong drink."

The Major's eyes flashed, his face shone and he became younger by a score of years as he said:

"No subject on earth is so dear as the one you have come to talk with me about, no man is so precious to my memory as Lincoln and no work so dear as that in which we were engaged so intimately together. You will do me a personal favor if you will take anything I may say to-night, or anything that I may have said at any time, and give it to the audience you will have in your book, and let my humble life go on with its mission of service after I shall have been gathered to my fathers.

"The tidal wave that swept so many States into Prohibition about 1850 carried me into the warfare on liquor," the Major continued. "As a young man I felt as greatly called to give my life to the work of saving the young people from the ravages of drink as any minister could be called to the task of preaching the Gospel; and I began my mission, which I considered from God, actively in the contest in the State of Connecticut. Though prepared for Amherst, circumstances prevented my going to college, and under this new divine call I became editor of the "Fountain," a temperance organ printed in Hartford, and corresponding secretary of the Connecticut Temperance Society. After the Maine law had been passed we undertook to have a similar law passed in Connecticut, and I led in the nonpartisan and interdenominational fight to secure that law. I enlisted among our corps of speakers Henry Ward Beecher, Horace Greeley, P. T. Barnum, and others; Neal Dow himself appeared before our Legislature, and after a fierce fight the Prohibition Law was passed.

"At an enthusiastic meeting, before the passage of the law, a citizen of Springfield, Illinois, who either happened to be in the audience or was sent by the temperance people of Illinois for the purpose, heard me speak at the meeting, and at the close of the exercises he said to me, 'When this work is over, if you will come out to Springfield and make just the same kind of an address to our citizens that you made to-night, I will not only be responsible for your expenses, but will see that you have proper compensation for your time as well.'

"After we had won out in Connecticut I went out to Springfield, Illinois, and my coming had been widely prepared for; it was heralded in the papers, great care was taken to announce the meeting by handbills, and as the Legislature was not in session, the hall of the House of Representatives of the State Capitol was secured. The hall was filled with people, and I thought I had a measureably good time describing the substance of the Maine law, the fight we had made at our State capital, the damage of drink to the community, and especially to the young, and the necessity of having a law that would put an end to the vice rather than license it to do its destruction for cold money. My address at the close was heartily applauded, and as I supposed the meeting was over, there came a call here and there, all over the house, 'Lincoln! Lincoln! Lincoln!' and it grew louder until there was universal demand for 'Lincoln.' Not knowing the gentleman that was called for, I wondered what he would look like, but did not wonder long, for just to my left a homely, tall man got himself up out of a very low chair. As he unfolded his long arms and longer legs and walked to the platform I shall never forget the feeling that came over me, and when this unique, unkempt individual took his place to speak, I was more than half afraid he was out of the enemy's camp and going to tear what I had said to pieces, or that he was some man who had invited himself to tone down and temper something that had been said. All doubt fled from my mind when, as he placed his hands on the secretary's desk, he began a talk which lasted twenty minutes, taking as his theme the law, its majesty, and its necessity in protecting the home, the Church and the State. He said law was never made for the protection of wrong but for the protection of the right and the prevention and punishment of the wrong. He said that splendid public sentiment had been made by the Washingtonian total abstinence movement, which he had so heartily commended in his public addresses, and rejoiced that while some had broken the pledge and gone back to their bad habits, numbers had also remained faithful. 'But,' he said, 'we have come to the place in the history of this movement where it is necessary to have the powerful hand of the law to keep back this giant evil and protect the men, the women and the children against the damages of the liquor traffic.' Greeley had made level-headed and convincing Prohibition speeches in our campaign in Connecticut, and Henry Ward Beecher with his fervid eloquence had carried everything by storm in our great gatherings; but I never had heard till that night in Springfield, nor do I ever remember to have heard since, anything so powerful as Lincoln's twenty minutes on the necessity for a prohibitory law in the State of Illinois.

"The silence was so great that the heartbeats of the audience could almost be heard, and the impression on the audience was profound beyond expression. At the close of this address, this same Mr. Lincoln, of whom I had never heard, but who was pretty much of a character to me by the hour's experience, came up to me, thanked me for my message, expressed the hope that I might find permanent employment in leading the campaign in Illinois as I had done in Connecticut, and asked me if I would not go home with him and he his guest for the night, which invitation I gladly accepted. We were both so full of the subject of temperance and so anxious for its success in the country and State that we talked and talked and talked until about daylight before we went to bed.

"The fight was conducted by the Illinois State Maine Law Alliance, and it was under the auspices of that Association and as secretary of it, that I went into the campaign, in which I had Lincoln as my strong right arm. I got Lincoln to write the prohibitory bill that was to be voted upon. After he had drafted it he said, 'There, I think that will hold water, but what I want to know is whether it will hold whisky'; and he named twenty or twenty-five of the finest lawyers of the State and had me go to them with the draft he had made to see whether the law would be declared good by the courts in case the people should vote for it. Lincoln was a great campaigner, and among other speakers whom I booked for the State contest we had none so strong as Lincoln, who made at least thirty addresses in favor of Prohibition. There is this to say about Mr. Lincoln's speeches: they were never vituperative, never bitter in personal denunciation. He did not pour out volleys of hatred against saloonkeepers; he claimed that society was equally guilty in licensing them to do their evil work, but he emphasized the danger of drink, the complete ruin it would effect in the case of those who tampered with it, the tremendous evils of the institution of the saloon in destroying health, usefulness, happiness and life itself, and made an argument which was positively unanswerable.

"Lincoln was so deeply interested in the fight that he helped me raise money for it. In fact, it was through his personal influence mostly that the funds necessary for carrying on the campaign were raised. I recall well this incident: Mr. William B. Ogden, then president of the Chicago and Northwestern Railroad, and a man of tremendous influence, who was deeply enlisted in the fight for no-license in the State, asked me to bring Mr. Lincoln into his office for a conference as to the most efficient method of carrying on the contest. I took Mr. Lincoln to his office and we entered seriously and heartily into the discussion of the problem, at the close of which Mr. Ogden wrote out his personal check for $2,500 and, handing it to Mr. Lincoln, said: 'If you need more money come back to me and I will duplicate that check cheerfully. No greater moral warfare could be conducted than that in which you are engaged, and I am so anxious to see you succeed.' In those days, you will remember, $2,500 was as much in proportion as ten or even twenty-five thousand dollars would be now.

"Lincoln personally commanded not only respect but the most perfect confidence, and money flowed into our treasury, through him as the channel, sufficient for all our purposes.

"Will you not be surprised when I tell you that in that early period we came within 15,000 votes in a popular election of carrying Illinois for Prohibition?"

I said to him, "Major, I have seen you exhibit the gold watch which you received as a souvenir at the close of that great State campaign in Illinois of which you have just spoken. Have you it handy? I should like to see it at close range."

He called for it and passed it over to me. I opened one side of the watch and found Lincoln's picture in it; I also opened the other and found this inscription cut into the case: "Presented by the friends of temperance in Chicago to J. B. Merwin, Corresponding-secretary of the Illinois Maine Law Alliance, as a token of their confidence and regard for his untiring energy and perseverance in its campaign of 1855 for Prohibition."

Tears came into the old man's eyes as he said, "Doctor, just to think that Lincoln wrote that inscription himself without any solicitation or prompting upon the part of any one else, and I have reason to believe that it was his own suggestion, personally, that led to the gift of the watch and the little ceremony of presentation."

"Major Merwin, please tell me about your association with Lincoln in temperance work during the period of the Civil War."

"At the beginning of the Civil War I was agent of the Michigan State Temperance Alliance, with my headquarters in Detroit. I received a letter from Mr. Lincoln, asking me to come to Washington and see him. He said to me, 'Merwin, you have done important temperance work, and I know what its quality is and I know what you are, and I want a man of your type on the ground here at Washington to promote the cause of temperance amongst our soldiers and sailors. There will be opportunity for you to make addresses here and there at the soldiers camps and other places, but I want you especially to deal personally with the men, talk to them like a brother and try and protect them against the drink habit, which would so lessen their efficiency and spoil their character.' And for four years I was engaged in that specific task. Lieutenant-General Winfield Scott, who, next to Lincoln, was the head of the army, gave me a letter officially authorizing the specific task to which Mr. Lincoln had called me. I preserved a fac-simile of that letter, which I have in a drawer there, and I will let you read it."

I took the letter and read:

I esteem the mission of Mr. Merwin to this army a happy circumstance, and request all commanders to give him free access to their camps and posts, and also to multiply occasions to enable him to address our officers and men.

WINFIELD SCOTT.

"That was in 1861," Major Merwin continued. "General Scott told me that Mr. Lincoln had made a special request of him for this official commendation. General Scott died early in the contest, as you know, and the generals did not seem to want to pay much attention to his old order to give me the right of way for temperance work among the soldiers, and, in fact, rather put barriers in my way, as they presumed I was, perhaps, a crank, and, maybe, in the way. I told Mr. Lincoln about this and he said, 'I will fix it so there will be no difficulty in the premises,' and he issued this commission:

The Surgeon-General will send Mr. Merwin wherever he may think the public service may require.

A. LINCOLN.

Major Merwin sent for the original order, and I held it in my fingers, signed, "A. Lincoln."

"You see it is written in Lincoln's own hand," the Major said, "and signed with his own pen; and there is not money enough in all the States of this Union to buy it. At my death that is to go to the Anti-Saloon League to be deposited in its archives as an immortal heritage.

"Lincoln said to me one day, 'Merwin, your work of temperance is so benovelent and so nearly like that of the Christian ministry, that I think you ought to be ordained a minister, and that will give you the special right of way to the hospitals and hearts of men in a little more intimate and sacred way.' He had a special friend in

Adrian, Michigan, to whom he wrote and asked him if he would not bring about my ordination, and in the letter he added this little piece of humor, so like him: 'When you ordain him, be sure and do not spoil him.' You understand that I was a full-fledged chaplain, with rank as such in the United States army, and I did the work of a chaplain often and have official endorsement of that branch of my work, but Lincoln said to me, 'Do not forget that your one work is to hammer into the minds of the boys the necessity of total abstinence; do not stop short of anything else than total abstinence.' One of the sweetest memories of my life is the fact that Lincoln treated me as a chaplain as well as a temperance reformer, for many a time, in his private office, we have bowed down and prayed to the God of Heaven; sometimes I would lead in prayer and sometimes he would lead in prayer himself, and oh, such prayers, as that giant lifted a whole nation up in his arms and laid it upon the bosom of the Almighty, and how agonizingly did he ask God to lead him as he led the nation."

"Major Merwin," I said, "I have heard you say from the platform several times that the last time you saw Mr. Lincoln he told you that as General Lee had surrendered, and slavery had been destroyed and the Union preserved, the next great national issue would be the destruction of the liquor traffic."

"I can give you the substance, and about the words, that Lincoln spoke to me that day," the Major replied, "they made such a deep impression upon my mind that I never shall forget them: 'Merwin, we have cleaned up with the help of the people a colossal job. Slavery is abolished. After reconstruction, the next great question will be the overthrow and abolition of the liquor traffic; and you know'—for I had known him since 1852 intimately—'and you know, Merwin, that my head and my heart and my hand and my purse will go into that work. In 1842—less than a quarter of a century ago—I predicted, under the influence of God's Spirit, that the time would come when there would be neither a slave nor a drunkard in the land. I have lived to see, thank God, one of those prophecies fulfilled. I hope to see the other realized.'

"It struck me as so important a statement that I said to him: 'Mr. Lincoln, shall I publish this from you?' He instantly replied: 'Yes, publish it as wide as the daylight shines.'

"One more thing I would like to have you speak about, Major Merwin," I suggested, "is that Internal Revenue Act—I might honestly say, 'Infernal Revenue Act,—which was passed by Congress during the war to tax the liquor business in this country for a war revenue. You have said publicly that Lincoln signed that bill with great hesitation."

The Major said: "I heard Salmon P. Chase, Secretary of the Treasury, one of the best men the country has produced, say to Mr. Lincoln: 'We have got to have the resources of evil as well as good to end this rebellion, and we must have the resources.' The President hesitated and hesitated, and said, 'I don't want to sign it.' Mr. Chase said, 'Mr. Lincoln, the strain is so great we cannot stand it much longer, and this is an actual necessity.' 'Very well,' said Mr. Lincoln to Henry Wilson and Mr. Chase in my presence, 'I had rather lose my right hand than sign a document that shall perpetuate the liquor traffic, but as soon as the exigencies pass away, I will turn my whole attention to the repeal of that document,' and that I know was his design, for he told me so, and he never would have signed it had he not had the promise of the members of the Cabinet and the committees of the Senate and House, having the matter in charge, that the law should be repealed at the close of the war."

I said, "Major, it was a great pity that that pledge was not kept after Mr. Lincoln's sudden death, for that Act was one of the greatest blots on the page of our American life, and one of the greatest curses to the civilization of our country. The brewers and distillers paying such a large amount into the treasury each year to support the Government, had a mortgage on it so large that they thought they owned it, and acted as though that were the case; and the pity to the nation was that their ownership was so absolute and so necessarily recognized that it seemed the people could not get out from under that despotism, and it is only just now that the Congress of the United States, echoing the voice of the voters of the nation, are declaring their independence from this tyranny and their determination to utterly destroy it."

His parting message to me was this: "The beginning of the end of the liquor traffic is near. I do not have to stay to see it. With prophetic eye I see it is in the immediate future. I feel now like saying with Simeon of old: 'Now, Lord, lettest thou thy servant depart in peace, for mine eyes have seen thy salvation.'"

He went into the realm and reward which his spiritual vision beheld only a few days after that. I took up a New York paper and read a full column article with this heading:

Major Merwin Dies. Friend of Lincoln. President Appointed him to Temperance Work in Union Army. Famous as a Lecturer. Campaigned with Lincoln in 1855, for State-wide Prohibition in Illinois.

I was not greatly surprised, but was very sad, and I seemed to hear a voice from the White Throne saying, "Well done, good and faithful servant; thou hast been faithful over a few things,

I will make thee ruler over many things; enter
thou into the joy of thy Lord."

WILLIAM O. STODDARD

Lincoln had three private secretaries at the beginning of his administration, John Nicolay, John
Hay and William Osborn Stoddard. I made a
pilgrimage to see Mr. Stoddard at his home in
Madison, New Jersey. I found a man in latest
cut of clothes, tall, straight as an arrow, gentle
and polite in voice and manner. It was a bene-
diction to meet with his sunshine and cheer, his
ready wit, his constant flow of humor, and, best
of all, his knowledge of and love for Lincoln.
I told him I was very glad of an opportunity to
get from his lips some evidence of Lincoln's
habits of total abstinence, and the unspeakable
eloquence of his voice and example against the
liquor habit and traffic. I said, "Please tell me
a little bit about your private secretaryship to Mr.
Lincoln. How did you come to be appointed?"

He said, "I was editor of a paper in Cham-
paign, Illinois, called the 'Central Illinois Gazette,' which had the honor of presenting Abraham Lincoln for the first time in public print as
a candidate for the Presidency of the United
States."

"What kind of a paper was it?" I asked.

"It was the most fanatical temperance paper

of Eastern Illinois," he answered. "Such papers were exceedingly scarce. I can recall hardly any between where I lived and Chicago. Prohibition was not as popular then as it is now, and those of us who espoused it were accounted cranks to the utmost limit. I was the crank editor myself, and wrote everything that went into it. The paper was also violently anti-slavery and friendly to the Free Soil (Republican) party."

Mr. Stoddard showed me his two articles first naming Lincoln for the Presidency. The local article read:

PERSONAL

Our Next President. We had the pleasure of introducing to the hospitalities of our sanctum a few days ago the Hon. Abraham Lincoln. Few men can make an hour pass away more agreeably. We do not pretend to know whether Mr. Lincoln will ever condescend to occupy the White House or not, but if he should, it is a comfort to know that he has established for himself a character and reputation of sufficient strength and purity to withstand the disreputable and corrupting influence of even that locality. No man in the west at the present time occupies a more enviable position before the people or stands a better chance for obtaining a high position among those to whose guidance our ship of State is to be entrusted.

The editorial in the same issue, nominating Mr. Lincoln, closed with the following:

No man will be so sure to consolidate the party vote of the State, or will carry the great Mississippi Valley with a more irresistible rush of popular enthusiasm than our distinguished fellow citizen, Abraham Lincoln. We in Illinois know him well, in the best sense of the word; a true democrat, a man of the people, whose strongest friends and supporters are the hard-handed and strong-limbed laboring men, who hail him as a brother and who look upon him as one of their real representative men. A true friend of freedom, having already done important service for the cause, and proved his abundant ability for still greater service, yet a staunch, conservative, whose enlarged and liberal mind descends to no narrow view but sees both sides of every great question, and of whom we do not fear will lead him to the betrayal of any trust. We appeal to our brethren of the Republican press for the correctness of our assertions.

"Doctor Stoddard," I asked, "did Lincoln's temperance proclivities have anything to do with your friendliness to him as a candidate?"

He said, "Most certainly they did. Lincoln was known far and near as a total abstainer and one not afraid or ashamed to acknowledge it. His voice had frequently been raised in the campaigns against the saloons, and his writings against them also were well known. You might be sure that as cranky a Prohibition paper as the 'Central Illinois Gazette' was, would not have nominated him if he had not been radically right on the temperance question. We were sure of that and knew we made no mistake in making him our representative. Besides, he was radically right on the slavery question and gave me good reason, as a Republican as well as crank temperance editor, to name him as our leader. I had two hundred extra copies of the paper containing the editorial naming Lincoln as a candidate for the nomination, and sent them to various newspapers and leading politicians in the State. I sent a special marked copy to Mr. Lincoln, who was greatly pleased, and told me afterward how kind a thing it was in me to do so. After Lincoln's election I went over to Springfield to see him. I had hardly gotten home when I received a letter from him appointing me as one of his private secretaries, and he instructed me to go before him to Washington and see that things at the White House were in readiness for him, 'and be ready to meet me when I come.' I did so, and from that time on I was with him in the office and at the White House daily, you might say hourly, to within a few months of Mr. Lincoln's death. The terrible excitement and heavy strain, and some virus I caught somewhere, threw me into typhoid fever, which took me down to nothing and disqualified me for further service; but I would not take a million dollars for those years I had of pleasant personal companionship with the immortal Lincoln, and service with him for my country."

"Doctor Stoddard," I said, "the object of my visit to you to-day is to get your views fresh from your own lips as to Lincoln's total abstinence habit, and his relation to the liquor business."

He said, "Lincoln was a total abstainer of total abstainers. You can't put it too strong in your book; double-lead it, emphasize it; there is no debate nor doubt about it. I never saw him take a glass of the lightest wine or ale, much less the whiskies and brandies and stronger beverages. I have been at the White House times without number, and have eaten there, and never saw a glass of liquor and never saw a glass of wine on his table. I have seen him at public functions and I never saw him put a drop of strong drink to his lips. He was down on the whole 'pisen' business, and said that nothing that had alcohol in it should pollute his lips or corrupt his body and mind. I never heard him say a harsh word about a brewer, distiller or saloonkeeper in my life; I never heard him say a rough word about a drunkard, only words of sympathy and love and hope; but his colossal will never set itself down firmer than it did when he said 'No' to any form of temptation to use liquor. What an example he was to me as a young man and to others of my class, and to the great nation of which he was the illustrious head! But he carried his idea of the danger of liquor into his own life at the White House, and did the unusual, the startling thing of banishing wine from the White House. This was a social revolution in Washington, and attracted the notice and comment of the whole nation. He effected the social change as to liquor in so quiet and modest a way, and yet with that firmness with which he did all things, that he thought were right."

I said, "You have touched a vital historic point in our temperance national movement. Tell me a little more about the circumstances of the time, and what he did in the White House as to serving liquors."

"I have it here in a nutshell," he said, "in one of my books, 'Inside the White House'; and I will read it to you and you can take bodily what I read to you."

This is what he read:

The first of the regular series of Friday evening public receptions at the White House was held March 8, four days after inauguration. There was at least this difference between the pack of 1861 and the memorable rush in Andrew Jackson's day in that all these handshakers were apparently well-behaved and entirely sober. It was hardly so in 1829, if historians have correctly pictured the effects of the "superabundant refreshments" provided according to the ideas of hospitality prevailing at that day. A great deal of that old idea survives, lingering upon the sideboards of old Washington families, in the cupboards of professional offices, under the desks of officeholders, civil, military and naval; over all of the hotels, meeting everybody in the street whenever he meets anybody else; and it is powerfully entrenched under each of the two Houses of Congresss at the Capitol, and its very citadel is the famous "Hole in the Wall," convenient to the Supreme Court rooms and operating as a half-way social house between the two legislative houses. Sometimes one can understand the old times better after a late-in-the-day inspection of the sociability going on in the "Hole in the Wall." There is nothing of the sort in the White House at present, for Mr. Lincoln is strictly abstinent as to all intoxicating drinks. His first printed paper, written while a mere boy, was a vigorous denunciation of the evils produced by whisky among the settlers in the backwoods of his own State. And yet some of the newspapers of the North, in company with other slanderous falsehoods, claimed that the funny jokes he told, and acts unfriendly to them which he performed, were while he was under the influence of liquor.

I said, "Doctor Stoddard, I have read with deep interest and not a little amusement the episode of the sending of liquors to the White House by friends in New York, and of your settling the dilemma by suggesting to Mrs. Lincoln that they be sent to the hospitals for the sick."

"Oh, yes," he said, "that incident is as fresh in my mind now as it was at the time it occurred." Then going to his shelf and taking down a volume, "Lincoln at Work," written by himself, and turning the pages, he said: "That account in full is here, and I will read it to you and you can take it down as part of this interview:

Precisely what was the new order of things may be illustrated by an incident which was almost amusing. Among Mr. Lincoln's warm admirers in the city of New York were several gentlemen with social tendencies; they knew little of his personal habits and prejudices; but they were aware that he was from the West, and believed that he was familiar with the social customs. They were also aware of the costly exactions of White House hospitality, and they determined to aid him in bearing that part of the tremendous burden put upon him. Their intentions, according to such light and knowledge as they had, were patriotic, and their performance was liberality itself. They made out a "wine list" which omitted hardly anything supposed to be required by the sideboard or locker of the Commander-in-Chief, and the supply included even his dinner table. Everything sent was choice of its kind, and it was expressed, prepaid, with warm declarations of good will. The first that I heard of it was a sudden, peremptory summons to me from Mrs. Lincoln to come and see her at once. I hurried down stairs to her reception room, the historic Red Room, somewhat anxious to know what might be the matter. There was enough, indeed, for serious consultation; for she rapidly unfolded to me the story of the New York contribution.

"Now!" she exclaimed, in a very comical perplexity, "what are we to do? I don't wish to offend them, of course, but Mr. Lincoln won't have it in the house. He never uses any. I never touch it myself. And oh, there is so much of it!"

"Where is it, Mrs. Lincoln?"

"Why, it is all downstairs in the basement. I haven't

GOSHEN COLLEGE LIBRARY

told Mr. Lincoln, and I don't wish to bother him about it. I wish you would just decide the matter, and tell me what to do. What answer shall I give to these gentlemen? What am I to do with all the liquor and wines?"

Her dismay had set me laughing, but I thought I could see a way out of her very serious dilemma.

"As to them," I said, "Madam, all you need to do is to send an entirely informal acknowledgment to whoever has acted as their agent. Only a business-like receipt for parcels duly delivered. As for the wines and liquors, don't let them stay in the house at all. Do not worry the President about it, either. Make a fair division of the whole lot among the army hospitals, and ship 'em right away; the surgeons and nurses will know what to do with them. Put all the responsibility upon the scientific people. If any of the sick soldiers need it, there it is."

"That's exactly what I will do!" she exclaimed. "Every bit of it shall go out, right away; then if anybody ever says anything about it, all I need to do is to tell what we did with it."

This was very nearly at the beginning of the Lincoln administration, and the kind of moral testimony which it represents went on in silent power, year after year. Men did not feel like drinking before going to call upon Mr. Lincoln. Officials of all sorts felt the unseen pressure, and it was all the while aided, added to, by the precept and example of several prominent statesmen. The tone of official conduct and life underwent a gradual change.

"How do you feel, Doctor Stoddard," I asked, "now that you are an old man, about this temperance question, on which you were such a 'crank' in your early life?"

He said, "I have the same views today I had then, and I am very thankful that I had the example of Lincoln to encourage and strengthen my right resolutions." He said, "If I had toyed with the poison of alcohol I should not now be upon the earth at eighty-two. I greatly rejoice at the tides of Prohibition sentiment and legislative action that are sweeping away the whole business, and it looks now as though I might possibly see the end of this great enemy."

CHAPTER VII

THE ATTITUDE OF LINCOLN (Continued)

IT was my good fortune to enjoy the warm personal friendship of Noah Brooks, who was on the editorial staff of the "New York Tribune" for years, and on the editorial staff of the "New York Times" a longer term. My friendship began with him when he was chief editor of the "Newark Advertiser." I preached a sermon on Lincoln in the Central Methodist Church, of which I was pastor, and Mr. Brooks printed it in his paper. He said to me one day, "You have related a number of incidents of Lincoln that you got from his old friends and clients in the West that had never been printed in the magazines and books; I can give you some new ones if you would like to have me do so, as I was one of the closest friends Lincoln had in Illinois and afterward in Washington."

We had a good long talk on Lincoln. Mr. Brooks had just written a "Life of Lincoln," the preface of which he read to me, showing how intimate was his knowledge of the subject:

It was my good fortune to know Lincoln with some degree of intimacy. Our acquaintance began with the

Fremont campaign of 1856, when I was a resident of Illinois, and continued through the Lincoln-Douglas canvass two years later. That relation became more intimate and confidential when, in 1862, I met Lincoln in Washington and saw him almost daily until his tragical death. This preliminary egotism may be pardoned by way of explanation of the fact that many things relating to his early life, herein set down, were derived from his own lips, often during hours of secluded companionship.

"Mr. Brooks," I said, "I should like to have from you some facts about Lincoln's temperance habits and his stand on the drink question."

He said "Lincoln was a consistent, persistent total abstainer, and foe of the liquor traffic. That chapter of his life is very clear and bright. I shall take that subject up with you in a moment or two. Before I do so, I want to tell you what a devout man Lincoln was. He turned his heart inside out to me, and I saw in it how deep his piety was. I will give you this illustration: I was at the White House one day when the fate of the nation hung in the balance, and a decisive battle was then raging. Lincoln walked back and forth in the room anxiously. He took out his watch and said to me, 'Twelve o'clock, and no word from the battle.' One o'clock came, and two, and he said, 'No news is bad news. I fear we have been defeated.' Three o'clock came, and the suspense was unbearable. Four o'clock came, and a courier rushed in with a telegram. Lincoln tore open the envelope and read it. He turned ashen pale and handed me the message. Sure enough, the Union army had suffered a terrible defeat. I shall never forget his wail of agony as he cried aloud, 'O God! What in the world are we going to do? O God, help me!' An old gray-headed man, a relative of the family, was the only other person in the room. He cried like a child; and though I am not much given to tears, I cried, too at the insufferable agony of Lincoln. It seemed a veritable Gethsemane, where 'a man of sorrows and acquainted with grief' wrestled with the sins and the woes of the world. Then stretching himself up and looking right into heaven, and taking the nation in one arm, and the hand of the Almighty with the other, he cried, 'O God of Israel, God of our native land, my God, do not let our nation die. Save us, oh, save us! Give us wisdom to plant, but, O God, come down to our battlefield and lead our armies to victory.'

"His mother's teaching and the awful examples of drunkenness in his neighborhood, awakened sympathy and a hatred of drink in the boy, and, when he became old enough to write compositions, he tried his best on one on the evils of strong drink. He carried it over to the home of a friend and asked him to read it and see if he thought it good enough to print in the paper. The man said he thought it was, but did not know what the publisher might say about it. He said, 'Abe, let me have it and I will see what can be done about it.' The friend got a Baptist preacher to send it to Ohio, where it was published in a paper. Lincoln was proud to see his first piece in the paper, and happy in the hope that it might do the people some good. Ward Hall Lamon, in his 'Life of Lincoln,' gives a detailed report of the writing of this essay on temperance."

"Mr. Brooks, the first line to the public from the pen of the immortal Lincoln, then, was an arraignment of the liquor evil, was it not?"

He answered: "It was."

I asked Noah Brooks about the incident that made such a sensation at the time Mr. Lincoln refused to serve liquors or allow others to serve them, on the occasion of his notification by a committee of his nomination for the Presidency the first time.

"The incident is historically true," he said. "I have made a record of it in the book I have written. More than once Mr. Lincoln spoke to me about it. He said at first he was not a little worried, as he did not wish to offend those who were so insistent, and had been such loyal friends, but, said he, 'I do not know how to be inconsistent with myself. After a long life of total abstinence, and of opposition to the drink habit, it would have been a thing unthinkable for me to drink or allow wines to be drunk in my house. By so doing I should have forgotten all the things

I had said and written against drink, the many pledges I have induced others to sign, and my own self-respect. I felt that the situation, not made by me but by my friends, with the best of intentions, furnished me an opportunity, in the eyes of the nation, to put myself on the right side of this great moral question."

Charles Carlton Coffin, as a member of the press, accompanied the committee to notify Mr. Lincoln of his nomination. In his "Life of Lincoln" Mr. Coffin says:

The clock had struck eight o'clock in the evening of May 17, 1860, when the party from Chicago proceeded to the house of Mr. Lincoln in Springfield. Mr. Ashman, president of the convention, made a brief address. The reply was equally brief. Smiles rippled upon Mr. Lincoln's face as he then addressed William D. Kelley of Pennsylvania: "You are a tall man, Judge Kelley. What is your height?" "Six feet three." "I beat you," said Mr. Lincoln; "I am six feet four without my high-heeled boots on." "Pennsylvania bows to Illinois. I am glad we have found a candidate for the Presidency whom we can look up to, for we have been informed that there were only *little giants* in Illinois," a graceful allusion to Mr. Douglas.

"Formalities laid aside," Mr. Lincoln said, "Mrs. Lincoln will be pleased to see you in the other room, gentlemen. You will be thirsty after your long journey. You will find something refreshing in the library."

In the library were several hundred volumes arranged upon shelves, two globes, one of the earth, the other of the heavens, a plain table, a pitcher of cold water and glasses, but no liquors.

Artist Carpenter, who painted the celebrated picture, "Signing the Emancipation Proclamation," says in his book, "Six Months in the White House," that a friend who attended the convention and the notification told him that when the party entered the library Mr. Lincoln said, "Gentlemen, we must pledge our mutual healths in the most healthy beverage God has given to man. It is the only beverage I have ever used or allowed in my family, and I cannot conscientiously depart from it on the present occasion. It is pure Adam's ale from the spring." And taking a tumbler he touched it to his lips and pledged them his highest respect in a cup of cold water.

The next morning a citizen said to Coffin: "You did not find any great spread of liquors, I take it."

"No, I did not," said Coffin.

"Thereby hangs a little story," said the man. "When we knew you were on your way, a number of us called on Mr. Lincoln and said that in all probability some of the members of the committee would need some refreshment, wines or liquors. 'I haven't any in the house,' he said. 'We will furnish them.' 'Gentlemen, I can not allow you to do what I will not do myself,' came the reply. But that was not the end of it. Some of our good citizens, feeling that Springfield had been highly honored by the nomination, sent over some baskets of champagne, but Mr. Lincoln sent them back, thanking them for their intended kindness.' "

Senator Shelby M. Cullom, of Illinois, has made this reference to the incident: "I recall distinctly when the committee of citizens, including myself, called at Lincoln's home after he was nominated for President to talk over with him the arrangements for receiving the committee on notification. Lincoln said, 'Boys, I have never had a drop of liquor in my life, and I don't want to begin now.' That part of the entertainment was provided for elsewhere."

This incident, denied so stoutly by the liquor men, is verified by Lincoln himself, who came, the new figure on the stage and in the eyes of the nation and the centuries, proclaiming himself a total abstainer, the inveterate foe of intoxicating liquors. Mr. J. Mason Haight, hearing of the incident, wrote Lincoln to know whether it was true or not, and received this answer, dated Springfield, Illinois, June 11, 1860:

I think it would be improper for me to write or say anything to or for the public upon the subject of which you inquire. I therefore wish the letter I do write to be held as strictly confidential. Having kept house sixteen years, and having never held the "cup" to the lips of my friends there, my judgment was that I should not, in my new position, change my habit in this respect. What actually occurred on the occasion of the committee visiting me, I think it would be better for others to say.

In my visit and interview with Noah Brooks, he said: "There never lived a more consistent total abstainer than Lincoln, nor one who felt more deeply the damage drink was doing to the individual and to society. He used to point out to me some of the most brilliant and promising men in public life and lament the fact that their usefulness and life had been cut short by strong drink. Time and time again he told me that he attributed much of his strength of body, vigor of mind and moral courage to the fact that he had never allowed alcohol to poison his body, muddle his mind or soil his soul. He had no harsh words for the drunkard, only the deepest pity for him, nor bitter condemnation of the liquor dealer, claiming that society, which demanded and legalized the traffic, was responsible for its curse and wreckage. He expressed the hope and belief that in some good time in the future the people would arise and destroy the cruel despotism of rum. Close as I was to Lincoln before and after his election, I never saw him touch a drop of liquor. I ate at the White House dozens, I might say scores, of times. I never saw a drop of beer or the lightest wine on his table, and at public functions I noticed that he either turned his glass down or pushed it aside untouched."

Noah Brooks's "Life of Lincoln," in style, clearness, fulness and reliability, is one of the standard works of American literature.

Colonel William H. Crook, who had experiences at the White House under five administrations and who was one of Lincoln's bodyguards, gave me a number of incidents illustrating Lincoln's total abstinence. He said Lincoln was a hearty eater, although he never took on much flesh, but that he never touched a drop of intoxicants. He never allowed them on his table at the White House, not even the mildest forms of alcoholic drinks, and at the public functions he never used a drop. "Mr. Lincoln ordered me to go with him on his trip to Richmond, which he entered thirty-six hours after the Confederate army had retired from it," said Colonel Crook. "It was a dangerous and rash thing, but Lincoln knew no danger. He went to the Federal headquarters, which was the old Jefferson Davis home, a large house of gray stucco with a garden at the back. I asked the old colored servant if they had anything to drink there. He said: 'Oh, certainly, marster,' and went down cellar and brought up a long black bottle of whisky. It was passed around and, if my memory serves me correctly, every person in the company took a swig but Mr. Lincoln, who, shaking his head and waving his hand, said, 'None for me.' This is an illustration of a hundred times I have seen Lincoln refuse

liquor when his friends and associates did not
hesitate to take it."

THE LINCOLN-LEE LEGION

The Rev. Howard H. Russell, D.D., founder
of the Anti-Saloon League of America, in taxing
his fertile brain to organize a Young People's
Auxiliary to the League, naturally turned his
thoughts to Lincoln, the ideal man and pronounced temperance advocate, as a character
around whom the institution could be built. In
search of historical data he went to Springfield,
Illinois, early in 1900. He found at Mr. Diller's
drug store in Springfield an old desk which Lincoln used when he was a member of the State
Legislature, and on which he had written in plain
letters, "A. Lincoln." Diller told Russell that
there was a farmer by the name of Cleopas
Breckenridge living in Sangamon County, about
sixteen miles away, who knew a great deal about
Lincoln's temperance proclivities, and he was sure
that Russell would be deeply interested in getting
data from him. A few months later Doctor
Russell wrote Mr. Diller, asking him if he would
not request Mr. Breckenridge, if possible, to meet
him at a certain date. The arrangement was
made and Breckenridge drove into Springfield
upon a stormy day and met Russell at the Leland
Hotel in that city, when he told Russell the following story:

"When I was a boy," said Breckenridge, "I lived with my father upon the same farm which I now own in Cotton Hill Township in this county. One day in the summer of 1846 or 1847, when I was about ten years old, my father came home and told us that there would be a temperance meeting held at the new schoolhouse, and that we could all go to the meeting if we wished to do so. Most of the family attended the meeting. The speaker on the occasion was a young lawyer from Springfield, who already had gained a reputation as a public speaker, and the announcement of the fact that he was to speak called out a large crowd, almost all the families in that part of the county being represented. The speaker made a very earnest appeal for total abstinence from the use of all intoxicating drinks. He gave reasons why he was in favor of total abstinence, and why he thought others should become total abstainers. He said, 'Let us make this meeting one of strong and lasting value. Whether we have been in the habit of drinking or not, let us here set an example to others by enrolling in the ranks of pledged abstainers. I have signed this pledge myself and would be glad to have as many of my neighbors who are willing to do so sign the same pledge with me.' The pledge was passed from one to another and was signed by a good many of those present.

After a number had signed, the first thing I
knew the speaker was standing in front of
me. He said to me: 'Sonny, don't you want
your name on this pledge?' I said: 'Yes, sir.'
He said: 'You know what it means, that you
are not to drink intoxicating liquor?' I said:
'Yes, sir.' He asked me my name and I told
him, 'Cleopas Breckenridge.' He wrote my name
on the paper, then he transferred the pencil to
his left hand, and holding the paper and pencil
in his left hand, he leaned over and laid his right
hand upon my head and said: 'Now, Sonny, you
keep that pledge, and it will be the best act of
your life.' The speaker who addressed that
meeting, and who wrote my name on the pledge,
was Abraham Lincoln."

The more the auxiliary to the League occupied
his mind the more Russell felt that Lincoln must
be the center of it, so he made another trip to
Springfield, Illinois, and drove out to the farm of
Cleopas Breckenridge, where he was entertained
admirably overnight, and where he had an opportunity to get more definite data. He asked Breckenridge whether he could recall any others who
were at that meeting at South Fork schoolhouse
when he himself had signed the pledge. At first
he could not be sure, but the next morning he
said to Russell that there were two men living at
Edinburgh, Christian County, Illinois, who he
thought were likely to have been there, and so

Russell went over with Breckenridge that same day and luckily found the two men in town, R. E. Berry and Moses Martin. He took them to the notary public, where they both made affidavit that they were present at the meeting, remembered Lincoln's address, and signed the pledge that Lincoln had written and signed himself with them. Martin in his affidavit says:

Among those who signed the pledge in that meeting were George, William, and Uriah Hughes and their mother; Preston Breckenridge and his children, and R. E. Berry, now of Edinburgh, Illinois. I myself signed then and there—my first pledge—and I have kept it until now. I further remember and state that after Mr. Lincoln had spoken and the pledge had been signed, Mr. Lincoln asked if any one had anything to say for or against the movement, and Mr. Preston Breckenbridge rose up and spoke of the importance of parents taking an interest in the matter. The wife of the said Breckenridge had recently died, and he pointed to his motherless children and spoke of his anxiety for them, and as he spoke the tears ran down his face. Afterward at various times and places the said Preston Breckenridge held Washingtonian meetings and I went with him and acted as secretary and helped enroll the signers to the pledge.

The meeting above referred to conducted and addressed by Abraham Lincoln was the beginning of a series of Washingtonian meetings which did great and lasting good in this section of the country.

After Russell's return to New York he received a letter from Cleopas Breckenridge, stating that he had found another person who when a child, signed the same Lincoln pledge—Mrs. Almarinda Bell Galloway. These four survivors of that historic event went to Springfield, had a reunion, went to the photographers and had their picture taken, and present a very intelligent and dignified quartet of veterans.

This is the text of the pledge which Lincoln wrote with his own fingers and signed with the grown people and children at South Fork schoolhouse:

Whereas, the use of alcoholic liquors as a beverage is productive of pauperism, degradation and crime, and believing it is our duty to discourage that which produces more evil than good, we therefore pledge ourselves to abstain from the use of intoxicating liquors as a beverage.

A Southerner suggested to Doctor Russell that the name of Robert E. Lee be added to that of Lincoln, making it the Lincoln-Lee Legion. Russell agreed to the suggestion, and the name of Lee, one of the ablest, purest, truest and best men personally this country ever produced, who was a total abstainer, was added to that of Lincoln; the abstinence pledge of the Lincoln-Lee Legion has been signed by 4,000,000 people.

LINCOLN'S ADDRESS AT SPRINGFIELD

We will now call to the witness stand Lincoln himself to testify in the case of Lincoln vs. Alcohol. From the great address he made in Springfield before the Washingtonian Society which on February 22, 1842, we take copious quotations as follows:

Although the temperance cause has been in progress for near twenty years, it is apparent to all that it is *just now* being crowned with a degree of success hitherto unparalleled.

The list of its friends is daily swelled by the additions of fifties, of hundreds, and of thousands. The cause itself seems suddenly transformed from a cold abstract theory, to a living, breathing, active, and powerful chieftain, going forth "conquering and to conquer." The citadels of his great adversary are daily being stormed and dismantled; his temples and his altars, where the rites of his idolatrous worship have long been performed, and where human sacrifices have long been wont to be made, are daily desecrated and deserted. The trump of the conqueror's fame is sounding from hill to hill, from sea to sea, and from land to land, and calling millions to his standard at a blast.

But when one who has long been known as a victim of intemperance bursts the fetters that have bound him, and appears before his neighbors "clothed and in his right mind," a redeemed specimen of long lost humanity, and stands up with tears of joy trembling in his eyes, to tell of the miseries *once* endured, *now* to be endured no more forever; of his once naked and starving children, now clad and fed comfortably; of a wife, long weighed down with woe, weeping, and a broken heart, now restored to health, happiness, and renewed affection; and how easily it all is done, once it is resolved to be done; however simple his language, there is a logic and an eloquence in it that few with human feelings can resist.

But I have said that denunciations against dram sellers and dram drinkers, are *unjust* as well as impolitic. Let us see.

I have not inquired at what period of time the use of intoxicating drinks commenced; nor is it important to know. It is sufficient that to all of us who now inhabit the world the practice of drinking them is just as old as the world itself,—that is, we have seen the one just as long as we have seen the other. When all such of us as have now reached the years of maturity first opened our eyes upon the stage of existence, we found intoxicating liquor recognized by everybody, used by everybody, and repudiated by nobody. It commonly entered into the first draught of the infant, and the last draught of the dying man. From the sideboard of the parson down to the ragged pocket of the houseless loafer, it was constantly found. Physicians prescribed it in this, that, and the other disease. Government provided it for its soldiers and sailors; and to have a rolling or raising, a husking or hoe-down anywhere, without it, was positively insufferable.

So, too, it was everywhere a respectable article of manufacture and of merchandise. The making of it was regarded as an honorable livelihood; and he who could make most was the most enterprising and respectable.

Large and small manufactories of it were everywhere erected, in which all the earthly goods of their owners were invested. Wagons drew it from town to town— boats bore it from clime to clime, and the winds wafted it from nation to nation; and merchants bought and sold it, by wholesale and by retail, with precisely the same feelings, on the part of seller, buyer, and bystander, as are felt at the selling and buying of flour, beef, bacon, or any other of the real necessaries of life. Universal public opinion not only tolerated, but recognized and adopted, its use.

It is true that, even *then,* it was known and acknowledged that many were greatly injured by it; but none seemed to think that the injury arose from the use of a *bad thing,* but from the abuse of a *very good thing.* . . . The victims to it were pitied and compassionated, just as now are heirs of consumption and other hereditary diseases. Their failing was treated as a *misfortune,* and not as a *crime,* or even as a *disgrace.*

If, then, what I have been saying be true, is it wonderful that *some* should think and act *now,* as *all* thought and acted *twenty years ago*? And is it *just* to assail, condemn, or despise them for doing so?

But if it be true, as I have insisted, that those who have suffered by intemperance, *personally,* and have reformed, are the most powerful and efficient instruments to push the reformation to ultimate success, it does not follow that those who have not suffered have no part left them to perform. Whether or not the world would be vastly benefited by a total and final banishment from it of all intoxicating drinks, seems to me not *now* to be an open question. Three-fourths of mankind confess the affirmative with their *tongues,* and I believe all the rest acknowledge it in their *hearts.*

Ought *any,* then, to refuse their aid in doing what the good of the *whole* demands? Shall he who cannot do *much* be for that reason excused if he do nothing? "But," says one, "what good can I do by signing the pledge? I never drink even without signing." This question has already been asked and answered more than a million times. Let it be answered once more. For the man suddenly, or in any other way, to break off from the use of drams, who has indulged in them for a long course of years, and until his appetite for them has become ten or a hundred fold stronger and more craving than any natural appetite can be, requires a most powerful moral effort. In such an undertaking, he needs every moral support and influence that can possible be brought to his aid and thrown around him. And not only so, but every moral prop should be taken *from* whatever argument might rise in his mind to lure him to his backsliding. When he casts his eyes around him, he should be able to see all that he respects, all that he admires, and all that he loves, kindly and anxiously pointing him onward; and none beckoning him back to his former miserable "wallowing in the mire."

But it is said by some that men will *think* and *act* for themselves; that none will disuse spirits or anything else merely because his neighbors do; and that *moral influence* is not that powerful engine contended for. Let us examine this. Let me ask the man who would maintain this position most stiffly, what compensation he will accept to go to church some Sunday and sit during the sermon with his wife's bonnet on his head? Not a trifle,

I'll venture. And why not? There would be nothing irreligious in it; nothing immoral, nothing uncomfortable. Then why not? Is it not because there would be something egregiously unfashionable in it? Then it is the influence of *fashion;* and what is the influence of fashion but the influence that other people's actions have upon *our own* actions; the strong inclination each of us feels to do as we see all our neighbors do? Nor is the influence of fashion confined to any particular thing or class of things. It is just as strong on one subject as another. Let us make it as unfashionable to withhold our names from the temperance pledge as for husbands to wear their wives' bonnets to church, and instances will be just as rare in the one case as in the other.

"But," say some, "we are no drunkards; and we shall not acknowledge ourselves such by joining a reformed drunkards' society, whatever our influence might be." Surely no Christian will adhere to this objection. If they believe, as they profess, that Omnipotence condescended to take on himself the form of sinful man, as such, to die an ignominious death for their sakes, surely they will not refuse submission to the infinitely lesser condescension, for the temporal, and perhaps eternal, salvation of a large erring and unfortunate class of their own fellow creatures. Nor is the condescension very great.

In my judgment, such of us as have never fallen victims have been spared more from the absence of appetite than from any mental or moral superiority over those who have. Indeed, I believe, if we take habitual drunkards as a class, their heads and hearts will bear an advantageous comparison with those of any other class. There seems ever to have been a proneness in the brilliant and the warm-blooded to fall into this vice. The demon of intemperance ever seems to have delighted in sucking the blood of genius and of generosity. What one of us but can call to mind some dear relative, more promising in youth than all of his fellows, who has fallen a sacrifice to his rapacity? He ever seems to have gone forth, like the Egyptian angel of death, commissioned to slay, if not the first, the fairest born of every family. Shall he now be arrested in his desolating career? In that arrest, all can give aid that will; and who shall be execused that *can* and will not? Far around as human breath has ever blown, he keeps our fathers, our brothers, our sons, and our friends prostrate in the chains of moral death. To all the living everywhere we cry, "Come, sound the moral resurrection trump, that these may rise and stand up, an exceeding great army." . . . "Come from the four winds, O breath! and breathe upon these slain, that they may live."

If the relative grandeur of revolutions shall be estimated by the great amount of human misery they alleviate, and the small amount they inflict, then, indeed, will this be the grandest the world shall ever have seen. Of our political revolution of '76 we all are justly proud. It has given us a degree of political freedom far exceeding that of any other of the nations of the earth. In it the world has found a solution of that long-mooted problem as to the capability of man to govern himself. In it was the germ which has vegetated, and still is to grow and expand, into the universal liberty of mankind.

But with all these glorious results, past, present, and to come, it had its evils too. It breathed forth famine, swam in blood and rode on fire; and long, long after, the orphan's cry and widow's wail continue to break the sad silence that ensued. These were the price, the inevitable price, paid for the blessings it bought.

Turn now to the temperance revolution. In *it* we shall find a stronger bondage broken; a viler slavery manumitted; a greater tyrant deposed. In *it,* more of want supplied, more disease healed, more sorrow assuaged. By *it,* no orphans starving, no widows weeping. By *it,* none wounded in feeling, none injured in interest. Even the dram-maker, and the dram-seller, will have glided into other occupations so *gradually* as never to have felt the shock of change; and will stand ready to join all others in the universal song of gladness.

And what a noble ally this, to the cause of political freedom. With such an aid, its march cannot fail to be on and on, until every son on earth shall drink in rich fruition the sorrow-quenching draughts of perfect liberty. Happy day when, all appetites controlled, all passions subdued, all manners subjected, *mind,* all-conquering *mind,* shall live and move, the monarch of the world. Glorious consumation! Hail, fall of Fury! Reign of Reason, all hail!

And when the victory shall be complete—when there shall be neither a slave nor a drunkard on earth—how proud the title of that *land,* which may truly claim to be the birthplace and the cradle of both those revolutions that shall have ended in that victory! How nobly distinguished that people who shall have planted and nurtured to maturity both the political and moral freedom of their species!

The historical fact of the delivery of this address is attested by Lincoln himself in letters written to friends on the subject, and one of those was to George E. Pickett, who afterward became the famous Confederate general who led the charge at Gettysburg, and whose mother a few years ago, in a letter to one of the American magazines, gave the letter in full, which is as follows:

The fact is, truth is your truest friend, no matter what the circumstances are. I have a congenital aversion to failure, and the sudden announcement to your Uncle Andrew of the success of your "lamp-rubbing" might possibly prevent your passing the severe physical examination to which you will be subjected in order to enter the Military Academy. You see, I shall like to have a perfect soldier credited to dear old Illinois. No broken bones, scalp wounds, etc. So I think it might be wise to hand this letter from me in to your good uncle through his room window after he has had a comfortable dinner, and watch its effect from the top of the pigeon house.

I have just told the folks here in Springfield, on this 111th anniversary of the birth of him whose name, mightiest in the cause of moral reformation, we mention in solemn awe, in naked, deathless splendor, that the one victory we can ever call complete will be that one which proclaims that there is not one slave or drunkard on the face of God's green earth. Recruit for this victory.

Now, boy, on your march, don't you go and forget that "one drop of honey catches more flies than a gallon of gall." Load your musket with this maxim, and smoke it in your pipe.

Another letter on the subject is to Joshua F. Speed, one of the dearest and best friends Lincoln ever had in his young manhood and in Washington:

You will see by the last Sangamon Journal that I made a temperance speech on the Twenty-second of February, which I claim that Fanny and you shall read as an act of charity to me, for I can not learn that anybody else has read it or is likely to. Fortunately it is not very long, and I shall deem it sufficient compliance with my request if one of you listens while the other reads it.

It would be thought that the liquor dealers would never dare mention the name of Lincoln as in any way friendly to them, but they have persisted in their audacity in dragging him into their support even up to the present time. Not very long ago, at a hearing in Albany on a local option bill for cities of the third class, the attorney of the State Liquor Dealers' Association made an eloquent speech against the measure, using as his peroration a part of this speech of Lincoln at Springfield which referred to personal liberty, and using that speech to claim Lincoln as an ally of his cause. The liquor dealers, who were out in large numbers, and brewers and distillers leading in the fight, cheered the gentleman lustily for such a capital hit in his speech. I sent a little slip to the one having charge of our side of the hearing and said: "I want just three minutes at the close;" and in those three minutes I said: "My able friend closed his address most eloquently by a quotation from the address of Lincoln at Springfield, Illinois. I want to finish that address for you." And then, having read the address over so many dozens of times, and knowing it almost by heart, I recited the part where Lincoln pleaded for the cause of total abstinence, referring to the cruel slavery of rum to the body and mind, and how he hoped and prayed for the day when there would be neither a slave nor a drunkard on the face of God's green earth, and the friends on our side of the house burst out into the wildest enthusiasm. The ruddy-faced brewers turned redder in the face, and they set on their attorney in great anger with their complaints that he should so have left himself open to criticism. In great excitement and discomfort he said, "That part that Doctor Iglehart recited is not in Lincoln's speech at all; Lincoln never said anything of the kind," reaching his hand toward his pocket he said, "I have the book and you can read it for yourselves; it is not there." This occurred after the hearing was over. Of course he did not have that part against his business in his liquor dealers' book which was printed for general circulation. It was the business of the liquor men to misrepresent him as they always do; it was their business to take a piece of what he said that they could distort into endorsement of themselves, and to leave out this terrific arraignment of their business by so great a man.

CHAPTER VIII

Pioneer Prohibition States

ABOUT sixty years ago a wave of Prohibition swept over the Northern States. Maine, New Hampshire, Vermont, Rhode Island, Connecticut, New York, Delaware, Michigan, Indiana and Iowa adopted statutory prohibition. One State after another dropped out of line until in 1907 Maine, Kansas and North Dakota were the only ones of the eighteen States that had tried the experiment of Prohibition that retained it, they having adopted constitutional Prohibition.

In 1907 a wave of popular indignation set in which has moved with steady, swift, merciless fury against the saloon.

Ten years ago, after fifty years of fighting, there remained but three dry States. In a short decade twenty-three more States have been added to them, making more than a majority of all the States, embracing two-thirds of the geographical area, and over a half of the population of the country.

MAINE

Col. Fred Dow, son of the great General Neal Dow, known throughout this country and the wide world as the father of prohibition in modern times, the worthy successor of his father in the realm of business, moral reform, and warfare on the liquor traffic, has furnished me this immensely important information on Maine and Prohibition.

In 1851 Maine adopted Prohibition. The novel legislation became widely known and famous as "The Maine Law." Of that enactment its author said: "More than any other measure it will bless the people who adopt it." The immediate benefits in Maine traceable to Prohibition were so great as to justify the prediction of its author, and to lead twelve States, within five years, to adopt laws largely patterned after that of Maine; and to-day the principle of "The Maine Law" finds wide approval in this and other lands. All this testifies to the wisdom and virility of the leadership of the early movement. Few have so deeply impressed themselves upon the legislation of so many lands as did Neal Dow.

Through that law Maine became the leader of a reformation destined to influence many States. But though honor be accorded leadership, danger always attends it. Maine incurred the hostility of the liquor interest, drew all the criticism and condemnation which opposition to Prohibition could bring to bear upon her, became from that day a target for unmeasured misrepresentation on the part of paid and volunteer agents of the liquor propaganda, and has suffered in reputation because some honest people thus misled have believed and repeated it.

Space will not permit notice and refutation of those misstatesments in detail. Such of them as are not merely the mouth-froth of a kind of moral delirium tremens are founded only on isolated instances, sporadic as to time and place, exploited as evidence of general conditions. Such tests and reasoning, used to discredit Prohibition in Maine, might show as effectually that the prohibitions of the Decalogue would better be permissions, and that civilization is a curse and not a benefit to mankind. Though my opportunities for observation in Maine and for acquiring knowledge of her people are quite up to the average, I know of no justification for much of the disparagement to which I refer. The liquor trade is not entirely eliminated from the State. Sixty years has been scant time for that. So also some of the Ten Commandments, though hoary with age, are yet violated. But where the traffic drags its intermittent existence it is under the restraint of the fear that the halter of the law about its neck may at any moment be tightened to the choking-point.

To the same effect may be quoted substantially all of the men of Maine who won national fame in the fifty to sixty years following the enactment of Prohibition. They were competent and reliable witnesses, none better to be found anywhere. They were such that Maine men have held in Washington, at one and the same time, the positions of Secretary of State, Speaker of the House, Presidency pro tem. of the Senate, chairmanships of the committees of Ways and Means, Commerce, Appropriations, Navy, and Public Buildings; while a Maine man born and matured was the Chief Justice of the United States Supreme Court. Among the nation-known men from Maine who during their lives testified to the efficacy and benefits of Prohibition in Maine I mention Hannibal Hamlin, William Pitt Fessenden, Lot M. Morrill, James G. Blaine, Eugene Hale, William P. Frye, Thomas B. Reed and Nelson Dingley. Who knows not of them must be himself unknown. Many others only less known to fame might be cited for the same purpose.

Neal Dow advocated Prohibition among other reasons because, as he claimed, it would be of economical benefit to the State. Maine adopted his views in 1851. The census of the preceding year had shown Maine, judged by her per capita wealth, to be the poorest of the Atlantic Seabord States. Sixty years after, her per capita wealth had increased by a larger percentage than that of any, save one, of her seacoast sisters. The great Empire State of New York, into whose coffers the commerce of the world was pouring tribute during all those years, escapes inclusion by less than two per cent. But between 1900 and 1910 the percentage of Maine of the increased value per acre of all farm property, land, buildings, implements and live stock was much larger than that in New York.

Maine in 1910 had a less percentage of mortgaged farms than any of the New England, Middle States and Maryland, save one. That State, under Prohibition nearly as long as Maine, leads her by one per cent. The average amount of farm mortgage debt in Maine is less than in any of the States mentioned save her Prohibitory companion, and there it is only three dollars less; while the percentage of the value of the equity in all mortgaged farms is larger in Maine than in any of those ten States.

Nor has Maine neglected the productivity of her farms. From 1899 to 1909 she increased the amount paid for fertilizers by a much larger percentage than did any of the States mentioned. The excess she paid for them in ten years, over an average for the period equal to the amount paid in 1899, would have discharged all her farm mortgages, with seven millions of dollars over.

I claim to know something of Maine and of her people. I was born there, have always lived within her borders, and, please God, I expect to die there. Time and again I have traversed her territory from Kittery to Quody and from Katahdin to the sea. I have fished in her streams and lakes, have hunted in her woods. I have worn overalls, carried a dinner pail and worked with her mechanics. I have been with her lumber men in their camps and with her fishermen on their smacks, with her business men in their counting-rooms and their marts of trade, have served with them in the directorates of manufactures and banking and railroad corporations. I have met her people in their schoolhouses, their churches, their halls, on their farms and in their homes. I have held elective and appointive offices among them, and feel that I am familiar enough to express an intelligent opinion of them. And I do not hesitate to declare, without fear of successful refutation, as the result of a most careful investigation, in substantially the language of James G. Blaine, used by him a few years before his death, that nowhere in the Anglo-Saxon world can be found an equal number of people better founded in all the essentials of good citizenship and consuming a smaller quantity of intoxicating liquors than the people of Maine. And I think, as do thousands of her citizens, that the State in indebted to Prohibition for much of this.

A short time before his death, my father was speaking of the possibilities of a nation free from the evils pertaining to a legalized liquor traffic. And I said to him, "father, you surely cannot expect to live to see that." With eyes brilliant with the light of his glorious belief in immortality which he cherished to the last, he said: "I surely do, but it will be from the other side."

SENATOR FERNALD

Prohibition has done much for Maine. This was true even in the period before the present era of enforcement, when in many sections of the State the law was ignored. It was true, even in the territory where the most flagrant nullification existed. True, because in those sections one did not find the open saloon and open drinking. By the very manner in which the saloons were conducted under the systems, known variously as the Peters plan, the Bangor plan, the Androscoggin plan and the Pennell plan, there was thrown about it an atmosphere of shame. The youth of our State, unconsciously imbibed the idea that drinking was disgraceful; that it was something to be hidden from the public.

But there is far more to it. Our State has grown under Prohibition. Examine the banking reports of Maine and compare the savings per capita of its citizens with those of license States and the finding will be in our favor.

Visit other States and examine the personnel of its men, its leaders, if you please. I care not whether you look to members of the legal profes-

sion or to that of medicine or to the business men,
you will find men from Maine constitute these
leaders. You will find them everywhere and you
will find them in the forefront of affairs; judges
of courts, engineers of great undertakings, heads
of larger mercantile and manufacturing establishments. No State has furnished so many men of
brains and leadership to the other States as has
Maine. We have sent our young men and our
young women out into the rest of the country to
help in its upbuilding, to pilot those other States,
and yet we have not lost in population, but have
gradually increased.

And, now, look at Maine as an industrial State.
Go into our manufacturing centers and what do
you find? No such slums as one so easily locates
in similar centers of license districts. You do not
find the want and squalor or the degeneracy
in Maine that you find in wet States.

Prohibition has given our boys and girls a
greater stamina, a better intelligence, a greater
regard for sobriety, morality and honesty. It has
helped to make the citizenship of Maine the best
in the Union.

GOVERNOR MILLIKEN

Few will deny that Prohibition prohibits at the
present time in Maine. Under the brave and determined administration of Governor Milliken
the law is respected and enforced,

In a letter addressed to me, July 17, 1917, Governor Milliken says: "It goes without saying that we believe in the advances of Prohibition for the State of Maine. I am doing my utmost for a thorough, honest, and State-wide enforcement of the law, and the results, as a rule, are very satisfactory."

The bootleggers whose wares are confiscated, as well as the district attorneys and sheriffs who if they dared would wink at the non-enforcement of the law, know full well how strictly the Prohibitory law is administered.

A gentleman told me the other day that a prosecuting attorney of a certain Maine county went to Augusta at the call of the Governor. He had his resignation already written out and handed it to the Governor, who accepted it. He had been playing false with the State, forgetting his oath and betraying the people in shutting one eye to the illicit traffic in intoxicants. The day when any sheriff or district attorney can make himself judge and jury and allow the liquor law to be nullified has gone by.

KANSAS

Governor Arthur Capper of Kansas gave me the following:

When I first went to Topeka there were fifty or sixty saloons. The jails were filled most of the time. The

"Daily Capital" rarely had enough men to do its work the day after pay day. Indeed, I got my first job on that paper because too many of the printers were absent from drink and the foreman was willing to take any one. It was a wide-open town. Even up to fifteen or twenty years ago I believe a majority of the leading business men favored high license, under the impression that saloons were needed if the town was to be a live place, and especially for the revenue they contributed.

But ultimately, through a period of observation, of education, these business men learned that they might as wisely license morphine or cocaine. They discovered that their fears about revenues were groundless and that the town lived and prospered amazingly under the rule of decency.

When I went to Topeka the men in my trade never had anything except trouble and unpaid bills and headaches. Now the majority of the printers own their homes, many have motor cars; they have their vacations now, with their families; they are good citizens. A few months ago a printer in the "Daily Capital" plant received a check for $10,000 from the Ætna Building and Loan Society, representing his savings and interest. In the same plant, of which I am the owner, we have a savings society with more than a hundred members, which includes printers, pressmen, and stereotypers, all of whom save a certain part of their wages every week. The number of arrests in Topeka for drunkenness has constantly decreased, though our population is steadily increasing.

As a strictly business proposition Prohibition has paid big dividends in Kansas. Its strongest advocates in the State are the large employers of labor, the managers of the big railroad properties, and the labor organizations. More than 4,000 men are employed in the Santa Fe railway shops at Topeka—the dryest city of its size in the world. Those shops maintain the highest degree of efficiency of any on the Santa Fe system. The books show that they turn out more work, consistently and promptly the year round, than any other railroad shops. Seventy-two per cent. of the married men in these shops own their homes—a showing that cannot be equaled by any other railway town in America.

On a dollar basis, merely, Prohibition has paid. As to the domestic side, the records of a survey show that the families of the shopmen are, of course, in very much better condition than those in license States. Naturally they have more money to spend. There is far less family trouble. There are fewer divorces. The children and the wives wear better clothes; they live happier lives. The fathers' earnings go to the family support instead of to the saloons.

We are not paying dearly for this decency. The State tax in Kansas in only $1.30 per thousand, the lowest, with two exceptions, in the United States. Compared with like cities, Topeka's taxes are no higher and certainly are not sufficiently burdensome to bring a protest from the people. Any student of such facts knows that no saloon ever contributed enough taxes to pay for the trouble it caused. No one ever heard of the liquor interests producing enough revenue to pay for the police and the jails and the courts needed to hold the criminals the saloons create. It is still the custom of wet communities, in wet or semi-wet States, to pave the streets and roads with fines from vice resorts, while these resorts pave the way to perdition for the young people; but the cities of Kansas that have received no revenue whatever from vice have a lower tax rate than those cities which in the old days stuck to the last to the license-fining system. More than five million dollars was spent by the cities of Kansas in the year ending June 30, 1916, for paving, electric light, parks, waterworks and other improvements, but not a dollar was contributed by the liquor traffic or commercialized vice. To-day there is no such thing as a slum or licensed red-light district in any city in Kansas. Nowhere in all the civilized world are moral conditions cleaner and better than in Prohibition Kansas.

Prohibition has been in operation thirty-six years in Kansas. If the people were not satisfied with the law and the conditions it has produced they certainly could have changed them long ago. It seems to me, as the lawyers say, that the people themselves are the best evidence. The surest way to bring about the repeal of an objectionable law is to enforce it. We enforce the prohibitory law in Topeka and in the State and I have seen no disposition to repeal it. Certainly not on the score of taxes.

The last defense of the saloon is the plea that its revenue helps to pay the taxes. It does, but it does it at a cost of blood, of broken hearts and wrecked homes as well as of dollars and cents. The saloon, wherever it exists, is our greatest public debt-maker, our greatest public burden.

Kansas sends more boys and girls to public schools, to the university and the colleges, in proportion to population, than any other State in the Union. Kansas is one of the two States in the Union having the smallest number of persons who cannot read and write—less than two per cent. of its population. According to an investigation completed in 1914 and authenticated by the Federal Health Department, Kansas has a death rate of 9.8, the lowest of any State in the Union comprised within the registration area recognized by the government.

Kansas is one of the few States in the Union without bonded indebtedness. The last outstanding bond was taken up January 1, 1916.

I have laid stress upon the testimony of the people of Kansas themselves. Let me give this testimony in a little detail:

Every Governor of Kansas for twenty-two years has said over his signature that Prohibition is a great success.

Every member of the Supreme Court of Kansas and every State official says that Prohibition succeeds.

More than 700 of the 780 Kansas editors in State convention, including newspapers of every political faith, unanimously endorsed Prohibition.

Every political party in Kansas favors the prohibitory law, and has endorsed the law in its platform.

No minister in Kansas ever opens his mouth in favor of returning to the licensed saloon, nor any teacher.

From our experience of successful Prohibition in Kansas we stand for and demand Prohibition for the nation.

SENATOR CHARLES CURTIS

United States Senator Curtis of Kansas gave me the following facts:

There are many and substantial benefits from Prohibition, which is now a settled policy in the State. The people are well satisfied with the law and are insisting upon its rigid enforcement. The many legislatures since its first enactment in 1881 have strengthened the law, and the sentiment in favor of the law has grown stronger and stronger each year. Our people believe it has been a great success and that many benefits have resulted from the Constitutional amendment and the legislation enacted since the adoption of it.

The official reports of the various counties in the State show a decrease in crime and a great reduction in the number of the poor supported by county authorities. In 1914 there were twenty-eight counties in Kansas that did not have a single prisoner in jail during all of that year; there were forty-eight counties in which there were no convicts sent to the State Penitentiary during the year; in twelve counties no jury has been required to try a criminal case in a number of years. In 1914 there were twenty counties without a prisoner in the State Penitentiary, and of the 740 prisoners in the State Penitentiary in that year, forty per cent. of them were non-residents of the State; thirty-eight county poor farms had no inmates, and there was only one pauper in the State to every three thousand of its population.

There are thousands of young men and women in the State who never saw a saloon, and there are thousands who have never seen a drunken man within the State. It seems to me that these facts, presented from the records, are the best evidence of the success of Prohibition in Kansas, and they are the best answer that can be made to the many false claims that have been sent out by the liquor interests.

WILLIAM ALLEN WHITE

I wrote to Mr. William Allen White, known throughout the nation as editor and author, for facts about Prohibition in Kansas and he sent me these:

Prohibition is not responsible for all the good things in Kansas. Our soil is rich; our people are the native American stock with a strong infusion of blood from the north of Europe. Our climate is equitable, and our rainfall on the whole dependable and plenteous. And we have made Prohibition succeed somewhat because of these things rather than that Prohibition has brought these things. Yet there are certain earmarks of Kansas that are distinctly Prohibition earmarks.

I should say that the first thing for which Kansans are to be grateful, as a distinct result of the abolition of the saloon, is a clean State politics. There is practically no corruption or bribery in the State. That doesn't mean that there is no corruption or bribery. Our voters are not all "just men made perfect;" but corruption and bribery are as negligible here as leprosy is in our social order. We have built up a whole race of politicians who are not afraid of the liquor interests, because there are no liquor interests in Kansas. That does not mean that there is no liquor sold in Kansas, for there is plenty of it—more of it than there should be. This is a town of ten thousand people, and I have no doubt whatever that at the Christmas time a hundred quart bottles of whisky were sold in violation of the law the night before Christmas, which means, of course, that the bootlegger fram Kansas City brought down in his suit case or had shipped to him, disguised as nails or whatnot, this liquor in small bottles; that he went skulking around the dark corners of the town Friday and Saturday nights before Christmas, beckoning such wayfarers as he thought might buy his wares, and that he sold his wares. But one hundred quarts of liquor divided among ten thousand people is not an important violation of the law. It would be as wise to say that our marriage laws were a failure because of the occasional violation of the statutes against adultery, as to say Prohibition fails because an occasional bootlegger, flitting up an alley, disposes of an occasional quart of liquor.

The bootlegger has no place of business. He can only be found by those who are willing to labor and wait, and he can have no influence on our politics. His whole force combined in this town would consist of half a dozen colored men and one or two mangy, half-starved white men, and that wouldn't be any liquor interest that any politician would not be glad to kick in passing. So that, as I said, the net gain we have received from Prohibition is clean politics. When a man runs for office a good man is not beaten because of his belief in Prohibition and a bad man is not elected because of his friendship for the liquor interests. Liquor is "out on the hills away" from our politics, and that is an unquestionable gain.

It seems to me also that the abolition of the saloon has reduced crime in Kansas, and that it has something to do—not everything, but something to do—with our phenomenal prosperity. We do not patronize savings banks. We are an agricultural people, but we have a large comparative per capita of wealth—larger than any other agricultural State of our age, in this part of the West—and I think Prohibition has helped. But the thing Prohibition has done is to improve the tone of the State; to make it possible to appeal to the people on moral issues and to make possible a response from the people to moral issues.

Now these opinions on Prohibition are not mine alone. I took occasion recently to address various representative heads of the various organized activities of the State— political, professional, agricultural, commercial and industrial—receiving from them all the positive statement that Prohibition does prohibit, and that Prohibition is an unmixed blessing to the material, mental and moral welfare of the State.

NORTH DAKOTA

Hon. Charles A. Pollock, ex-United States Judge of Fargo, North Dakota, has given me a history of the war against the saloon in North Dakota and of his relation to it. His testimony will be taken as authority on any question, judicial or moral, anywhere in this country. Judge Pollock writes:

Prohibition refers to a governmental method of dealing with an admitted evil; total abstinence to the habit or personal practice of the individual. It often happens that a heavy drinker is in favor of Prohibition simply for personal protection. He is perfectly consistent in so acting, although he may meet with much criticism. It was by keeping these distinctions before our people, in the fight which began over thirty-five years ago, that we were later, in the year 1899, enabled to secure the adoption of the Prohibitory clause of our constitution against the manufacture, sale and keeping for sale, of intoxicating liquors as a beverage.

During Territorial days I was the prosecuting officer under the license system and for the past twenty years have been the sole presiding Judge of the Third Judicial District, which includes the counties of Cass, Traill and Steele. It is from the standpoint of experience in courts, as well as my general information concerning the development of Prohibition in the Territory of Dakota and State of North Dakota, that I now speak.

To properly understand what is possible in the future permit me just a word as to what has been done by the past generation, of say, thirty-five years in this Territory and State. Those who came in the early eighties will tell you, "Rum was king." It ruled our politics. It stalked abroad in council chamber and legislative hall. City, county and Territorial governments were under its grasp. The saloon boss controlled the polls. The absence of a legally constituted ballot under the Australian system and a secret polling booth enabled the bogus single ballot, in the hands of the licensed saloonkeepers and their allies, to determine who should receive the majority vote. Every village and hamlet had its full quota of saloons. Farmers in the proper control of their help were embarrassed, delayed and annoyed. The rainy day was a terror. Stabbing affrays and murders were of frequent occurrence. Scant police protection could not afford relief. Business men were clamoring for no change, lest their sales would be injured, rents decrease and general stagnation follow. Young men were growing up, feeling that the business of the saloonkeeper was respectable and the open sesame of political preferment. There was, of

course, here and there, the occasional mortgage fore-
closure—for then the country was new—because the
owner of the farm had squandered all in drink. Business
and professional men generally drank. In Fargo, with
few exceptions, the followers of Blackstone, numbering
about forty, were regular members of more than one bar.
Many became habitual drinkers, and most of them were
among the so-called moderate class. Six of the most
brilliant now fill untimely graves—the direct result of the
liquor habit.

Now, exactly the reverse condition exists. In Cass,
my home county, there are sixty-five men entitled to
practice. All of our leading lawyers, with rare exceptions, are total abstainers, and only three or four can be
classed even as moderate drinkers. When we consider
the influence which the lawyer can exert for good or evil,
fortunate indeed is that community whose legal fraternity
is composed of sober men.

Some facts may help to show that Prohibition as a
method of dealing with the traffic helps instead of hurts
the true development of the State. For example, when
admitted as a State both with Prohibitory clauses in their
Constitutions, South Dakota, with about 1,000 more
square miles of territory, had about 250,000 population,
while North Dakota had but 190,000. South Dakota
went back to license in 1894 and has been under it until
recently. She now has less than 600,000, while North
Dakota, continuously under Prohibition, has about 650,-
000 inhabitants.

In North Dakota the per capita wealth was increased
from $1,114 in 1890 to $2,000 in 1910. In the Penitentiary were found at the end of the same period only

1.4 prisoners for every 5,000 inhabitants. The products of our soil, mines and farming industries in 1915 were over $250,000,000. We have 650 State and 151 National banks, carrying a total deposit for March, 1916, of $116,062,027. The combined resources of the banks in Fargo alone are $13,000,000.

It is interesting to study the combined statement of the State banks alone, as showing the prosperity of our people. From December 31, 1915, to March 7, 1916, there was an increase in time certificates of deposit of $3,506,157.67, thus showing the savings of our people. More might be said did the length of this article permit. The fact that sporadic cases of law violation occur argues nothing against the system. Prohibition, both constitutional and statutory, in this State has come to stay, not only because it is morally right, but because it is also economically the better system of dealing with a traffic which undermines the health and happiness of the community.

GOVERNOR FRAZIER

In answer to a letter of inquiry, Governor Lynn J. Frazier of North Dakota, has sent me this brief but unequivocal testimony to the success of Prohibition in his State:

I have no hesitancy in writing you that Prohibition has been a clearly defined success in North Dakota. This fact is so well established that it is not questioned by any one familiar with conditions in our State.

The saloon was thrust out of our midst many years ago. Its record while here was not such as to commend it for further consideration at the hands of our voters, and resubmission has never been a live issue in any political campaign.

I take pleasure in recommending Prohibition to all considering its enactment into law.

SENATOR GRONNA

United States Senator Gronna of North Dakota has given me his opinion as an expert witness on the success of the fight against the saloon in his State and his efficient relationship to it. This is the clear, able and unanswerable testimony he gave to the effect that Prohibition prohibits in North Dakota:

Having lived in the Territory of Dakota and in the State of North Dakota for thirty-seven years, I know the country from its infancy; and I also know that Prohibition has been the most potent factor in our rapid growth and advancement.

The early pioneers of that Territory consisted mainly of poor people who took possession of it when it was known as a barren waste. At any rate, it was altogether undeveloped some forty years ago. It has been changed from a wilderness to one of the most productive areas on the American continent. The pioneer, or the homesteader, soon discovered the need of man power in order to cultivate and develop the millions of acres of virgin soil, where for centuries the Indian and the buffalo had roamed. The early pioneers consisted of young men and young women, who in the early Territorial days realized the importance of conserving human energy. To accomplish this a temperance revolution was necessary; control of the mind and the appetites of man was necessary. All poisonous matters had to be subdued. The saloon had to be eradicated; the great tyrant, John Barleycorn, had to be deposed; the dram-maker and the dram-seller had gradually to find other occupations where they could be more useful to themselves and their families, ready to join all others in the universal song of gladness, because of the opportunity to rear their families in the wholesome atmosphere of temperance.

In production and resources our State has made the most wonderful progress; in education and intelligence the most marvelous advancement has been made by our people. A second generation has grown to manhood and womanhood and consists of a healthy, virile, and intelligent class of young men and women. The abolition of the liquor traffic and the temperance habits of the first generation already manifests its effect upon the second, or new generation.

A great many progressive reforms have been enacted into law, and in no State in the Union has more progressive legislation been written into law than in our State.

Our people are not extremely wealthy, nor are they extremely poor. It is true that we have very few millionaires; neither have we a single poorhouse in the State. Our condition is not yet perfect, but with our sober and enlightened people, the march of a mighty people will in the near future make greater progress. Prohibition will manifest itself as a distinct blessing for the improvement and the betterment of mankind.

CHAPTER IX

ROOSEVELT AND THE SUNDAY SALOON

IN no form of lawlessness have the saloons been more flagrant than in the infraction of the Sunday closing law. Few things have so stirred the American conscience to a hatred of the saloon and a determination to destroy it as has its persistent assault upon the Lord's Day. In no place has there been such open and notorious and shameful violation of the Civil Sabbath by the saloons as in New York City, the wettest spot in America.

Theodore Roosevelt, when Police Commissioner of New York, gave an order that on the next Sunday all saloons were to be closed, and that if the proprietors did not close them they would be arrested by the police and prosecuted for an infraction of the State law. As pastor of the Park Avenue Methodist Church, New York City, I preached a sermon on that Sunday morning asking the people of our church and Methodists generally, and the ministers and members of all denominations, Protestant, Catholic and Hebrew, and the citizens who were members of no church who loved law and order, to stand behind Mr. Roosevelt in his effort to compel the law-defying and crime-breeding saloon to close on Sunday. Sure enough, some of the liquor dealers, who had always been stronger than the law and authorities, considered the threat a joke and kept open. And, of course, the Commissioner was in dead earnest and not joking, and with his strong intellect and determined will put six thousand policemen on the job of detecting and arresting these lawbreakers. He scared the brewers, distillers and saloon-keepers till they fairly shivered and their teeth chattered with fear.

On the Monday morning following I went down to the police headquarters to see Commissioner Roosevelt. I said to him, "Mr. Roosevelt, you do not know me; I never met you; I saw you once. It was at the National Republican Convention in Chicago which named James G. Blaine for the Presidency and John A. Logan for the Vice-Presidency. You were in the New York delegation, in the group with George William Curtis. You had on a little straw hat and were not so fleshy as you are now. You were young, had not been long out of Harvard, but were one of the notables of the Convention and was pointed out to me as such. I did not speak to you nor have I seen you since that day. I have come down this morning to introduce myself to you, and to congratulate you on your courage in determining to close the Sunday saloons. The town has waited for twenty-five years for the coming of such a man. It ought not to be counted a heroic thing for a man to keep his oath solemnly made and to earn his salary by the discharge of his official duty, but the moral sense of the community is so low through the polluting influence of the liquor dealers, and their collusion with corrupt officials, that a man is counted a hero who dares keep his oath to enforce the law or earn his salary by so doing. I will stand by you till the last hour in the day; you are in a fight for the people and for God, and I belong in it and am proud to have such a leader. Our church will stand by you, too. In my sermon yesterday morning I asked all good people to sustain you in this crusade against the Sunday saloon."

The Commissioner said: "I saw what you said in your pulpit in the report of this morning's papers, and thank you very much."

I continued: "I am only one, and an humble one at that, but you may count on me to stand with you on the front of the firing-line. Whenever you shoot your big gun down here in Mulberry street just listen and you will hear its echo in the crack of a little fine-bored pistol on the corner of Park Avenue and Eighty-sixth Street, and that little pistol will be in my hand and I will be shooting at the thing at which you aim."

He said enthusiastically, "You're the stuff! I

am looking for you as much as you are looking for me;" and, taking my hand warmly, he added, "I will stand with you in the fight till the end." Then he continued: "Do you know that you are the first man whose opinion I count of any value who has commended my action in closing the Sunday saloons? Do you see those letters and telegrams on that table? There are perhaps fifty of them. Every single one criticises me; some abuse me bitterly. These are some of the quotations from them: "What an ass you are"; "You are the biggest crank and fool in the world"; "You have wrecked the Republican Party"; "You have killed yourself politically, you will never be heard from again"; "You are the deadest political duck that ever died in a pond."

"Commissioner Roosevelt," I assured him, "I do not believe a word of them. For every enemy you make you will gain ten friends. In the long run, the most popular thing a man can do politically is to do the right thing morally. In my opinion you are not dead, but have just begun to live politically."

He answered with considerable feeling, "I have entered this fight with no idea of making friends or fearing enemies; that has nothing to do with the question. It is simply a question of duty. That law is on the statute books and I have taken an oath to enforce it with the rest," and looking up he continued, "With the help of

God I intend to do so. Whether my course will
bring friends or foes, promotion or relegation to
the rear, does not enter an instant into my cal-
culation. It is mine only to do present duty which
is plain to me."

On taking his hand to leave I said, "In your
vision of righteousness and moral courage in pur-
suing it you show stuff of which I think a good
President could be made. I should like to vote
for you for that office some day." And I did!

I spoke with Commissioner Roosevelt in halls
and other public places, visited the ministers'
meetings and used the press to arouse a militant
spirit among church members and good citizens
generally. I also contributed to the magazines
in the support of the Commissioner in his war on
the Sunday saloon. In digging amidst the rub-
bish of my study I have just come upon a copy
of the "North American Review" of October,
1895, containing an article by myself on "The
Saloon and the Sabbath," backing Mr. Roosevelt's
efforts.

In the "Atlantic Monthly" for September, 1897,
Commissioner Roosevelt wrote of his stormy experience as the head of the Police Department.
In the article he thus arraigns the liquor traffic:
"Any man who studies the social condition of the
poor knows that liquor works more ruin than any
other one cause. The liquor business does not
stand on the same footing with other occupations.

It always tends to produce criminality in the population at large and lawbreaking among the saloonkeepers themselves." In referring to the forces that opposed him in closing the saloons on Sunday he said: "The rich brewers and liquor-sellers who had made money rapidly by violating the excise law, with the corrupt connivance of the police, raved with anger, and every corrupt politician and newspaper in the city gave them clamorous assistance; but the poor man and, notably, the poor man's wife and children, benefited very greatly by what we did. The one important element in good citizenship in our country is obedience to law. This we gave."

We shall never forget the scene at the beginning of the fight, when the frenzied brewers, distillers, saloonkeepers and their hired representatives appeared at a hearing they had called before Mayor Strong, and how bitterly they denounced Mr. Roosevelt and how insolently they demanded a change in his policy. They said it was a cosmopolitan community, that the Sunday closing feature of the law had never been observed, and they insisted that the Mayor require the Commissioner instantly to stop his insane policy and give a "liberal" enforcement of the excise law.

When the liquor men had finished their say Commissioner Roosevelt made his reply. I shall never forget it. I was standing just against him when he spoke. He said: "Your Honor, these gentlemen have savagely attacked me and my policy of Sunday closing, and they have demanded of you that you require me to give a 'liberal' enforcement of the excise law." With vehemence and biting sarcasm he continued: "These men want me to enforce the law a 'little bit,' to enforce it a little, tiny bit. Your Honor, I do not know how to do such a thing and I shall not begin to learn now. I did not take an oath to enforce the law a little, tiny bit. The great Empire State did not put that law on the statute books to be enforced a tiny bit, and so long as I am at the head of the Police Department of the city I shall do all in my power to enforce the law honestly and fearlessly."

The terrible assault of the liquor dealers and others of great influence scared Mayor Strong almost out of his wits, and the Commissioner had to brace up the Mayor's backbone with one hand while he hammered the saloons with the other.

General Francis V. Greene has this to say of Theodore Roosevelt's administration as Police Commissioner: "He held this office for two years, and though subjected to much criticism from certain quarters for enforcing the liquor license law, yet it can be said, in a word, that during his administration he placed the department on a thoroughly efficient basis, broke up the system of blackmail which had hitherto prevailed in the department, and gained the affectionate admiration of the members of the force to an extent which has never been equaled by any Police Commissioner before or since."

Since Col. Roosevelt's time the Sunday saloon has continued with no official protest, thriving fully as well under the reform administrations of Low, Gaynor, and Mitchel, as under Tammany Hall, in defiance of the laws of God and man. It is likely that it will not be six years till there will be no Sunday saloon in New York, Chicago, San Francisco, or any other city or town, and no saloon on any other day, either.

At the close of Mr. Roosevelt's two years' experience as President of the Police Board, President McKinley, on taking office in 1897, appointed Mr. Roosevelt Assistant Secretary of the Navy. He spent nine months putting the ships in good shape for the Spanish-American War, and then determined to go out to the field himself. I wrote him a letter suggesting that as it was to be largely a naval contest he could serve his country better by staying in the Navy Department. He wrote me that there was just cause for the war; that he had helped bring it on; and that he intended to go out into the field if he had to leave his dead body there. He, with his Rough Riders, after Dewey, was the most significant personality of the war.

He returned from the short war of a few

months, just before the meeting of the Republican State Convention in September, 1898, and his name was considered a possible candidate for the nomination for Governor. Taking up a New York paper one morning I noticed that Senator Platt had stated that Colonel Roosevelt would not be nominated, but that Governor Black would be renominated for a second term. Senator Platt was the "easy boss," and I knew that unless there was a change in the situation the Colonel would not be nominated.

That same day I took a train down to Manhattan Beach to the Oriental Hotel to see the Senator. I told him I had come down to see him about the nomination of Colonel Roosevelt for the Governorship. He was cold on the subject and discouraged me.

"What are your objections to the Colonel's candidacy?" I asked him.

"Well, he is rash and impulsive," said the Senator.

"Yes," I said, "he is impulsive, but his impulses are good, and if you will notice, he is running in the right direction."

"But he slops over," the Senator continued.

"Yes, he does," I replied, "because there is so much of him to slop. He is so large that he often fills the vessel to overflowing. He has an overplus of vitality and manhood."

The Senator said, "He made such a dismal

failure in the administration of the Police Commissionership that his unwisdom and unpopularity, in the judgment of many, take him out of serious consideration for the nomination. He has provoked the violent hostility of the liquor people of the State."

"Senator," I persisted, "I disagree with you entirely. The moral heroism he manifested in his fight against the Sunday saloons of New York will be an asset to the Republican Party. Remember, there are a good many people in the State who live above the Harlem and who have no love for, nor even patience with, the saloon on Sunday or on any other day, and, besides, I believe the number of voters in New York City who are unfriendly to the saloon is often underestimated. Are you not too smart a man and leader to attempt to compete with Tammany Hall for the saloon vote? The liquor dealers may promise to vote for your ticket, but on election day they will vote for Tammany Hall, which they count a friend to be relied upon. You can run Theodore Roosevelt and win without the saloon vote. You can win in spite of it. So able a man as David Bennett Hill—so great a national figure that, backed by his party in the State, he surely would have received the nomination for the Presidency on the Democratic ticket in 1892, if Cleveland had not taken it from him—made the fatal political mistake of overestimating the saloon vote

in this State, and was driven from power largely
on account of his supposed friendliness to the saloon. When he ran for the Governorship in
1894 it was reported that he said he would rather
have the votes of the saloonkeepers than of the
preachers. Whether he ever made the statement
or not, it was so generally believed that the
preachers took him at his word and fought him,
and the church people of both parties turned
against him and beat him by more than 100,000
votes. On account of that mistake you are in
Mr. Hill's place in the United States Senate and
have displaced him as the dominant political
figure of the State. If you make the mistake he
did and punish Roosevelt for having fought the
Sunday saloons it will so anger the church people
that they will bury your ticket under an avalanche
of 150,000 majority; you will step down and out,
and Mr. Hill will return to the political leadership of the State. There are many people who
are not total abstainers who count the saloon a
bad institution and will knock it at the polls, and
many more who resent the impertinence and im-
piety of the Sunday saloon and will work actively
against your ticket. I have always voted a straight
Republican ticket; but, Senator, if you depose
Colonel Roosevelt for having done his sworn duty
as Police Commissioner I will bolt the ticket this
fall, and you will find my ballot in that avalanche
of votes. I never made a political speech in my

life, and yet if you turn down Roosevelt because you fear the saloon power will beat him, I will take the stump and make a score, or if need be fifty, speeches from here to Buffalo between now and election day and tell the people how it happened, and ask them what they think of it. There is especial reason for caution this fall. You will be handicapped by the fact that this is an 'off' year, not a Presidential one, and by the severe criticism on the Republican policy for its administration of the canals of the State; and you will need Roosevelt's physical, mental and moral enthusiasm to pull your ticket through."

It had gotten to be 5:30 o'clock in the afternoon, and I bade the Senator good-by and walked over a short distance to take a train for home. Who should get off the train I was to take but B. B. Odell, Jr., Chairman of the Republican State Committee, Joseph Dickey, Mr. Bain and others of Newburgh, my personal friends. Mr. Odell said: "Hello, what are you doing down here?"

"I came down to see Senator Platt," I replied, "to try to persuade him to nominate Colonel Roosevelt for the Governorship. I saw in the paper this morning that he had told you boys last night that the Colonel would not be nominated."

Mr. Odell said, "I am glad you came down. I am for Roosevelt myself and so are my friends here. I think he is the logical candidate as a war hero and reformer, and would poll a heavy vote and be elected. The Senator has faith in your judgment, thinks that you reflect the moral sentiment of the State pretty accurately; I wish you would stay down and have another interview with Mr. Platt. Suppose you go back to the hotel and have dinner with me and see him again tonight."

I went back and sat down as a guest at his table. After dinner I had another talk with the Senator, in which I said: "Senator, do not think for a moment that Colonel Roosevelt sent me down to see you in the interest of his nomination. He does not know I am here. I have never spoken to him on the subject. While I have corresponded with him ever since he was Police Commissioner, even since he came back to Montauk Point to be mustered out, the matter of the Governorship has never been mentioned by either. I am here because I have seen Theodore Roosevelt at close range for two years and know him to be a man of great ability and all-daring moral courage, and believe that as a leader his administration would work for righteousness."

I went home thoroughly discouraged, the Senator was so cold and keen in answering my arguments and unresponsive to my warm appeals. Before going to bed I sat down and wrote a letter to the Colonel at Montauk Point, in which among other things I said: "I had thought the Republican leaders would have had wisdom enough to offer you the nomination for the Governorship, but in a morning paper I saw that Senator Platt had said you would not be the candidate. I knew that settled the matter, if that opinion continued. So, without your advice or consent, I hurried down to the Oriental at Manhattan Beach today and have had two long, earnest interviews with the Senator, in which I tried to convince him of the wisdom of your nomination. But I feel discouraged. I fear I have made no impression on him whatever. Whenever I would come around to the plea that he be friendly to your nomination, a Sphinx is eloquent compared to the sudden silence of his lips. Unless he shall change his mind I fear your nomination will be impossible."

The Colonel was nominated. I never knew I had made the least impression till some time after the Convention, when one of the men with whom I went back to the hotel for dinner, the day of the interviews, told me that when I left that night the Senator called the group of State leaders who were stopping at the hotel and said that he had told them the night before that Governor Black would have to be renominated or there would be a split in the Republican Party. But Doctor "Inglehart" (he always put an "n" in my name) had been down to see him and had given him four reasons why Colonel Roosevelt should be nominated, three of which he considered valid. On the strength of them had concluded to reverse his opinion and favor Mr. Roosevelt's nomination. The gentlemen said from that moment that Roosevelt was as good as nominated. Chairman Odell worked loyally and successfully with the Colonel, who was elected by about twenty thousand majority.

Theodore Roosevelt was made Governor, and consequently Vice-President and President, because he closed the saloons of New York on Sunday. He would have doubtless become President later by another route, but it was the plan of Providence to lead him through this gateway of moral heroism to the White House.

In my interview with Senator Platt I made the moral element in his availability paramount and insisted that while he would run well as a war hero, he would run still better as a moral hero. It was because, scorned by the Democrats, ridiculed by the Republicans, hissed at by hell, he put his giant hands against eight thousand saloons and shut them, in spite of hundreds of millions of dollars back of the brewers and the distillers and the enormous vote of the municipal underworld.

During Mr. Roosevelt's candidacy for the Presidency on the Progressive ticket he made some speeches in Ohio at the time the wet and dry proposition in that State was being carried on, and in several of his speeches he said that the liquor people were entirely to blame for pushing the question to the forefront of politics at that time, and that if he were living in the State he would vote for Prohibition.

Just about that time I received a telegram from my personal friend, Mr. J. Frank Burke, Superintendent of the Oregon State Anti-Saloon League, dated March 15, 1912, stating that on the platform and in the press it was charged that Colonel Roosevelt was on his way rapidly to a drunkard's grave and a drunkard's hell and asked me as the Colonel's friend to wire a denial of the slanderous statements to be used at a political meeting to be held in Portland that same night.

I immediately sent this telegram in reply:

Statement diabolical falsehood. Roosevelt never claimed total abstainer. Drinks almost nothing. No alcohol in eye or muscle. Not a spot on him, body, mind or soul. The bloom of best American civilization. Idol of people. Christly McKinley suffered same villainous slander from same source. Hell is not far from lying scandalmonger.

Though corresponding with the Colonel regularly, I did not say anything to him about this telegram or my answer at the time. I felt a little delicacy in doing so, as the slander was so foul and false that I did not care to irritate him with it, but in a letter of mine to him of May 11, 1912, I gave him the text of the telegram received and of the one I sent in reply. His answer was the following:

En route Pullman private car Oceanic,
May 14, 1912.

My Dear Friend:

You are a trump! I am very glad you sent precisely that telegram. You are absolutely correct. I have never claimed to be a total abstainer, but I drink as little as most total abstainers, for I really doubt whether on an average, year in and year out, I drink more than is given for medicinal purposes to many people. I never touch whisky, and I have never drunk a cocktail or a highball in my life. I doubt whether I have drunk a dozen teaspoonfuls of brandy since I came back from Africa, and as far as I now recollect, in each case it was for medicinal purposes. In Africa during the eleven months I drank exactly seven ounces of brandy; this was under our doctor's direction in my first fever attack, and once when I was completely exhausted. My experience on these two occasions convinced me that tea was better than brandy, and during the last six months in Africa I took no brandy, even when sick, taking tea instead. I drink just about as much as Dr. Lyman Abbott—and I say this with his permission.

Faithfully yours,
Theodore Roosevelt.

Colonel Roosevelt nursed his wrath until he could nail the lie, which he did in his successful suit against an editor, in which he got the complete vindication which he demanded and deserved. On the rendering of the verdict I wired the Colonel: "Supremely happy at victory and complete vindication." To this Mr. Roosevelt sent the following response: "Heartiest thanks for your telegram. Naturally I am pleased with the way things went in the libel suit."

Never since that day has any person of responsibility dared repeat the foul slander, and Theodore Roosevelt stands as a superb personality against the iniquity of the saloon and its intimate partnership with corrupt politics.

On January 4, 1917, I called by appointment on Colonel Roosevelt at his office with the "Metropolitan Magazine," and said to him: "I am writing an anti-alcohol book, and I have come to ask you to give me a little something from your pen which I may put bodily as a gem into that book."

"Well, on what phase of the subject do you want those words?"

"I would like you to give me in condensed form your views against the saloon as you have so often done to me in private conversation, and especially on the collusion of corrupt politics with the saloon. Your fight in New York City was tragic and epoch-making, and you might make that the basis of what you say."

He called his stenographer and began:

"MY DEAR DOCTOR IGLEHART: It has been my good fortune to be associated with you ever since the days——"

I halted him and said: "Colonel, cut out the compliments to me and put in your knowledge of the badness of the saloons and of their partners,

the rum politicians." He waved his big arm toward me and said, "Just hold on. I know better
what I want to say than you do," and continued
to the stenographer:

My Dear Doctor Iglehart: It has been my good
fortune to be associated with you ever since the days
when I was President of the Police Commission of New
York, when I worked hand in hand with you, and with
the Ministers' Association that you represented on behalf
of temperance, and of doing away with the evil of the
saloon power in New York City. At that time our fight
was for a proper observance of the Sunday law. There
could have have been no more practical illustration of
the hideous evil wrought by the liquor traffic than was
afforded by the results of its stoppage for the few Sun-
days during which we were able to keep the saloons absolutely closed. During this period the usual mass of
individuals up in the courts on Monday morning, on
charges of being drunk and disorderly and committing
assaults, diminshed by two-thirds or over. The hospitals,
such as Bellevue, showed a similar diminution of persons
brought to them because of alcoholism and crimes due to
drunkenness. On the other hand, the healthy Sunday resorts in the neighborhood of New York showed a great
increase in business. Men who would otherwise have
stayed in New York drinking, while their wives and
children suffered in the heated tenement houses, took
these same wives and children for a Sunday holiday in
the country. Unfortunately, by the end of that time, the
decisions of the courts and juries had so hampered our
action that, to a very large extent, the old system was

reinstated. While this was partly because public opinion had not been educated to sustain us, it was partly because of the alliance between the saloon power and the politicians. Any man who fails to take into account both of these facts is blinding himself to two of the prime factors in the misgovernment of our citizens and in the misery of our city populations. If you care to know my views more fully, as written at the time, I refer you to my chapter on the subject printed in a book called "American Ideals." The only change I have since to record is a constantly growing appreciation of the wide-reaching evil of the liquor traffic, and of the need of extending, by every method possible through our country, a full understanding of what this evil is.

Sincerely yours,
THEODORE ROOSEVELT.

In "American Ideals," to which Colonel Roosevelt referred me, I find this reference to criminals who were office holders, and political leaders. There was one case of an assemblyman who served several terms in the Legislature, while his private business was to carry on corrupt negotiations between the Excise Commissioners and owners of low haunts who wished licenses. The president of a powerful semi-political association was by profession a burglar, while the man who received the goods he stole was an alderman. Another alderman was elected while his hair was still short from a term in State Prison. A school trustee had been convicted of embezzlement and was the associate of criminals. A prominent official in the Police Department was interested in disreputable houses and gambling saloons and was backed politically by their proprietors.

In urging National Prohibition as a war measure, Colonel Roosevelt said:

When we are threatened with a shortage of foodstuffs, when it is our duty to supply food to our allies to our utmost ability, we should see that needed food necessities are not diverted from their proper use. Most of the belligerent nations of Europe have taken up this problem and settled it. Let us begin at once to see to it that our grain is kept for food and not put into alcoholic beverages.

I sent Colonel Roosevelt a copy of the first edition of this book and received from him the following letter:

"MY DEAR DR. IGLEHART: I thank you for your book and appreciate your sending it to me and I wish to congratulate you on what has happened in Congress and the success that is crowning your long fight against alcoholism. The American saloon has been one of the most mischievous elements in American social, political and industrial life. No man has warred more valiantly against it than you have, and I am glad that it has been my privilege to stand with you in the contest.

Faithfully yours,

THEODORE ROOSEVELT."

This letter was dated December 19, 1917. On December 17, 1917, only two days before, the House passed the National Prohibition resolution, and on the day following the Senate adopted the amended measure. This is the Congressional action to which the Colonel refers in this letter written the day after that action had been taken.

CHAPTER X

THE SOUTH ABOLISHES THE SALOON

WITHIN eight years, from 1907 to 1915, nine of the Southern States rebelled against the authority of King Alcohol. By the action of their legislatures and the people's ballots they declared their independence of his despotism in a voice that stirred the nation and attracted the attention of the world.

GEORGIA

Georgia was the first of the Southern States to abolish the saloon, by the passage of a law in July, 1907. For forty years good men and women had been planting the seeds of hostility to drink that came to the harvest that day. Georgia not only achieved the first victory in the modern anti-drink crusade, but gave to the movement one of her most gifted sons to be perhaps the most conspicuous and potential leader in stirring the solid South into the banishment of alcohol. It was Sam Jones, a minister of the Methodist Episcopal Church, South, who spent twenty years as a traveling evangelist in the South and other parts

of the country.   He was as noble in his character
as he was keen in his intellect, eloquent as an orator and powerful as a preacher.   His biting sarcasm and terrific invective made the cold chills
run up and down the back; his inimitable wit and
humor convulsed his audiences with laughter,
while his pathos melted them into tears.   He
was called on to speak almost everywhere, on all
occasions, and was always the able, fearless, persistent and inveterate enemy of the liquor traffic.

He spoke in a village of twelve hundred people
one night, and said:

"You have a nice village, with lovely residences
and grounds and gardens; you have good streets
and stores and public buildings; but you could not
get along without three saloons to damn your
boys.   What license do they pay?"

One spoke up: "A hundred dollars a piece."

Jones continued: "The three would make three
hundred dollars.   You have twelve hundred inhabitants.   If you were each to walk up to the
treasurer and pay forty cents you would have
your revenue and no saloon.   What does a hog
bring in this neighborhood?"

A man called out, "Twelve dollars."

"That is about what I thought," said Jones.
"Hogs worth twelve dollars, folks forty cents a
head, around here.   You have sold your boys and
girls to hell and yourselves to the devil for forty
cents a head; and as far as you are concerned the

devil has got the worst of the bargain, for those
of you who would sell your sons and daughters to
damnation for forty cents each are not worth five
cents a head. And when at the last day the overthrow of your children will be charged on you
and you are called upon to answer what you sold
your boys and girls to hell for, look the Judge in
the face and tell Him the truth: 'For forty
cents.' "

For twenty years Sam Jones went up and down
the Southland, hammering with his merciless logic
into the minds of the people, and burning with a
divine flame into their hearts, the great fact that
no money consideration in the form of a license
fee can weigh for an instant in the balance against
the bodies, minds and souls of the precious boys
and girls. The people of the South believed what
he said and acted accordingly in saving the boys
and girls, the men and women, and scorning the
license fee.

Such is the seed sowed broadcast which appears
in the white harvest of today; it is the dynamite
that charged the mines that wrecked the saloons
of the South. The method of saloon elimination
he preached, he practised. He drove the saloon
out of his home town of Cartersville, in the
county of Bartow, and for fifteen years compelled
a rigid enforcement of the law there. But one
night in October, 1906, he died of heart failure
on a railway train in Arkansas. His funeral was

a State event in Georgia. But the liquor people of Bartow, his home county, were jubilant at the thought of a return to license, with their greatest enemy out of the way, and early in June called a new election. The temperance people were in consternation at first without their great leader, but they organized, prayed in the churches, paraded the streets and made a hand-to-hand campaign. When the ballots were counted there were eighty-five votes for the saloon and 1,687 for no license. The ghost of Sam Jones had come back to Cartersville to lead the fight.

The marvelous victory in Bartow county was the torch of Prohibition that set all Georgia on fire. Lowndes County, a rum stronghold, cast her vote resulting in 1,684 for Prohibition to 406 against it. The legislature was in its summer session. Its members had not been elected on the issue of State-wide Prohibition. But the victories of Bartow and Lowndes Counties had set the whole State wild with temperance enthusiasm, and the Anti-Saloon League, Women's Christian Temperance Union, Prohibitionists, Good Templars and other temperance societies were well organized and united, and, seeing that the psychological moment had come, pressed the measure. The Hardman-Covington Bill was backed by its authors and by Williford, Knight, Neal, and Seaborn Wright championing the measure. After a long and desperate fight in which

Mrs. Mary H. Armor and the "Daily Georgian" were important factors, the bill was passed in the Senate by 34 to 7, and in the House by 139 to 39. A scene of wildest enthusiasm followed. Men and women, old and young, sang and cried and laughed and shouted for joy. Above all was the hymn of praise to God for victory.

Though the adoption of Prohibition by the Legislature was sudden, there had been years of preparation for it. At the time of the passage of the law the saloon had been driven by local option from 135 out of the 150 counties of the State. The law went into effect January 1, 1908.

In search of the very best authority on the subject of Prohibition in Georgia, my mind turned to United States Senator Hoke Smith, who had been a successful lawyer in Atlanta, proprietor of the "Atlanta Journal," a member of President Cleveland's cabinet, twice elected Governor of his State, and twice United States Senator. Senator Smith delivered a speech in the Senate, January 9, 1917, on the District of Columbia Prohibition Bill, from which I make the following quotations, which are so powerful and convincing as to leave very little room for debate on the subject:

During the summer of 1907 the State of Georgia, which I represent here in part, adopted State-wide Prohibition. There has been some effort to criticize the manner in which the law is enforced in Georgia. I do not claim that it is completely enforced and that the use of intoxicating drinks has been entirely suppressed in Georgia. But, having approved that law as Governor of the State, I watched the effect of it in the city of Atlanta, my home and the largest city in the State. I can say that in many an humble home after its passage, and even with partial enforcement, there was more food and better clothing for the women and children, and in many a home there was gentleness and kindness instead of coarseness and brutality from an intoxicated husband and father.

I have the report of the chief of police of the city of Atlanta, a city of more than 225,000 inhabitants. He gives the relative effect of the open barroom in the city of Atlanta for six years before Prohibition and for six years afterward. The statistics which he furnishes show that the number of cases made for intoxication in proportion to the population was about one-half in the city after Prohibition, as compared to the number before, and that the number of arrests for crime was at least one-third less in proportion to population after the adoption of Prohibition than before.

My own observation throughout the State satisfies me that Prohibition has been beneficial and helpful to the people of the State. I was a local optionist before the passage of the law, but promised in my campaign for Governor that if the State passed State-wide Prohibition I would approve it. Today any influence I might have in the State would be thrown against returning to local option and in favor of the maintenance of State-wide Prohibition. I would pursue this course as the result of the beneficial effect, in my judgment, of the legislation.

Coming to the economic side of the question, I am sure that the general business of the city of Atlanta has prospered as a consequence of Prohibition; that the legitimate business of the city has largely received the money that was before wasted on liquors in the saloons. There has been a rapid accumulation of deposits in the banks, not, of course, entirely due to this subject, but in part. There has been an improvement in the business of the general retail stores and the department stores of the city, in part, in my judgment, due to Prohibition.

We have one city in Georgia which was very much opposed to Prohibition, the second largest city in the State, and for a long time the enforcement of the law was resisted there. I refer to the city of Savannah; but within the past twelve months the law has been enforced there; and I hold in my hand an editorial from the "Savannah Morning News" dealing with the business condition of that city during the Christmas holidays, in which the editor rejoices that the merchants have done the best business in the history of the city. The editor, though never, I believe, a prohibitionist, further attributes at least a part of that improved business to the fact that money was going into legitimate lines, instead of being wasted for intoxicating spirits.

I wish to see barrooms driven from the District of Columbia; I wish to see the sale of intoxicating liquors for beverage purposes stopped in the District of Columbia. I believe a majority of the Senate is in favor of stopping it. Here come, every day almost, thousands of visitors, young and old, to all of whom the lessons of patriotism from a visit to the Nation's Capital result in a higher type of citizenship, and the pride of participation in the

affairs of our Government grows stronger with the realization of its latent power and outward dignity and
grandeur. Let me stop a moment to say that as they
come I want them to see that the National Congress at
the National Capital has closed barrooms, has forbidden
the sale of liquor, and I want them to go back from here
with the inspiration of knowing that their national legislators are helping them in the fight which, pray God, will
close such places everywhere, from ocean to ocean, and
from the Lakes to the Gulf. I wish to see the barrooms
closed; I wish to see the sale of liquor for beverage
purposes stopped here, and to my constituents at home I
hold myself responsible, and I vote what I believe to be
their wishes, accepting the responsibility myself and de-
clining to refer it to anybody else.

Senator Reed of Missouri asked Senator Smith
this question: "Are not the citizens of the Senator's own State permitted to import liquor for
their own use under the laws of the State?"
Senator Smith answered:

That is true. The bill was passed, I think, under a
misapprehension of the meaning of the Webb Act. They
were of the opinion, so I was advised, that they could not
absolutely prohibit it and remain within the Constitution; but I feel perfectly sure that this summer they will
stop it. At least I hope so. In other words, I am in
favor of stopping men from using it, not simply playing
with it. I want to say that to the Senator. I am in
favor of trying to make our State bone-dry. With me
opposition to the use of spirituous and intoxicating drink

has been a gradual growth. When I leave myself free to think about it and realize the skeletons found in almost every home as a result of its use, I have reached the place where I am willing in my State this next summer to help make it absolutely dry, and I hope the people of the State are ready to give up entirely the use of intoxicating drinks.

But Georgia could not, would not, wait till the summer, but went dry at once, only a few weeks after the Senator had spoken.

Governor Nat. E. Harris of Georgia, in reply to a letter of inquiry from me, has written me the following letter:

I am in sympathy with every one in the American Union who is traveling the pathway that your letter indicates you to be on. In my State I am thinking of calling a session of the Legislature to cut off the monthly shipments of two quarts allowed to each individual. This has been our Trojan horse, but the sentiment here is so strongly in favor of a "bone-dry" program that there will be no difficulty in changing our law and adjusting ourselves to the present trend of affairs. It looks like Prohibition is going over the world.

Very sincerely and fraternally yours,

N. E. HARRIS, *Governor.*

Precisely this thing the Governor did. He called a special session of the Legislature to pass a bone-dry law, which it did, and then adjourned and went home, rejoicing in having done the work of a generation in a day. Now the rich man in his palatial home cannot have a glass of champagne, nor the negro a drop of his alcohol in his river street joint.

Why need we multiply witnesses? Senator Smith and Governor Harris ought to know as much about the situation in Georgia as the brewers, the distillers, the saloonkeepers and their hired mercenaries in the editorial sanctum, in municipal and legislative halls, who bellow out their loud lament, and shed their crocodile tears at the "failure of Prohibition in Georgia."

OKLAHOMA

Oklahoma was the next State to adopt Prohibition. Congress, in the enabling act of 1906, required Prohibition for twenty-one years in the Indian Territory section of the new State. In the election of delegates to the constitutional convention the liquor question was one of the foremost. Then the pressure was made by both sides on the delegates to incorporate or leave out of the constitution a prohibitory provision. The convention prepared a constitutional provision, but made it necessary for the people at the polls to determine whether they would make it a part of their constitution or not. After an exceedingly excited contest the prohibitory provision was adopted at the election in November, 1907, by a majority of 18,000. And thus Oklahoma, the youngest of Columbia's fair daughters, entered the sisterhood of States adorned with garments unstained by wine or beer, unfouled by the fumes of alcohol, clad in the pure white robe of Prohibition. The following fall the liquor forces surprised and alarmed the temperance people by a demand for a new vote on a technicality, but the measure for the repeal of the Prohibition amendment was defeated, November, 1910, by a majority of 23,000 votes.

The legislature of 1913 passed severe measures of law enforcement. It included a penitentiary sentence for keeping a place for the sale of intoxicants, made a felony of the second offense against any feature of the prohibitory law, and rendered amenable to impeachment and dismissal any State officer charged with drunkenness or the excessive use of intoxicants.

A young physician at the head of a hospital in one of the cities of Oklahoma, said he went to that State a few years ago with favorable notions of beer and with a positive prejudice, if not contempt, for Prohibition as a remedy for the evils of drink. But he said the practical working of the law had changed his mind on the subject, had entirely converted him. He said that the drastic features of the law, even sending men of influence to the penitentiary for terms long enough for serious reflection for an infraction of the law, had been salutary to public morals. He said that no one acquainted with the facts would deny that Prohibition in Oklahoma prohibits.

ALABAMA

The wires had scarcely carried the word that President Roosevelt had accepted the new State of Oklahoma, with its prohibitory amendment, when the Legislature of Alabama passed a State Prohibition law, to take effect on January 1, 1908.

The original excise law had been amended from year to year, allowing privileges of local option to special localities, till the saloon had been driven out of twenty counties. As the sessions of the Legislature were only quadrennial, the anti-saloon people determined to make the best use of their opportunities at the winter session of 1907 to press radical temperance measures. Laws were passed allowing local option for counties, preventing the shipment of liquors from wet into dry territory, compelling temperance instruction in the public schools, and forbidding the sale of "hop-jack" and other drinks containing a smaller percentage of alcohol.

In November of the same year Governor Comer called a special session of the Legislature to consider the differences between the railroads and the State. He did not make any mention of the temperance question in his message, as he did not intend that it should be considered until the regular session, three years thence. Because he did not make mention of it in that call a two-thirds majority was required to carry such a measure. When the members arrived at Montgomery, they were blazing with the enthusiasm that had fired the law-makers of Georgia, and they would not give a single thought to railroads till they had "expressed" the saloon out of the State by the adoption in the Senate of the House Bill prohibiting the manufacture and sale of liquors as a beverage by a vote of 32 to 2.

Soon after the passage of the measure Governor Comer, coming out of his executive chamber, said to a friend, "Did you see that woman go out of the door just then?"

"Yes."

"Hers was a pathetic mission. She came to ask me to pardon her husband for having killed her brother. Both were honest men, good workmen, personal friends. They got to drinking one night till they were drunk, got into a fight over nothing, and her husband killed her brother, and was sent to prison for life, and she and her children are destitute, and she has come crying to me for a pardon. There are many widows and orphans down in the wiregrass of Alabama, caused by strong drink, and we expect the new prohibitory law to greatly lessen the number of such tragedies."

The passage of the Prohibition law was followed instantly by a fierce reaction. The officers of the law in the cities were not in sympathy with it; the compactly organized liquor-dealers exerted their powerful influence in politics to discredit it; they sowed the State with blind tigers, and then made many temperance people believe it was the law that was responsible for them, instead of themselves who had created them by breaking the law. Amidst this riot of nullification a special session of the Legislature in August, 1908, submitted the question of a Prohibition amendment to the constitution, to be voted upon November 29. The amendment was lost by a large majority. The church people innocently believed the statement of their enemies before the election that the State Prohibition law would be sufficient and would not be touched. But immediately the liquor men put into power officers of State, including the Governor, who did their best to undo the statutory law. The anti-saloon leaders, the day after the election on the amendment, claimed that the defeat was only temporary, and with wisdom, courage and hope continued a relentless warfare till they elected a friendly legislature and passed a State-wide Prohibition law in January, 1915, which was vetoed by the Governor and promptly passed over his veto, and went into effect July 1, 1915. As deep as was the humiliation and disappointment of the no-license workers of the State and Nation at the defeat of the constitutional amendment, so high was their enjoyment that after seven years of the baleful rule of rum Alabama had returned to the ranks of Prohibition.

MISSISSIPPI

Mississippi has always been good ground for Prohibition seed. Its citizens are mostly farmers. Of the 1,797,114 inhabitants of the State 1,585,-802 live in the country; only 207,311 dwell in the cities. Meridian is the largest city; has less than 24,000; Jackson about 22,000; and Vicksburg 21,-000, with Natchez and Hattiesburg coming next with less than 12,000, and all the rest of the cities under 9,000 in population. Difficulties, however, confronted the temperance people. The colored people have, from the close of the Civil War until now, outnumbered the whites, and the relation of the negro to the saloon became a serious problem to be solved. The problem became acute in wet districts like Aberdeen in Monroe County, center for a cotton-planting country, which has 18,000 blacks to 12,000 whites, and in Leland in Washington, where the blacks outnumber the whites nine to one. The country saloon was spoiling the negro and the white man as well, and instead of a three mile limit, as in Alabama, the people pushed the saloon five miles away from a church or school, which cleared the farm districts of the cross-roads groggery.

When the public sentiment of this rural State

against the saloon was crystallizing into restrictive legislation there appeared on the stage one of the most powerful enemies the liquor traffic ever had in Mississippi or in any other State, who became the brains, the heart, the powerful right arm of the Prohibition forces. He was the Rev. Charles B. Galloway, a young Bishop of the Methodist Episcopal Church, South. He was six feet high, every inch a Southern gentleman, a fine writer, an able speaker, a brave, manly man. He had an intense interest in the spiritual welfare of the church, and also a genius for taking the principles of his religion into the affairs of everyday life, including the field of politics. For a whole generation he fought like a hero against the rum traffic. With rare prophetic vision he saw the solution of the saloon problem in Mississippi and for the whole nation. Long before the Anti-Saloon League was dreamed of he adopted the identical methods which have become so powerful in the hands of that organization in the destruction of the liquor traffic. He claimed the saloon had to be voted out, and devoted himself to practical politics for that purpose. He held that the voting ought to be done in small units at first, and increased to larger ones as fast as public sentiment would sustain it, working all the while to educate and create that friendly sentiment. The radicals insisted that he went too slow, and the conservatives that he went too fast. But with one hand he held the radicals back, and with the other he pulled the conservatives forward, and allowed the movement to go only as fast as public sentiment would sustain it. His notion was that local option by counties as a unit would pretty nearly clean the saloons out of the State, and he was right. After using the township option law for a while he made a fierce fight before the Legislature of 1886 for his cherished county local option law, and secured it. And after twenty-two years of hard labor and wise use of that law he saw the saloon driven from sixty-nine of the seventy-six counties, which included ninety per cent. of the territory of the State, and, according to his prophecy, the question of State-wide Prohibition took care of itself.

It became almost a matter of form only for the Legislature of 1908 to pass a State-wide Prohibition bill, by almost unanimous vote of both houses. Bishop Galloway used the modern methods of the Anti-Saloon League in bringing the pressure of the church upon the wet and dry campaigns and upon the sessions of the Legislature. The Women's Christian Temperance Union, under Miss Frances Willard, with many in coöperation, devoted men and women, did much to arouse Mississippi to hostility to and action against the saloon, and was in a large degree responsible for the introduction and passage of the State-wide Prohibition bill in 1908.

Bishop Galloway attracted attention outside of his State by his spirited newspaper controversy with Jefferson Davis, who had attacked Prohibition as a political theory. "Jeff Davis prides himself on having always the last word," said Bishop Galloway, mildly. "Well, I'm a somewhat younger man than he is, and I propose to have the last word in this." And so he did. And it was almost his last word, for he died the year after the State-wide bill was passed, the one in which it went into effect. The last battle fought, the last word said, the hero laid down his sword and went to his reward.

Governor Bilbo of Mississippi sent me a letter telling what a success Prohibition is in his State, and inclosing a copy of an address made before a Baptist convention, from which I quote:

Year by year the use of alcohol is being gradualy abandoned by a greater number of our people; social usages are adjusting themselves to the new gospel of total abstinence, and the business world has joined with society and the Church in putting its ban upon whisky-drinking. All of these forces and influences are daily growing stronger and stronger in support of our Prohibition laws. We have lost no ground; every year adds new areas to the territory conquered to Prohibition; the great movement has taken no backward step; its way has been always and unwaveringly onward, and the march has gathered greater confidence and celerity with each forward step.

But the best fruits of our battle for temperance do not

lie in our present possession and enjoyment; they lie in
the assurance of to-morrow. Under the rule of the saloon
and common use of alcoholic beverages, habits of drinking
were readily and easily formed, which led to intemperance
and its multiplied progeny of woe. The elimination of
the saloon under Prohibition removes both the temptation
and the opportunity to form what we call the drinking
habit; while the abolishment of the social practice and
custom of wine-drinking has also gone to restrict the
development of this habit; Prohibition unquestionably re-
stricts and must ultimately eliminate the habit which
produces drunkenness. Thus the new generation is rescued; the young are protected against intemperance.

NORTH CAROLINA

North Carolina went dry in 1909 by a majority
of over 40,000, securing constitutional Prohibition. The Governor, the two United States Senators, the members of Congress and other leaders
rolled up their sleeves and drove the rum traffic
out. Ex-Governor Glenn rendered invaluable service in the campaigns.

I sought a meeting with Congressman Edwin
Y. Webb, the able and efficient leader of the Prohibition forces in the lower house, for information with reference to Prohibition in his State and
the nation, and of his personal relation to it. He
said:

Prohibition in North Carolina has been a great success from any standpoint from which it might be viewed.

Those who were first opposed to its adoption used the approved arguments against it. Since the law has been tested, its effects have been so beneficial that a proposition to repeal it and go back to the laws in force prior to 1909, would not receive serious consideration. Capital and property which had been previously employed in the liquor traffic, soon found investment and were employed in other business that has aided the State in its great commercial progress, and the men previously employed in the traffic have turned their efforts to help develop the natural resources of the State. The State felt no crippling shock from the loss of taxes, which were quickly compensated for by greater commercial advancement and a more healthy, prosperous, and contented people.

TENNESSEE

It was according to the eternal fitness of things that the schoolhouse should drive the saloon out of Tennessee, as they represent directly opposite ideas: one, the education and salvation of the young, the other their destruction. It is generally admitted, even in communities with a weak temperance sentiment, that drinking-places should be pushed away from churches and schools, anywhere from a hundred feet to a mile or more. It was the law keeping a dramshop four miles away from a school that made Tennessee dry. The original law was passed forty years ago, and for this reason: The University of the South, under the authority of the Protestant Episcopal Church, situated at Sewanee in the Cumberland Mountains, fearing the contamination of the country saloon, secured from the Legislature an act forbidding the sale of liquor as a beverage within four miles of any incorporated institution of learning, located outside of an incorporated town. Ten years afterward, the clause, "an incorporated institution of learning," was cut out and these words substituted: "any schoolhouse, public or private, where a school is kept." This change at one stroke drove the dramshop out of almost all the rural districts of the State. In 1899 this "Four Mile Law" was made to apply to towns of two thousand or under; in 1893, as the Adams Law, it included cities of five thousand; in 1907, as the Pendleton Law, it applied to cities of 150,000; and in 1909, as the Holladay Bill, doing away with the charter repeal and reincorporation features and making it universally applicable, the whole State was made dry. The law did not leave a single spot in mountain or valley in the State on which to set a saloon, that would not be within four miles of a schoolhouse. If there had been such a spot a new school would have been built in twenty-four hours. In 1910 a companion law was passed, forbidding the manufacture of intoxicants anywhere in the State.

As the saloon and anti-saloon forces were grappling in the supreme struggle a shocking tragedy occurred, the worst in the history of temperance

warfare in America, in the murder of Senator
Edward W. Carmack, one of the most brilliant
and honorable members the United States Senate
ever had from the South. He was the acknowledged champion of the anti-saloon cause and died
as a martyr to his active and efficient leadership.

In 1908 Senator Carmack entered the primary
contest for the Democratic nomination for the
Governorship of the State against Governor M.
R. Patterson. Both being able and influential
and fine orators, the campaign was a sensational
and memorable one. State Prohibition was the
paramount issue, Carmack favoring and Patterson opposing it. Patterson received the nomination and was elected. Carmack became editor of
the "Nashville Tennessean," continued his relentless war on the liquor traffic with his pen and
demanded of the Legislature a State-wide prohibitory law. One of his editorials offended a chief
political advisor and director in the gubernatorial
campaign, and he with his son waylaid Senator
Carmack on one of the most public streets of
Nashville and shot him to death.

The brewers thought that as they had elected
their Governor and the champion of their enemies
was out of the way, they would certainly be able
to defeat State Prohibition. They were mistaken.
The shot that killed Carmack killed the saloons
of Tennessee, and aroused the temperance people
everywhere, and two months after the Legislature

assembled, they rushed to the capital from all parts of the State and demanded State Prohibition. A company of them marched to the spot in the pavement made red with the blood of their champion, kneeled about it and prayed to God for wisdom and help, and made a new vow of loyalty to the cause for which he had laid down his life. Carmack's ghost was the chief guest and influence in the Legislature. Under his inspiration the "Four Mile law," meaning State Prohibition, was passed, and though Governor Patterson vetoed it, it was passed over his veto and is now the law.

Judge Cooper and his son were sent to the penitentiary for twenty years for the murder of Carmack. Governor Patterson pardoned them. Carmack's spirit dominated the next gubernatorial campaign. Patterson did not stand for a third term. Ben W. Hooper, who ran on a fusion ticket of Republicans and Independent Democrats, was elected, on a platform of the maintenance and rigid enforcement of the new Prohibition Law, over United States Senator Robert L. Taylor, thought to be personally the most popular man in the State. Hooper served two terms of two years each. He had to call a special session of the Legislature three times before he could secure any law-enforcement measures. At last he got some, the chief one being the "Nuisance Law."

Toward the close of his last term Governor Hooper in an address said:

Five years ago yesterday Senator Carmack, the leader of the fight for decent government, was murdered on the streets of Nashville. The crying of his blood from the ground rallied the forces of good government in the Legislature of 1909, and, beside the State prohibitory law, there was an election law which deprived the liquor interests of their control of the ballot boxes of the people.

The Legislature of 1915 passed the "ouster" bill, removing officers for non-enforcement of the no-license law, and the Soft Drink Stand Act, which have aided in making and keeping Nashville, Memphis, Chattanooga and other large cities dry.

The "Anti-Shipping" law passed under Governor Hooper's administration was declared unconstitutional by the Supreme Court of the State. But the Legislature of 1917 and the decision of the United States Supreme Court declaring the Interstate Commerce Amendment Bill effective made the State bone-dry.

GOVERNOR PATTERSON'S CONVERSION

The contest in Tennessee furnished not only the most horrible tragedy of the temperance reform movement in America in the murder of Carmack, but one of its most dramatic and potential incidents, the conversion of Ex-Governor Patterson. It was a staggering blow to the liquor power, when the one who had been the most brilliant and powerful advocate of their cause in Tennessee, if not in the nation, publicly confessed his mistake, fault and sin and his profound sorrow, and dedicated the rest of his life to the destruction of the drink traffic. Patterson's address announcing his change of heart before the twentieth anniversary of the foundation of the Anti-Saloon League, held in Columbus, Ohio, November 10-13, 1913, is one of the best specimens of temperance literature to be found. Among other things he said:

The Anti-Saloon League and I have not always been friends. The paths we traveled were wide apart. They seemed so parallel that it looked incredible that they should ever meet. But they have met, and we now find ourselves in the same road, marching in the same direction, under the same flag, actuated by the same desire to destroy the traffic in liquor and redeem a nation from its curse. I am neither ashamed or abashed to stand before this great audience, and acknowledge the wrong when I once advocated policies which would have made legal a trade which I have come to look upon as having no rightful place in the scheme and economy of Christian civilization. I grew up in the city of Memphis where saloons were numerous and regarded as permanent institutions. I can not remember to have ever heard of any movement to close them or recall any speech or newspaper article attacking them. I became a lawyer, was elected prosecuting attorney of the District, and during my incumbency saloons were open and licensed under the law and were without restriction as to numbers. I was afterward sent to Congress, where I served six years. At this time liquor was openly sold in the restaurants of both wings of the Capitol. The convenience and comfort with which intoxicating drinks could be obtained often interfered with my own attendance of the sessions, and that of other members, and distracted attention from the duties of our representation. While serving in Congress I became a candidate for Governor of Tennessee. I was elected on a platform friendly to local option, but against State Prohibition. In my message to the Legislature I declared that Prohibition as a governmental policy was fundamentally wrong, and that I would veto any bill providing for it. That message was published in the press of Tennessee, also in other States. It has been circulated as campaign material, published in liquor journals and in books, and used as arguments by those who were contesting the advance of the Prohibition sentiment. I say to you that if this message has encouraged lawlessness, or even been sought as a refuge for violators of the law, if it had to stand as my last expression on the liquor question, I would consume it in the living fires and erase it forever from the minds and memories of men. I have seen the trail of liquor in the criminal courts where I have prosecuted crime. I know and have been a participant in its paralyzing and corroding influence in the public and social life of our National Capital. Going through life I have seen it drag down many of the associates of my boyhood, blasting their hopes and consigning them to untimely graves. I have seen its forked lightning strike my firstborn, the child of my young manhood, and have borne with him the suffering and tried to help him in his brave but sometimes melancholy struggle for redemption. At last I have felt the foul and stealthy blow as it turned upon me in its deadly and shaming wrath—upon me, who had pleaded before the people for its very existence. Men have called me strong; and while I could see its harm in others, I thought myself immune, as thousands before my time have thought, and suffered for the thought. All this I knew and felt without a revelation of the deep pathos and meaning of it all. I needed help, for I was groping and my feet were stumbling in the dark. Deep in humiliation, tortured and condemned by my own esteem, which is the severest penalty a man may afflict upon himself, I thought of the oft-repeated phrases about personal liberty, of the power of the human will to resist temptation, with which I had beguiled myself, and I found them as unsubstantial as the fabric of a dream. When logic failed and reason gave no answer I cast aside all pride of opinion, all thought of what the world might say or think, and went to the throne of Almighty God. There, on bended knees, I asked for light and strength, and they came. The curtains of the night parted and the way was clear. I arose a changed man. An invisible hand has led me on to where the vision is unobscured, and the purposes of life stand revealed. From a critic of others, I looked within. From an accuser, I became a servant in my own house to set it in order. From a vague believer in the guidance of Divine Power, I have become a convert to its infinite truth. From an unhappy and dissatisfied man, out of tune with the harmony of life and religion, I have become happy and contented, firmly anchored in the faith and ready to testify from my own experience to the miraculous power of God to cleanse the souls of men. Out of this has come the profound conviction that on the questions with which I had to deal in my public career, all my arguments and all my conclusions, so far as they excused or justified the moral right or policy of the State to legalize the sale of liquor, and thereby gave sanction to the ravages on society, were only the empty and hopeless statements of propositions which had no verity or application to a thing wholly and essentially evil, and concerning which no principle of right or order or liberty should ever be invoked for its existence. Civilized society can offer no excuse for the temptations which it sets before humanity, for in itself and of itself drunkenness is a sin without a reason, a degrading crime without a recompense, a promoter and prolific parent of other sins and crimes which sap the strength and wealth of men and nations. Abstinence is, therefore, the only guarantee of safety, and the destruction of the liquor traffic is the only guarantee of abstinence.

After the personal part of the address given above Ex-Governor Patterson continued at length in an impassioned arraignment of the liquor traffic for its wrongs and crimes. Language can not adequately express the effect of this address on the audience. During its delivery the four thousand delegates frequently burst into applause, halting the speaker, and at its close there was a perfect tumult of enthusiasm. Round after round of cheers were given. The people stood on the chairs, the men twirling their hats on their canes, the women waving their wraps and handkerchiefs. Men and women, old and young, cried like children, and laughed while they cried for joy, and shouted praises aloud, and spontaneously broke out into songs of rejoicing and victory. The pen of history in recording the most eloquent scenes of American oratory can hardly omit this speech of Patterson before the Anti-Saloon League Convention. The Ex-Governor has been making good his pledge in touring the country, scathingly arraigning the liquor traffic, and pleading eloquently for nation-wide Prohibition. The bolt that killed Carmack and the vision that halted Patterson on his way to Damascus have been sad specters to haunt the rum power of Tennessee and the nation.

In February, 1917, I asked United States Senator Luke Lea of Tennessee for a brief opinion on the working and effect of the Prohibition law in his State, and at once received the following:

The oft-repeated argument was heard by those opposed to the passage of the Prohibition laws, that they could not be enforced, and that disrespect and contempt for law would be one of the results. It is true that in the larger cities of the State there was not the strong sentiment favorable to prohibitory legislation at the time of the passage of these laws that existed in the country districts. However, eight years have witnessed a steady growth of temperance sentiment in the State, so that to-day the four large cities of the State, Memphis, Nashville, Chattanooga and Knoxville, are almost completely "bone-dry." There is not an open saloon in any of these cities, and legislation supplementing the Prohibition laws which have been enacted by the present session of the Legislature, looking to the prevention of shipment into the State from "wet" territory, will completely destroy even the so-called "bootlegging" traffic, which has been in vogue to some extent among the lower elements of our city populations. I think Tennessee is better morally and economically because of Prohibition, and if left to a popular referendum at this time, there is no doubt that it would carry by an overwhelming majority.

Governor Tom C. Rye, of Tennessee, in a speech in the campaign of 1916 for the Governorship for the second term, said:

The Democratic Party stands committed to temperance, good government and law enforcement. The people have definitely and finally determined that the manufacture and sale of intoxicants as a beverage in Tennessee shall cease; we accept this as an accomplished fact, and declare our firm opposition to any movement or effort to repeal or impair existing laws for the suppression of the liquor traffic and the enforcement of the laws. This is the declaration of the last Democratic platform.

All laws for this purpose were endorsed by the Democratic Party in its last convention; for that reason, and for the further and better reason that I believe these laws are right and should be enforced, I take the same position now that I did as a candidate two years ago,

and solemnly declare that insofar as the efforts of the
Chief Executive of the State and the powers vested in
him and the authority given by legislative enactment will
authorize and permit, these laws shall be enforced so long
as I enjoy the distinction of being your Governor. I am
glad to announce that in the effort made along these lines
I have had the hearty coöperation of many of the officials
of the State charged with the duty of enforcing the law,
and I am encouraged to believe that in the future all, or
practically all, the officers charged with these responsible
duties will be found industriously exerting themselves in
upholding the law and maintaining the dignity of the
great State of Tennessee.

In a letter of February 16, 1917, sending me
Governor Rye's speech, his private secretary says:

Since this speech was delivered, Governor Rye has been
inaugurated for a second term, and in his inaugural address he took occasion to express his convictions as to the
necessity of the General Assembly passing the so-called
Bone-Dry Law, and expressing the pleasure he would
receive in having the privilege of signing it. This act
has since been passed, which forbids common carriers ship-
ping intoxicating liquors into the State.

CHAPTER XI

The South Abolishes the Saloon (Cont.)

WEST VIRGINIA

AFTER the tragical contest in Tennessee there was a lull of four years, which the liquor men claimed was a reaction in their favor, but which the temperance people said was a preparation for future victories. The lull was broken by West Virginia, which on November 5, 1912, achieved one of the most significant temperance victories America had had in the adoption of a constitutional Prohibition amendment by a majority of 93,342 out of a total vote of 235,843, to take effect July 1, 1914. Only two counties voted against the proposition of Prohibition. The strange part of the contest was that only one city in the State went "wet," while the oher cities and most of the country places went "dry." Parkersburg voted by a considerable majority for the amendment.

Rev. Doctor Thomas Hare, who led the allied forces in the contest, in accounting for the victory, said the church and temperance people were thoroughly united and fairly sowed the State with no-license literature.

Hon. H. D. Hatfield, Ex-Governor of West Virginia, who held the office four years, thus speaks of the workings of the law: "The general results thus far in the matter of Prohibition have been satisfactory. Many who were against the adoption of the Prohibition amendment originally and voted against it, have repeatedly told me that if an opportunity presented itself in the future they would reverse their action and favor the measure. Of the many letters sent to me on the subject I will quote this one from the manager of two of the largest and best collieries in the State: "Since Prohibition went into effect we have had comparatively no trouble with our men lying off from work, fighting, etc. The families of the fathers and sons who drank are better cared for and are perceptibly more prosperous. We are troubled a little with bootleggers, but I assure you there is not one pint used now to gallons before Prohibition went into effect."

VIRGINIA

Before the Civil war there was only a light traffic in intoxicating drinks in Virginia. Some of the planters got enough to hurt themselves and their promising sons, but the negroes were not allowed to have it. The law of the State made it a crime to sell intoxicants to a slave without a permit from his master. And the master was too smart to give to his slave that which would reduce

his earning power, create a criminal menace and
shorten his life, which was worth a thousand dollars in cold money. At the close of the war the
brewers and distillers, feeling that they had a
joint ownership in the Government because they
continued to pay the liquor war tax, with inso-
lence and energy pushed their business into all the
States, including the South, where they found in
the new-made liberty of the slave an especially
fruitful field. In the midst of the chaos and bitter
conflict of the reconstruction period in Virginia
the saloon was thrust as a new disturbing factor
and a grave menace to white and black alike. The
good people of the State sensed the danger and
began at once to resist it. Their first great victory was achieved in 1885, when the Independent
Order of Good Templars, that modest but efficient pioneer temperance organization, secured
the passage of a Local Option Law for counties,
cities, and towns as a unit, under which the saloon
was driven from three-fourths of the counties,
nine-tenths of the towns and one-half of the cities
of the State. The fight for Prohibition in 1914
was fierce. It is said the liquor people poured
$1,000,000 into the campaign. The temperance
and church people were united and organized
completely, down to captains of tens. It was
found necessary in the contest to establish a daily
newspaper, the "Richmond Virginian," which
Rev. Doctor James Cannon, Jr., leader in the

fight, claims had more to do than any other one thing in carrying Virginia for Prohibition. The vote, which was taken on September 22, 1914, resulted in a majority of 30,365 out of a total vote of 150,000 for Prohibition. The law went into effect November 1, 1916.

In an interview Governor Stewart of Virginia said that his State had one of the best prohibitory laws in the country and that he was doing his best to enforce the law and was succeeding.

Senator Martin, a leader in the Senate, told me that Virginia had a good prohibitory law, which was a great benefit; that it was enforced and that he did not believe the peole would ever think of going back to license.

ARKANSAS

For many years they had local option in Arkansas, and also the three-mile law, which forbade a drinking-place within three miles of a church or school on petition of a majority of all the inhabitants of the territory involved, which included mothers, wives, sisters, and daughters over eighteen years of age. As early as 1902 forty-four counties had been voted dry, leaving only thirty-one in the wet column. The Legislature of 1907 abolished crossroad country saloons, stopped liquor salesmen from going into Prohibition territory, and the wholesale houses from advertising liquors in the papers and circulars in territory where the sale of liquor was forbidden by law. The Legislature of 1915 passed a State prohibitory law which took effect January 1, 1916.

Hon. W. F. Kirby, United States Senator from Arkansas, who vouches for the success of Prohibition in his State and works actively for its adoption by the nation, in a letter to me says, "My position has been well defined on this question for a long time."

SOUTH CAROLINA

South Carolina, like the other Southern States, was moving along the road of local option to State-wide Prohibition when its progress was interrupted by the adoption of the Dispensary System of regulating the liquor traffic, which is a system of State control of the same. In 1896 United States Senator Tillman, who believed in the dispensary as a wise solution of the question, by his powerful personal influence had it incorporated into the State constitution. As a revenue-producer when honestly administered it was a success, but in places it was maladministered and became a scandal. As a moral measure the dispensary was a failure. Its record of vice and crime showed an increase over the license system. On September 14, 1915, South Carolina adopted State-wide Prohibition by a vote of 41,735 to

16,809, being a vote of two and a half to one. Every county in the State but one voted no license.

In a personal interview Governor Manning told me of the difficulties encountered in enforcing the prohibitory law, and how he had successfully overcome them. I asked him for his views on the liquor situation for publication, and he gave me the following:

When I became Governor of South Carolina, three years ago, the liquor business was regulated under a gallon-a-month act. I at once inaugurated a campaign of enforcement of the law, using county, municipal and State officers to enforce it. In places where the law had been most flagrantly violated, substantial improvement was made, and the amount of the illegal sale of liquor greatly curtailed. Last winter the Legislature of South Carolina passed a law reducing the amount to any person to a quart a month, for medicinal, scientific and sacramental purposes. Under this act, the sale of liquor was prohibited to minors, to students of college, to women other than the head of a family, and provision made for the enforcement of the law by State constabulary. Under the provisions of this act, an aggressive improvement has been waged against the use and illicit sale of liquor, with the result of greatly improved conditions.

My policy is to steadily tighten the hand of the law against offenders, and the result shows a condition better than even the most ardent advocates of the measure hoped for. I do not mean to say that the law is absolutely followed, but public sentiment has been aroused, convictions are had for violations, and the State is more nearly "dry" than we had hoped could be brought about in this short time. The public is realizing the advantage of these strict prohibitory measures, and public sentiment is now behind the measure.

SOUTHERN STATES WHICH HAVE NOT ADOPTED PROHIBITION

MARYLAND

State-wide Prohibition lost in the popular election of 1916 in Maryland, but quite an advance in dry territory was made the same day. But for the powerful influence of the liquor-dealers of Baltimore the State would have adopted Prohibition by this time. There is a wholesome public sentiment moving steadily toward State Prohibition.

KENTUCKY

There are few surprises to friend or foe greater than the temperance situation in Kentucky. There are 106 dry counties in the State and only fourteen that are wet. Old Bourbon County, said to have been the mother of the best whisky in the world, is in the dry column. J. C. W. Beckham was elected to the United States Senate from Kentucky on a Prohibition platform, and is one of the ablest anti-liquor leaders in that body. Kentucky would have been dry long ago but for the tremendously powerful distillery influence in Louisville and its corrupt alliance with politics.

The liquor people of Kentucky had just as well save their money, throw up their hands and surrender, as John Barleycorn has been killed, and the State in the immediate future will fairly skip into the Prohibition ranks.

MISSOURI

Missouri has for many years been under a local option law by counties, excepting cities of 2,500 population or more, allowing them voting units, and leaving St. Louis as a civic unit by itself. It would have been thought that the overwhelming defeat Prohibition received at the polls three or four years ago would have set the cause back a decade. It had a contrary effect, nerved the temperance people for more vigorous work, and now eighty-one out of the 114 counties are dry, including nearly fifty-one per cent. of the population. Of the 69,000 square miles of territory 53,000 are under no-license.

The State would doubtless have adopted Prohibition had it not been for the opposition of the Anheuser Busch Brewery Company of St. Louis, perhaps the most powerful enemy of Prohibition in America. When it looked as though the State Legislature were likely to pass a prohibitory law the representatives of this brewery, whose advertisements, carried to the ends of the earth, fill the sides of houses and long fences, played the baby act and pitifully pleaded for mercy and begged the members not to drive them out of the State. An anti-saloon leader told me the other day that the State would go no-license at the next election on the question.

Senator Stone, who astonished the nation by voting yes last summer on the National Constitutional Amendment proposition after having been one of the most efficient advocates of the liquor cause, did not imperil himself politically by doing so, taking into account the strong temperance sentiment in his State.

FLORIDA

Up to about thirty years ago a license could be taken out to sell liquor anywhere in the State of Florida. But in 1887 Article 19 was added to the Constitution. The people by the use of this law had by 1907 cleared the saloons from thirty-three of the forty-six counties of the State.

The temperance leaders secured from the Legislature of 1915 the passage of the drastic Davis Restrictive Law, which at one stroke killed 200 of the less than 300 drinking-places, leaving at this time only seventy-five mail-order and retail liquor-stores in the whole State. The temperance people charge that the millionaire owners of the palatial seaside hotels and pleasure resorts, determined to retain their bars for the accommoda-

:ion of their rich and ruddy guests, have been the most powerful enemies Prohibition has had, in their baleful influence at the State capital and in the popular elections. They may just as well save their money and adjust themselves to the temper and desire of the South, as the Legislature of 1917 granted a referendum, and it is morally certain the people will vote Prohibition. Florida adopted prohibition Nov. 5, 1918.

LOUISIANA

The liquor dealers have for many years dominated the politics of Louisiana. They have been entrenched in their headquarters in New Orleans, the stronghold of their cause in the South.

In New Orleans, with its many foreigners and pleasure-loving people, and in the other wet parishes as well, the rum rule has largely nullified the Gay-Shattuck Law. Notwithstanding the saloon's grip on politics, the people have by their parish local option voted the traffic from considerably more than one-half of the geographical area, and from fifty-one per cent. of the population, of the State of Louisiana.

TEXAS

Texas is an empire in itself. It is not only the largest State in the Union, but it is the most productive one agriculturally, having recently taken the primacy away from Illinois. It is an empire morally. From the dry territory in this State alone can be cut out Maine, New Hampshire, Vermont, Massachusetts, Rhode Island, Connecticut, New York, New Jersey, Pennsylvania, Delaware and Ohio, and then have 20,000 square miles left over. The number of its people living under no-license is 700,000 more than the combined population of all of the New England States with the exception of Massachusetts. Thus the "pepper-box," and "tooth-pick," the revolver and dagger of the pioneer Texan ranger, have given way in so short a time to one of the best civilizations known.

In 1875, eighteen years before the Anti-Saloon League was born in America, the United Friends of Temperance wrote into the constitution of Texas the local option provision now in force, and the next year the people ratified it by a popular vote. In 1887 a constitutional Prohibition amendment was defeated at the polls by 91,357. On July 22, 1911, there was another fierce fight over State-wide Prohibition, with 231,096 for the amendment and 237,303 against it, an adverse majority of 6,307.

The year following, Morris Sheppard was elected to the United States Senate, and a majority of the Congressmen to the House of Representatives on a Prohibition platform. The no-liquor candidate for Governor, however, was elected. I had a delightful interview with Senator Morris Sheppard, of nation-wide fame, as to the great success of Prohibition in the South and throughout the nation, in which he prophesied that the great State of Texas would take her place with her sister States of the South in the no-license column at the next election on the question. I asked the Senator if he would give me in small space his views on the relation of the liquor problem to State legislation, and he gave me the following:

Shall a State confess itself powerless by law to abolish the traffic in a drug that will sap the physical strength of its people, reduce them in ever-growing numbers to intellectual and moral ruin, affect their collective capacity for the exercise of free institutions to such an extent as to imperil the priceless gift of liberty, destroy all hope of further progress in the various lines of human endeavor, and, corrupting the very foundations of reproduction, convert posterity into a race of weaklings and degenerates? If a State has not the right to defend itself against such an enemy with the strong arm of statutory laws, it had as well dissolve. Is it not folly to assert that a State can not preserve its own existence? If the police power of a State may be invoked to take individual property without compensation, in order to prevent the destruction of other property, as in the case of a conflagration, or in order to preserve the lives and health of its citizens, as in the case of an epidemic, how much more justly may that same power be employed to stop a traffic that imperils the existence of the State itself and threatens the lives of multiplied thousands of its people? The appearance of

an invading army in a single county of our State would
bring to arms three-quarters of a million Texans to defend the honor and the existence of the Commonwealth.
The liquor traffic is a far deadlier enemy of the State
than an invading army could ever be. It is a perpetual
menace to the life of the individual and the existence of
the State. They tell us we cannot enforce a State-wide
prohibitory law. We tell them the people of Texas have
not lost the capacity of self-government or self-preservation. The adoption of the State-wide amendment is but
a step. The next step will be the election of men to
executive office in whom the spirit of Goliad and San
Jacinto still lives.

Texas adopted prohibition in 1918. Action
declared unconstitutional.

WHY A SOLID SOUTH AGAINST KING ALCOHOL

There are reasons why the South should take
the lead in this Prohibition movement. It was
necessary to remove the saloon from the negro
to save Southern industry and civilization.

The late Booker T. Washington said, "The
abolition of the barroom is a blessing to the negro,
second only to the abolition of slavery. Two-
thirds of the mobs, lynchings and burnings at the
stake are the result of bad whisky drunk by bad
black men and bad white men."

Besides, the South is intensely American. In
the fourteen Southern States there are but sixteen
foreign-born persons to every 1,000 inhabitants.
In Ohio, California, Pennsylvania, New York,
Illinois and Wisconsin there are 178 foreign-born

persons to every 1,000 inhabitants. In the mountain disticts of the South, where the foreign-born population is the least in America, there are almost no drinking-places. The "moonshiners" hide in some of the mountain dens, but there were scarcely twenty open saloons in the mountain districts of Virginia, West Virginia, Kentucky, Tennessee, North Carolina, Georgia, and Arkansas, even before any of these States had gone dry. It is not hard to get the liquor traffic away from so homogeneous a population.

The Southern people are sentimental and enthusiastic, and do what they do with an intense zeal. As a rule they have a deep religious instinct and the highest moral ideals; the territory is good ground for Prohibition. Thus there are other reasons than the race problem which have made for such local success in the South. The negro question has had nothing to do with Prohibition in Maine, Kansas, North Dakota, or other States of the North that have gone dry. The work of abolishing the saloon met least resistance in the plantation sections of the South and the rural districts of the North. It has now gotten into the cities and will sweep them. Much of the marvelous growth and glory of the New South, whose progress in some regards has outstripped that of any other section, can be traced to its inveterate hatred of and deadly warfare on the saloon.

CHAPTER XII

Prohibition in the West

THE fires of Prohibition burning in the cotton fields of the South crossed Mason and Dixon's line and caught in the prairies, cornfields and wheatfields of the West and, raging with merciless fury, wiped out the breweries, distilleries and saloons in its path. In one day, the 3d of November, 1914, four of these States went dry at the polls, thereby securing constitutional Prohibition. They were Arizona, Colorado, Oregon and Washington. We have not space for such detailed history of the war on the liquor traffic in the Western States as we gave of that in the South, but we will give room for the testimony of the highest possible authority on the successful working of Prohibition in the Northern States—testimony that would convict King Alcohol of high crimes and misdemeanors in any court on earth.

ARIZONA

The action of Arizona was a surprise, as hardly more than a fifth of the population was under no-license laws. There was harmony between the temperance forces, as well as organization and intense activity in the campaign. The law took effect January 1, 1915. Women's votes contributed to the result.

I wrote to Governor Thomas E. Campbell, asking him how Prohibition worked in his State, and received the following reply: "Arizona went into the 'dry' column of January 1, 1915, by constitutional amendment. Thus we have had a term of two years by which to judge the merits of the case as affecting this State, and for comparison with years in the bygone 'wet' history of the State. Merchants and bankers, regardless of their personal attitude to the use of liquor, unanimously report increased business, better credits and more cash from the savings of workers. The jails throughout the State are nearly empty, except in cases of men charged with unlawfully selling whisky; few commitments are of record for drunkenness, and many justices of the peace have practically nothing in the way of criminal business. Mercantile companies noticed a betterment in credits within six months after the 'dry' amendment went into effect, and the improvement continues. Money outstanding before January 1, 1915, represented a great sum and a huge economic waste. When it became impossible to obtain liquor in large quantities, this condition was bettered at once, and business men who had most bitterly opposed the Prohibition amendment rapidly became its best friends. A 'bone-dry' law, under which no liquor can be brought into Arizona for any but sacramental purposes, passed the Legislature on March 8 last. Arizona is satisfied. In the family the greatest improvement is seen. The wife and children of the Arizona wage-earner are better clothed and fed than ever before, and there is ample money for needed vacations. If the matter should ever be brought to vote, I am confident that bone-dry Prohibition would triumph by three to one."

COLORADO

The victory of the anti-saloon forces in Colorado was brought about by complete organization and persistent neyspaper advertising. The violence in the strike zone had its influence. Billy Sunday, the peerless evangelist, with his great revival in the State, made many Prohibition votes. Billy Sunday is one of the most bitter, relentless and efficient enemies of booze the generation has raised up. In a conversation I had with Governor Julius C. Gunter he spoke of some of the difficulties in enforcing the prohibitory law, but had great enthusiasm in its success and its benefits. I quote him from a statement made not long ago to the Woman's Christian Temperance Union for publication in the "Union Signal":

A prohibition constitutional amendment was adopted in the State of Colorado at the November election of 1914, by a majority of about 11,000 votes, to become effective January 1, 1915. After one year of Prohibition a large majority of those most radically opposed to the amendment at the time of its submission are its most ardent supporters to-day. Should the question of Prohibition be again submitted to the people of this State, the majority of 1914 would be manifolded. As an evidence of this, the beer amendment submitted to the voters at the November election of 1916 was defeated by a majority of 85,789. The practical benefits which are most conspicuous are the relief of suffering among women and children, the decrease in demand on charitable organizations, the great decrease in crime and consequent committals to state prisons, and increase in the number of new savings accounts opened by the various banks throughout the State, totaling 119,000. The Legislature, which is now in session, will doubtless amend the present statute, tending to a more effective and rigid enforcement of the law, as suggested in the inaugural address of the incoming Governor.

United States Senator Thomas told me that the prohibitory law of Colorado not only justified the action of its friends, but converted the views of many who voted against it. He said the benefits of the law were seen everywhere. He said the success in the cities surprised the friends as well as the enemies of the proposition. Senator Thomas expressed this sentiment in a debate in the Senate recently, when he said:

I interrupted the Senator from Washington also because the city of Denver is only a few thousand smaller in population than the city of Seattle, and the argument made in Denver against Prohibition—and I thought there was a good deal of it—was along the same lines on which it was made by the editor of the paper from which the Senator has read. The prophecies and predictions which were made of the effect of Prohibition upon large cities —it being conceded that it would not be the same in the smaller places—have all been unverified by the logic of events.

Senator John F. Shafroth, who takes pride in the victory over the saloon in his State, and is an active friend of Prohibition in the Senate, has sent me a little pamphlet, from which I take the following:

There was a time when there were less restrictions and when there were no licenses, and then when licenses required only a small payment. But as each step has been taken the realization of the people has grown that the greatest curse this country has ever had or the people of the world have ever had is the work of the saloon and the excessive use of intoxicating liquors. That is what has caused the sentiment and what has caused the change in the situation as to submission.

There was a time when legislators would not think of submitting the question of Prohibition to the people of a State. Oh, no. You must take it to a community; you must take it to a county. There was a time when a city council could not submit it to the entire city, but would submit it simply to a ward of that city or to a precinct of that city. But as the evil has been shown, as the detrimental effect of the use of liquor has been demonstrated, as its effect upon civilization has been made clear, there has developed this overwhelming sentiment against it.

OREGON

In Oregon all but two counties voted for Prohibition, and Portland, a city of 250,000, went dry by a majority of 1832.

I have the following letter from Governor James Withycombe:

Replying to your inquiry as to the progress of Prohibition in Oregon, I have to report that in 1915 at the general election the State went "dry" by a large majority. Under the law as subsequently drawn by the Legislature, in effect the past two years, the sale and manufacture of intoxicants was prohibited in the State, and two quarts of alcoholic beverage or twenty-four quarts of beer could be imported once in each 28 days. At the general election in November, 1916, an initiative measure was adopted by the people by an overwhelming majority, making the State "bone-dry." It is not legal to import any intoxicants whatsoever into the State, or to have the same in one's possession unless it was legally received prior to the enactment of the new law. I am free to say that there is every indication that Prohibition has been and is successful in Oregon, from an economic as well as a social and moral standpoint. I am confident that under no conditions whatsoever would the electorate of this State permit the return of the saloon.

Hon. George E. Chamberlain, United States

Senator from Oregon, sent me the following communication for publication:

The States of the Union are saying one by one that the saloon must go; and that means that alcohol in all its forms must cease to be used as a beverage. The reason for this is, first—and most important of all—the fact that in order to be efficient a man must be sober; and that does not mean merely that he must be sober at the time his hand is accomplishing a task, but that he must have been sober for some time prior, in order that there be a steadiness of head and heart and hand. In other words, efficiency has demanded these qualifications of men in every walk of life. Railroad corporations, great industrial and commercial organizations, whether corporate or individual, will not employ men who patronize the saloon or indulge in the use of intoxicants. They have found out that the use of these is inconsistent with efficiency, and in order to secure employment a man must either give up alcohol or give up the chance of earning a support for himself and those dependent upon him. What stronger argument was ever educed to sustain the position here assumed than the fact that the powers now engaged in the European War —the most terrible in the history of the world—put a ban upon the traffic in alcohol? This was necessary to efficiency in a fighting force. But, aside from the question of efficiency, the second reason for the change in public sentiment is the saloon. It has been instrumental in wrecking more homes, destroying more lives and bringing more sorrow into the world than any one instrumentality in the world. Instead of being outlawed, as its acts demanded that it should be, it has been recognized and licensed, and it has taken years to make the people understand the disaster that the saloon has wrought upon the moral fiber of our civilization. Neither youth, nor age, nor sex, nor condition has been exempted from the ravages that this curse has wrought. But its death knell is soon to be sounded, in America, at least. Forty years ago there was scarcely a village, or a town, or a city, in Oregon where the saloon did not exist, and the more prosperous the community the more numerous the saloons. But gradually the sentiment of the people of that progressive State has changed, and when once the people by constitutional amendment secured for themselves the right to enact legislation the saloon began to lose its power in politics, and now the State is absolutely Prohibition territory. Its effect will be to close the jails in the smaller towns, diminish crimes in the cities, and elevate the moral tone of the whole State.

WASHINGTON

Prohibition won in Washington by a majority of 18,632, carrying all but six counties.

Hon. Ernest Lester, Governor of the State of Washington, under date of February 19, 1917, wrote me as follows:

I have at hand your letter of the 12th inst., wherein you ask an expression from me regarding Prohibition in the State of Washington. Replying I may say that saloons in the State of Washington were closed on January 1, 1916, under the provisions of a law enacted by the people at the general election held in November, 1914. It would be too much to say that there have been no violations of the law. I am confident, however, that were the same law to be again submitted to the voters, it would be enacted by an even larger majority than was given to it in 1914. Sentiment in the State on this subject is best indicated by the vote given at the general election last November on two initiative bills submitted to the people, and which would virtually have nullified the dry law had they been enacted. Both of these measures were overwhelmingly defeated.

In my message to the Legislature, delivered on January 10, I recommended the enactment of a "bone-dry" law. Such a law has been passed by both Houses of the Legislature, and I now have it before me for consideration. I expect to approve it today.

There is no argument but that the State of Washington and its people are better off in every respect with saloons closed than they were when the saloons were in operation. The "bone-dry" law to which I refer will, in my opinion, be of great benefit and value to the citizens of the State as soon as it goes into effect.

Senator Wesley L. Jones, of Washington, in a conversation concerning the success of Prohibition in his State, gave me the following information and comment:

We have had Prohibition in the State of Washington since January 1, 1916. The predictions of dire disaster by those who opposed it have not come true. Beneficial business has not been destroyed, but has been stimulated and improved. Savings-bank deposits have increased, more comforts and necessaries have been brought to our homes than ever before. Women and children have been made comfortable and happy. Crime and poverty have been greatly lessened and our jails and almshouses have been emptied. Business men, professional men and laboring men who opposed the law now praise it most warmly and express the hope that it will never be repealed. Personally, I have long been in favor of Prohibition and of every step that would lead to it, and have done what I could to bring it about. I hope National Prohibition will soon come. It will promote the growth of business, the welfare of labor, the happiness of the home, the conservation of health and manhood, the strengthening of our citizenship and the prosperity and welfare of the nation.

Senator Jones also gave me a copy of an interview of Major Blethen, a Seattle editor, in the "Kansas City Times," who had been an opponent of Prohibition in the campaign, but who acknowledges his conversion and thus testifies to its wonderful success in Seattle:

My paper fought its hardest against Prohibition. We fought it on economic grounds alone. We believed that in a great seaport city with a population of upward of 300,000 Prohibition would be destructive; it would bring on economic disaster. We believed that under our system of licensing saloons we had the liquor traffic about as well controlled as it could be, and we wanted to let it alone, and so we fought as hard as we could fight. But, in spite of all we could do against it, Prohibition carried, and it went into effect in Washington, January 1. We have had a month of it now. And how has it worked out? We already know that it is a great benefit morally and from an economic standpoint. Its moral benefit has been tremendous. Seattle had 260 saloons and we had an average of 2,600 arrests a month for crimes and misdemeanors growing out of liquor-drinking. In January we had only 400 arrests, and sixty of those were made January 1, and were the results of hang-overs from the old year. That in itself is enough to convince any man with a conscience that Prohibition is necessary. There can be no true economy in anything that is immoral. And on top of that great moral result we have these economic facts: In the first three weeks of January the savings deposits in the banks of Seattle increased 15 per cent. There was not a grocery store in Seattle that did not show an increase of business in January greater than ever known in any month before in all the history of the city, except in holiday time. In all the large grocery stores the increase was immense. In addition to this, every dry-goods store in Seattle except one, and that one I have no figures from, had a wonderful increase in business. Each store reported the largest business ever done in one month, except in holiday time. I wished to know in what class of goods the sales increased so greatly, and so I sent to all the grocery and dry-goods stores to find that out. And to me it is a pitiful thing—and it makes me sorry that we did not have Prohibition long ago—that the increase in sales in all the dry-goods stores was in wearing apparel of women and children and in the grocery stores the increase was made up chiefly of fruits and fancy groceries. This proves that it is the women and children who suffer most from the liquor business, and it is the women and children who benefit greatest from Prohibition. Money that went formerly over the bar for whisky is now being spent for clothing for the women and children and in better food for the household. It is just like this: When you close the saloons the money that formerly was spent there remains in the family of the wage-earner, and his wife and children buy shoes and clothing and better food with it. Yes, sir; we have found in Seattle that it is better to buy shoes than booze. The families of wage-earners in Seattle are going to have more food and clothes and everything else than they had before.

Hon. Miles Poindexter, United States Senator from Washington, gave me for use his estimate of the liquor situation in his State, which is as follows:

Various influences through a number of years contributed to the movement to abolish liquor saloons in the State of Washington. The organized fight was conducted largely—towards the conclusion of it, especially—by the Washington Anti-Saloon League. The time-worn arguments were made against the entire movement, but with constantly lessening effect. The fight was first for the extension of local option to counties, and, when this was gained, the fight was extended in behalf of State-wide Prohibition. This came to an acute stage in the general election of 1914, at which there was submitted directly to the people, under our State initiative law, a bill abolishing the saloon and prohibiting the manufacture or sale of intoxicating beverages in the State. The influences which led up to this opportunity of the people to pass judgment directly upon the question reach back, in the gradual extension of popular government and the power of the masses of the people, through a number of years, including the granting of suffrage to women in the election of 1910 and the gradual development in the State of direct legislation, including the initiative, referendum, and recall. Actual results have converted thousands of the hard-headed business men of the State who formerly voted wet. It is not too much to say that the enactment of this law has added enormously to the general welfare and happiness of our people.

CHAPTER XIII

PROHIBITION IN THE WEST (Continued)

IDAHO

IN February, 1915, the Legislature of Idaho adopted statutory Prohibition, and also sent the question to the people at the polls, who at the November election in 1916 adopted constitutional Prohibition by an overwhelming majority.

Governor Moses Alexander is a Hebrew and a most efficient champion of the Prohibition cause. I wrote him for his views of the situation in Idaho for record here and received a communication signed by him with the M for Moses two inches tall by measurement, and the letters for Alexander all nearly an inch high, which looked very much as though he meant what he said. This is his message:

I am a Prohibitionist on account of believing in the brotherhood of mankind. To help the weak is our duty, and to throw our arm around our weak-willed brother and strengthen him to withstand the temptation of the demon Alcohol and build him up so that he may walk in the path of success. I am a business man, engaged in active business at several points, and my business success depends upon the number of my patrons, as does the business of every enterprise, and if a man consumes his earnings over the bar every legitimate business suffers, for he then has not the money to spend for food and clothing which are necessities, and certainly not for any of the luxuries of life. By the abolition of liquor a man is placed in position to enjoy the money he earns, and, more than that, we enjoy the abolition of crime from our communities. When Idaho became dry in 1916, there were some who doubted the wisdom of the enactment on account of business reasons, but there is none now, and the constitutional amendment submitted last fall received an overwhelming majority in every county in the State. Prohibition like every other good thing has to be tasted before it is liked, and, once a taste is acquired, you cannot do without it. Idaho is in the Prohibition line now and forever, and even the most ardent supporter of Alcohol in the past has changed his opinion. It is no longer a matter of sentiment, but a business proposition with us; we can figure out the benefits to the community in dollars and cents, and Idaho is becoming richer under Prohibition than it has been in the past.

A personal interview with Senator Borah of Idaho, one of the ablest of our American statesmen, elicited from him the most positive testimony as to the success of Prohibition in his State, and also his views on the value of Prohibition to the laboring man, which appear in another chapter.

IOWA

In February, 1915, Iowa, which had been constitutionally dry in theory but wet in practice, adopted Prohibition in fact.

Hon. Albert B. Cummins, United States Senator from Iowa, one of the strongest men in the Senate and country, who was backed by his State for the Republican nomination for the Presidency, in a conversation I had with him testified to the success of Prohibition in his State, and he predicted the speedy removal of the liquor traffic in America. He gave me this statement:

The one thing upon which the best minds of this country have reached a definite and unalterable conclusion is that the use of alcoholic liquor as a beverage shall cease. Its temperate use does no good and its intemperate use is the admitted cause of more suffering, hardship, poverty, disease, and crime than all other things combined. Those who use liquor temperately, even though they are not conscious of the harm it does them, must surrender their privilege in order that society may avoid the awful consequences of the intemperate use of alcohol. All the influences of safety, efficiency, health, happiness, and comfort are working day and night to destroy this evil thing. Mothers and wives are praying for the day that will banish it. Children who have a right to the enjoyment of pure minds and strong bodies are demanding its condemnation. The hosts of morality are fighting it, and the great army of industry is determined to drive it from the memory of mankind. There is no longer a doubt with respect to the outcome. It will not be long before a generation will appear that will look with as much surprise and indignation upon the taking of poison in the form of alcohol as this generation does upon the taking of poison in the form of prussic acid.

Iowa has another great Senator in the person of Hon. William S. Kenyon, who has gained national fame and a place in the permanent history of the country by the introduction of the Webb-Kenyon Inter-State Commerce Amendment Bill, forbidding the illicit transportation of liquor from wet into dry territory.

Iowa rejected Constitutional Prohibition by the smallest majority in October, 1917, but retains Statutory Prohibition.

FOUR STATES

On election day in November, 1916, just two years from the time the first Western States went dry, another group of four Western States voted no-license, thereby securing Constitutional Prohibition. They were Montana, Nebraska, South Dakota and Michigan. They went into the column by a non-partisan vote, Montana and Nebraska going for Wilson, South Dakota and Michigan voting for Hughes. That one day drove out of business 114 breweries and 6,528 saloons and put 5,000,000 people under no-license rule. It cleared the liquor traffic from a geographical area which could be set down over Great Britain, Italy, Holland, Denmark, Switzerland and European Turkey, and there would be 18,000 square miles left over.

MONTANA

I found in Hon. S. V. Stewart, Governor of Montana, a tall, strong, handsome man, a typical Westerner. I asked him how he felt about the prohibitory law in his State. He answered he ought to feel warmly toward it, as he had made the race for the Governorship on that issue the fall before, and that he intended to do all in his power to enforce the law. The Governor gave me a copy of a letter he had written to Rev. Joseph Pope, head of the dry forces in Montana, dated September 2, 1916, which is as follows:

I regard Prohibition as a purely moral question and one which ought not to be involved in politics, but rather should be determined by each voter irrespective of political affiliations and solely according to the dictates of conscience. Nevertheless, the question is a public one, and many voters feel that they have a right to know the attitude of public men on all public questions. In view of this general feeling and of the further fact that the next administration may be called upon to make Prohibition effective, I take this occasion to say to you that I personally believe in State-wide Prohibition and expect to vote for the pending measure at the forthcoming election. In the event of the adoption of Prohibition by the people I promise that if I am elected Governor of Montana I will do all in my power to enforce the law and make it effective.

In his message to the Fifteenth Legislative Assembly, on the second day of January, 1917, Governor Stewart called attention to the necessity of providing revenue to take the place of that which would be lost to the State when Prohibition becomes effective. He concluded his discussion of this feature thus:

In this connection I do not want to be understood as deploring the situation; rather would I commend the people for the advanced step along the lines of civic betterment and moral refinement, even though it has affected the revenues of the State.

NEBRASKA

I sought Hon. Keith Neville, Governor of Nebraska, to get from him the no-license situation in his State. He said, "I guess I am not the man you are looking for. I was elected Governor on the wet ticket."

"Your State accepted Prohibition so heartily," I said, "I supposed that it chose a Governor friendly to the proposition."

He said to me, "Though elected on a wet platform, I intend to keep my oath and enforce the law the best I can." "It is a free country, and you have a right to your opinion," I rejoined, "and you are no doubt honest in it. I am not so narrow that I will not listen to the advocates of all sides of the question. But my opinion is at right angles to yours on the subject, and you were correct in the notion that you are not the man I was seeking for testimony as to the blessing of State-wide Prohibition."

If the Governor will rigidly enforce the law, its benefits will be so apparent that they will probably convert him, as they have done hundreds of thousands—yes, millions—of those who formerly advocated license. For our purpose we will have to ask Nebraska to let her illustrious citizen, William Jennings Bryan, speak for her on the value of abstinence and State and Nation-wide Prohibition.

Governor Neville is the only one of the Governors of dry States whom I interviewed who was not an enthusiastic friend of Prohibition. It may be there are other liquor Governors of dry States. I have heard of at least one other, the head of a great commonwealth in the South, who got his State into a pile of trouble and got into a peck of trouble himself.

SOUTH DAKOTA

I was greatly pleased with my interview with Governor Peter Norbeck of South Dakota, a

ruddy-faced, hardy, level-headed, big-hearted man
of Scandinavian descent, on the return to constitutional Prohibition in his State. In compliance
with my request, he furnished me the following:

I am a native of this State and have for the second time
seen the people adopt State-wide Prohibition. Twenty-
seven years ago, when the State was admitted to the
Union, the people adopted State-wide Prohibition, only
to repeal it seven years later—after an unsuccessful effort
to enforce it, due to the fact that this State has practically
no authority in the enforcement of laws. In the localities where Prohibition was popular the law was enforced.
In the mining sections and other parts of the State where
the law was unpopular, it was openly violated. Public
bars were run seven days in the week, night and day,
without any restriction except in so far as the city council
saw fit to regulate it. This regulation consisted of permitting them to run in violation of the law and a fine
at regular intervals, which fine sometimes went into the
city treasury and sometimes into the pockets of the collectors. In one case the acting mayor of the town collected the fine and made no secret of the fact that he kept
the money himself. Next we tried local option, the people voting on the question of license at annual elections.
After twenty years of this, about two-thirds of the towns
became dry with a pretty good enforcement in the dry
territory, but that part of the State which violated the
Prohibition law is still permitting the sale under the local
option law. A constitutional amendment was submitted
by the legislature two years ago and was adopted in
November last.

Governor Norbeck sent me a copy of his inaugural address in a nicely bound booklet with the section on Prohibition marked, in which he calls for the passage of rigid enforcement measures among them, one to empower the Attorney-General in coöperation with the Governor to institute prosecutions and to remove sheriffs and State Attorneys for non-enforcement of the law.

MICHIGAN

Michigan was the fourth State that adopted Prohibition that November day, bringing with it into the column Detroit, with its 650,000 population, the largest dry city in the Western Hemisphere; Toronto, Canada, coming next with its 360,000.

Ex-Governor Woodbridge N. Ferris, an efficient leader against the liquor interests, wrote me the following about the situation:

I came to Michigan May 16, 1884. There was hardly a county in Michigan that was dry at that time. The city of Big Rapids, having a population of five thousand, had thirty-three saloons and two houses of ill-fame. The number of saloons diminished under a change in public opinion. The houses of ill-fame did not last long after 1884. From that day to this public sentiment has changed to the attitude of the dry. Nearly half the number of counties in the State were dry under local option when it held its election last November. In November the State voted dry by a majority of fifty or sixty thousand. Our legislators have hesitated about whether this meant that Michigan was really dry, or half dry, or spasmodically dry. The action of Congress, however, seems to have strengthened our weak brothers at Lansing. The results are going to work out all right, no question at all about that. The whole nation will become dry unless the "drys" themselves make some extraordinary blunders.

Hon. William Alden Smith, United States Senator from Michigan, selected for me an extract from his speech on the Dry District of Columbia Bill, as an expression of his views on the general situation. It is this:

And why should not the Capital of the Nation exalt this principle of morality and good conduct? Why should not the National Government within that part of the public domain which it absolutely controls exalt every civic and moral virtue and make of this Federal City the highest ideal of our national hopes and aspirations? I am glad to be privileged to vote in favor of the passage of this bill and give my approval to the principles here involved. If the National Government, with absolute authority in this District, ten miles square, is unable to enforce the law strictly and impartially, the sooner the country understands the weakness of our system of government the better it will be for our citizenship. I expect this law to pass; I expect it to be helpful to the cause of temperance everywhere, and I am glad to stand in my place as its advocate and defender.

Hon. Charles E. Townsend, United States Senator from Michigan, assured me of his gratification at the no-license victories in his State and in the country at large.

Governor Sleeper of Michigan has written me that he was expecting the Legislature to enact such workable laws as would enable him successfully to enforce the Prohibition provision the people had voted into the constitution.

INDIANA

These four made twenty-three dry States. It was expected that Utah would be the twenty-fourth, but Indiana beat her to the goal and early in the year 1917 adopted statutory Prohibition.

Governor Goodrich of Indiana, a vigorous statesman and fearless foe of the liquor traffic, told me he had made his race with a frank declaration of his hostility to the saloon and his determination if elected to do all in his power to free the people from its curse. He whispered in my ear in a confidential manner, "Wait and see what will happen at the session of the Legislature." I listened and heard.

Besides the powerful anti-saloon organizations that led in the conflict, Ex-Governor Frank Hanly, who while Governor and since as the head of the Flying Squadron has been such a foe of rum, rendered invaluable assistance in the campaign.

It is with peculiar personal pride and gratitude that I record Indiana's action, as I am a Hoosier, proud of the fact, and more so since my native

State has gone dry. This action seems like a miracle, for I remember when only a few years ago both political parties were owned bag and baggage by the brewers, distillers and saloon-keepers, when good conscientious Christian states-men turned pale as death with fear and speech-less as the grave, when the liquor question was raised. They had to keep their mouths shut or they could not be elected to any office, not even to that of "dog-pelter" in the town. But the change in the Hoosier State only measures the miracle of the movement in the whole country.

UTAH

Just after Indiana, Utah came in under the string by the adoption of statutory Prohibition, making the twenty-fifth, or one more than a ma-jority of the States adopting Prohibition.

I saw Governor Bamberger at a conference. It had been intimated that he was not as radical on the temperance question as some. But he said in the canvass in the fall that if elected and the Legislature were to pass a prohibitory law he would not only sign the bill but would put every ounce of strength he had, personal and official, to enforce the law. I saw by the look of sincerity and deep determination in his face that he meant what he said; and so he did, as will be seen from the following communication I received from him after he got back home:

The Prohibition law has only just gone into effect in Utah, and it is too soon to tell from experience just how the law will work out. However, I believe there is no law on the statute books of this or any other State behind which there is such general public approval. Every State official and every county official in Utah is in close sympathy with the law and is pledged to its rigid enforcement. I believe they will be aided by public-spirited citizens throughout the State. I feel that there will be very few to violate this law, and that these will be dealt with promptly and effectively. We believe that our Prohibition law is one of the best in the United States. While some few slight amendments are undoubtedly necessary, the law will certainly make the state "bone-dry." In the practical operation of the law, slight defects not now discernible will undoubtedly be discovered and these will be straightened out by the next legislature. There seems to be a splendid spirit toward the observance of this law by all classes of people within the State, and we expect assistance from the Federal Government in keeping liquor outside of the borders of our State. We believe that Prohibition will give us a happier and more prosperous people; that it will make many homes cheerful; that it will reclaim for society many persons now almost derelicts, will lessen the population of our penal institutions and insane asylums, increase our bank deposits, and give to many women and children a happiness they have never known before.

NEW HAMPSHIRE

The Legislature of New Hampshire at its session in 1917 adopted statutory Prohibition, putting the State back into the no-license column, from which it had fallen.

United States Senator Gallinger of New Hampshire is an especially conspicuous figure in this fight. The Senator is an old man with white hair and mustache, portly, genial, witty, with fine personal presence. I said to him, "You are an old 'Prohibition crank,' and that is why I have come to see you and ask a favor of you. For a generation I have been reading what you have said in the papers and in the halls of Congress against the liquor traffic, and I have been thrilled by what you have said no less than I have been proud of your moral courage in standing up in the Capitol building almost alone and fighting King Alcohol. I have come to ask that you will give me something on Prohibition in your State, in the Nation, and above all your personal relationship to it. Words from a man like you will make mighty good and helpful reading at this eventful, tragical time when King Alcohol is being dethroned and destroyed." He gave me the following:

The present awakening on the subject of State and National Prohibition, is especially gratifying to those of us who gave encouragement and support to the cause of temperance in the days when it was less popular than now. For myself, I have been a strong advocate of temperance from early boyhood, being one of a family of twelve children, no one of whom became addicted to the

NOTE.—Senator Gallinger, now deceased

use of strong drink. The fact that out of that number nine of the family still live in good health, the oldest being eighty-seven and the youngest sixty, would seem to justify the claim that a temperate life has much to do with good health and longevity. In my younger days I took great interest in temperance societies, such as the Sons of Temperance and similar organizations, and during my public service it has been my pleasure to advocate the cause of temperance and Prohibition, both on the public platform and in the halls of the two houses of Congress. I recall with special interest the fact that more than fifty years ago, at a time when I was engaged in the practice of medicine, I delivered an address in some of the leading cities and towns of New Hampshire on the subject of "The Physical Effects of Alcohol," and it is a matter of gratification to me that the leading physicians and scientists of the country have reached the conclusions that I then held and advocated. The wave of Prohibition, which for the past two years has been sweeping over the country with irresistible force, not only foreshadows the doom of the saloon, but also presages the day when the claims of the men who have advocated temperance as being essential to the well-being of the individual and the community will be fully justified and universally acknowledged.

Naturally I have taken a deep interest in the cause of temperance in the State of New Hampshire, where for twenty-five years I practiced medicine, and for the last thirty years have been permitted to represent the State in both houses of Congress at Washington. For forty years or thereabouts New Hampshire had a prohibitory law, which was very imperfectly enforced, giving the opponents of the law an opportunity to declare that it was a failure and ought to be repealed. The agitation along that line was persistent, and was actively aided by the saloon interests and financed by the money of the brewers, distillers and wholesale dealers in the large cities of the country. The result was that the prohibitory law was broken down, and a local option law put in its place, which law remained on the statute books for about fifteen years. Dissatisfied with the workings of the law, the Anti-Saloon League, the churches, the Women's Christian Temperance Union, and the men and women of the State who believed that the licensing of the sale of liquor was an immorality, marshaled their forces, and at the last session of the Legislature in 1917 repealed the license law and enacted a strong and efficient prohibitory law in its stead. There is every reason to believe that the awakening conscience of our people, and the determination on their part to see that the law is strictly enforced, will secure for our State a better condition of things than has existed at any period since the organization of the State Government. The people of New Hampshire are so aroused to the importance of the movement that it is safe to say that a large majority of them believe in National Prohibition, and stand ready to do their part toward bringing about that much-desired consummation. Whatever form the contest may assume in the future, I feel sure that New Hampshire, one of the original thirteen States, will be in the fore-front, doing valiant battle for the cause of humanity and temperance.

NEW MEXICO

New Mexico adopted constitutional prohibition November 6, 1917.

FOUR NEW DRY STATES

On November 5, 1918, Florida, Ohio, Nevada and Wyoming, voted for State-wide prohibition.

ALASKA

In 1916 the people of Alaska voted for no-license by an overwhelming majority and the National Congress ratified and fortified their action.

PORTO RICO

On June 16, 1917, Porto Rico voted for Prohibition by a majority of 37,000. It was the first of the Latin nations to go dry. The government, the press, the leaders were reported to be against prohibition, everybody but the people, who concluded to adopt it. In the campaign circulars the wets had a bottle at the top with this instruction written under it: "This is the way to vote in order to save our island from poverty." The drys had a cocoanut as their emblem, on account of the sweet, non-alcoholic, nutritious milk it contained, with this instruction written under it: "This is the way to vote. Our children would be saved from danger." The voters took the cocoanut in their hand and with it smashed the bottle into a thousand pieces.

In 1918, Congress gave Hawaii war prohibition.

CHAPTER XIV

BRYAN CHAMPIONS PROHIBITION

PERHAPS the most powerful individual enemy of the liquor traffic in America in recent years has been William Jennings Bryan.

To those who had long witnessed the domination of the Democratic Party, and the Republican Party as well, by the liquor people, it seemed almost incredible that the acknowledged head of the Democratic Party for nearly twenty years, who had been three times its candidate for the Presidency and who had thrown the Presidency to Woodrow Wilson, should publicly proclaim himself a total abstainer; and more incredible it would seem that as Secretary of State in Mr. Wilson's Cabinet he should have given a State dinner without intoxicating liquors, and that in their place he should have offered his distinguished guests only unfermented grape juice to drink, stating at the time that his wife and he were opposed to the use of intoxicants from principle, and that they did not wish to offer it to others.

The brewers, distillers, saloon-keepers and their apologists set up derisive laughter at such a "silly" exhibition, the press as a rule poured out ridicule, and the cartoonists had no end of fun at the expense of the one they counted a fanatic. But the millions of level-headed, determined enemies of the drink traffic, including the church members, generally commended his action, and congratulated him on his moral heroism.

While Secretary of State, on April 15, 1915, in Philadelphia, he addressed one of the most significant temperance audiences ever assembled in the history of the world; nothing approaching it had ever been seen in this country. It was held in the Billy Sunday Tabernacle. So magical was the address on total abstinence that 12,000 men, amid the wildest enthusiasm and deepest determination, arose to their feet and made a pledge of total abstinence from strong drink.

In the Anti-Saloon campaign in Ohio, in the autumn of 1915, Mr. Bryan made sixty addresses which were condensed into one and presented in the United States Senate by Morris Sheppard, January 25, 1916, as document No. 254, and ordered to be printed.

In December, 1916, an epoch occurred in Mr. Bryan's life and in the better life of the nation when he demanded that the Democrats adopt Prohibition as a party measure. That demand was on the occasion of a banquet given in his honor on December 6, 1916, at the Hotel La Fayette, in Washington, by more than 300 Democrats, United States Senators, members of the House of Representatives and others, including many of national prominence. President Wilson, who was unable to be present at the meeting, sent a letter which was read by the toastmaster and was as follows:

"Will you not be kind enough to convey my very cordial greetings to Mr. Bryan and to those who are assembled to do him honor? In the recent campaign no one rendered more unselfish service than Mr. Bryan, and I am happy to know that this dinner expresses the genuine admiration of all Democrats for him. May I not by this means convey to him my warmest congratulations and best wishes for his continued health and happiness?"

After covering a number of important subjects in his advice to his party, including the espousal of woman suffrage, Mr. Bryan made the climax of his speech on the necessity of opposing the rum traffic on the grounds of moral conviction and political expediency and of saving the party from being "buried in a drunkard's grave." And the subsequent action of Congress with its more than two-thirds dry majority indicated that many Democratic and Republican members of that body as well shared Mr. Bryan's opinion and followed his advice on the subject.

At the world-wide Conference at Columbus, November, 1918, Mr. Bryan said that one week contained two of the most important victories in human history, one the destruction of the Hun, the liquor traffic, on November 5th and the other the smashing of the Hun of monarchy by the armistice on November 11th. He predicted that forty-four states would ratify the Prohibition Amendment within thirteen months of the time the question was handed down to them, and that within five years the ratification would be unanimous.

REV. DOCTOR DAVID JAMES BURRELL

In an interview with Rev. Doctor David James Burrell, pastor of the Marble Collegiate Church, New York City, who has represented everything that is ablest and best in the American pulpit for a half century, I asked him to state as briefly as possible the results of his observation of and participation in the Temperance Movement for the past fifty years.

He said: "It was during my first pastorate in Dubuque, Iowa, that the campaign began for Prohibition in that State. My congregation was divided in sentiment and regarding discretion as the better part of valor, I, for a while, held my peace and kept out of it. But when George Haddock of Sioux City was waylaid one night after preaching a temperance sermon, and stabbed to death, my blood took fire and my coat came off. It was not long before I had the distinction of being burned in effigy by some of my fellow citizens; an honor which I esteem to-day above all demilunar fardels. Since then my interest in the temperance cause has never flagged. You ask for my conclusions in brief: here they are:

"*First,* the liquor traffic can not be regulated. No restriction statute has ever been enacted which the rum dealer has not defiantly violated. He is constitutionally a law-breaker and must be dealt with that way.

"*Second,* Prohibition does prohibit and nothing else will. Experience proves that laws prohibiting the sale and use of intoxicating drinks are as easily enforceable and as practically effective as laws prohibiting any other vice.

"*Third,* a prohibitory law in order to be effective must cover the whole field. They say that 'beer doesn't intoxicate.' Tell that to the marines. Beer makes more drunkards than whisky. And what's more, it involves a larger industrial drain. This is where our Food Commissioners are playing a screaming farce; shutting the distilleries and leaving the breweries wide open. What's the use? America has the opportunity of leading the world in the temperance reform and is allowing it to go by default. Who's to blame? Let the Church speak up. What does she propose to do about it?"

CHAPTER XVI

FEDERAL LEGISLATION

THE members of both Houses of Congress who have dragged out the doctrine of States' Rights to use as a weapon against Federal action on Prohibition in the District and Nation have shown their ignorance of the history of Federal action on the subject.

The first Congress of the United States, held in New York, at its second session celebrated the Declaration of Independence on July 4, 1789, by passing a bill which included the following duty on intoxicating liquors imported; on distilled spirits of Jamaica proof, 10 cents per gallon; on other distilled spirits, 8 cents; on Madeira wine, 18 cents; on other wines, 10 cents; on every gallon of beer, ale or porter in casks, 5 cents; in bottles, 20 cents a dozen. And the third Congress, held in Philadelphia, passed an act, June 5, 1794, which actually licensed men to sell liquor by retail. And Congress kept its hand on the liquor business till the close of the Civil War, when Uncle Sam went into partnership with it.

It was a long time after the people had voted

the saloon out of the towns, counties and States before there was any reflection of that action at Washington. The reason was that King Alcohol had such a powerful grip on the throat of Uncle Sam that he could not squeal. Little by little that grip was relaxed. Drink was taken away from the army and navy, including the wine mess, the Soldiers' and Sailors' Homes, the Government buildings, the Indian reservations, the Canal Zone, etc.

WEBB-KENYON BILL

On February 8, 1913, the Webb-Kenyon Interstate Commerce Amendment Bill was passed in the House and the next day by the Senate. Up to that time this was the most staggering blow which the liquor traffic had ever received since the foundation of the Government. It was then that the people took possession of their own Government, and took one of the hands of King Alcohol from the throat of Uncle Sam, and gave him more air to breathe and voice to speak.

There had been a halt in Prohibition for five years, between 1907 and 1912, caused by the nullification of the State prohibitory laws by the misuse of the Interstate Commerce Law in taking liquors illegally from wet into dry territory. By this law the Federal Government made it impossible properly to enforce the State prohibitory laws. The Webb-Kenyon Bill was designed to put an end to that Federal nullification of the State laws.

Senator Kenyon in the advocacy of the bill said among other things, "The partnership of the Federal Government with the boot-legger ought to be dissolved. The assistance of the Government in maintaining 'holes in the walls' and 'speak-easies' ought to cease. That is the purpose of this bill. It never was intended by the Constitution, in conferring upon Congress the exclusive power to regulate interstate commerce, to take away from the various States the right to make reasonable laws concerning the health, life and safety of their citizens, even though such legislation might indirectly affect foreign or interstate commerce."

The Webb-Kenyon Bill, passed early in February, was held by President Taft till about the close of the session and then returned with his veto, on the ground of unconstitutionality. It was instantly passed over his veto by the two-thirds majority necessary in both Houses, and became a law, which aided the States in enforcing their no-license laws, and encouraged new States to adopt Prohibition. That bill at one stroke killed one-third of all the liquor business of the country. By this bill the people took the other hand from the throat of Uncle Sam, removed from him the white apron of the barkeeper which he had worn so long, and set him free, the real

ruler of the nation instead of King Alcohol, dethroned.

THE YEAR 1917

The year of our Lord 1917 has been one of
the most eventful periods in the moral history of
the world. On January 8 the Supreme Court of
the United States declared the Webb-Kenyon
Law constitutional.

Chief Justice White in announcing the decision
said: "The all-reaching power of Government
over liquor is settled. There was no intention
of Congress to forbid individual use of liquor.
The purpose of this act was to cut out by the
roots the practice of permitting violation of State
liquor laws. We can have no doubt that Congress has completely authority to prevent the paralyzing of State authority. Congress exerted a
power to coördinate the National with the State
authority."

Mr. Wayne B. Wheeler, general counsel for
the Anti-Saloon League, who led the legal fight
which resulted in this Supreme Court decision, in
an address at the Central Branch of the Young
Men's Christian Association of Brooklyn thus
expressed the significance of this decision: "The
most conservative agency in American Government
decided that the people of a given community
have the inherent right to better their condition
without outside interference, and therefore held

that alcohol could not be shipped into a State where the people of that State opposed it. It held, second, that the health and morals of a people are essential to the life of a Government, and recognized that alcohol was therefore an enemy to the Government. The third point was the most startling of all. The court decided that there were no constitutional guarantees which applied to the liquor business. In other words, the liquor business had no right to exist at all, and if it did exist it was through privilege, which could be withdrawn by the people at any time."

Mr. Wheeler, when the decision was rendered, turned to the attorneys on the other side and said, "We have beaten you wholesale, retail and cocktail."

I asked Congressman Webb for a line on this Inter-state Commerce Amendment bill, which he fathered in the House, and he gave me the following:

"Prior to the enactment of the Webb-Kenyon Law, the laws of the States, passed to regulate and curb the liquor traffic, were practically nullified by shipments of liquor in original packages from other States. Under this law such shipments became subject to the State regulations as soon as it came into the State. In this fight which I made for the enactment of the Webb-Kenyon Law, I realized that we had arrayed against us the combined liquor interests of the country and all the anti-Prohibition sentiment. The complete victory did not come, however, until the Supreme Court of the United States handed down its opinion this year upholding its constitutionality."

DISTRICT OF COLUMBIA DRY

Knowing the strong fight Congressman Webb had put up to drive the saloons out of the capital of the nation, I asked him about the District Prohibition Bill. He said:

"The fight for Prohibition within the District of Columbia has been waged in Congress for a number of years. About five years ago I led the fight in the House of Representatives which resulted in reducing the number of barrooms from about six hundred to three hundred. A complete victory for Prohibition in the District of Columbia was achieved by the Act of March 4, 1917, which goes into effect on the first day of November of this year, and prohibits the manufacture and sale of liquors of all kinds for beverage purposes."

POSTAL AMENDMENT BONE-DRY BILL

Hardly less important than the Webb-Kenyon bill is the Jones-Randall amendment to the Post Office Appropriation Bill, providing for the exclusion of liquor advertisements from the mails, not only when directed to States having laws against such advertising, but when directed to places where the solicitation of liquor sales is forbidden. The Senate bill passed the House on February 21 by a vote of 321 to 72. The celebrated Reed Amendment to the advertising section of the bill, providing for the exclusion of liquors from interstate commerce in Prohibition States, made every Prohibition State bone-dry. That meant that the State would not let the people have any liquor from the inside, and the Federal Government would not let them have any from the outside. It is impossible to describe the smashing blow this law has dealt the liquor traffic. It was owing much to the masterly championship of this measure by Rev. Doctor Clarence True Wilson, secretary of the Methodist Church Temperance Society, that its passage was secured.

There are to-day over 8,000 newspapers in this country that will not take an advertisement of the liquor business. Their millions of readers object to having such temptation pushed into their homes and under the noses of their sons.

NATIONAL CONSTITUTIONAL PROHIBITION

THE VOTE IN THE HOUSE OF REPRESENTATIVES IN 1914

When in 1914 Doctor Baker announced that the Anti-Saloon League intended to stand for a National Prohibition Resolution, I said to him,

"I have faith in your wisdom, but I am just wondering whether the time has come yet to pass such a resolution. The theory of the League has been to go only so fast in legislation as public sentiment will sustain. Are you not afraid that a defeat now would mark a halt in progress, and maybe set back the reform a decade? I do not say it will, I am only asking the reasons for your bold policy."

He said, "I think the time has come for us to make the strike. I think we are strong enough to make it, and if we are not we shall get the strength we need by the stroke."

He said the powerful liquor lobbies in combination with the corrupt politicians in the dry States had rendered the enforcement of the prohibitory law so difficult that he feared timid friends would get discouraged and that other States would hesitate to come into the dry column. He had concluded that they would take the strong arm of the Federal law and wipe the whole thing out at once. "We shall get national agitation," he said, "which means saloon extinction. We shall do in this national contest what we do in that of the towns, counties and States—fight; and if we are defeated one season we shall appear fresher and more ready for the fight when the next year begins. Backed by the allied temperance forces we shall put the bill in this Congress, and if we are defeated we shall put it in the next Congress, and the next, and the next, till we win." I said to him, "That is the kind of talk I like to hear. Your arguments satisfy me of the wisdom of your action. I believe there is more good than evil in this Republic, that God is stronger than all his enemies, and that you will be victorious."

Big plans were laid for introducing the resolution, and a call for one thousand volunteers was made to join in the demand of Congress for the measure. Two thousand answered the call, and marched down Pennsylvania Avenue, from the New Willard to the Capitol. A finer set of men from every State and every calling never marched down that street. I was in that procession and proud to be in it. As we came to the turn at the foot of Capitol Hill, about one thousand women of the Women's Christian Temperance Union took their places by the side of the men in the line, and went up to the steps of the Capitol to unite with the Anti-Saloon League in a demand for national Prohibition. A policeman said that aside from inaugural occasions he had never seen so many people in front of the Capitol. The exercises, which were imposing and impressive, were held on the outer steps. The princely Richmond P. Hobson spoke eloquently for the measure he was to be responsible for in the House. He was as splendid in his moral heroism as he was in his bravery when he sank the Merrimac. Morris Sheppard, the young Senator from Texas, made a speech. I shall never forget the scene as I beheld his manly features, standing out in bold relief against the dark background of a sullen winter sky, and heard his great speech worthy of his great State and the great occasion.

The Hobson Bill came to a vote in the House of Representatives on December 22, 1914. The vote was 197 in the affirmative, 189 in the negative. That so drastic a measure, the first one of the kind ever allowed to be voted on in Congress since the foundation of the Government, should have eight majority when Mr. Underwood, the Democratic leader, and Mr. Mann the Republican leader, opposed it fiercely, was an astounding revelation to the people of this country. An amendment to the Constitution requires a two-thirds vote. The amendment fell sixty-three votes short of the required number, and failed.

The vote on the Hobson Bill in 1914 so inspired the temperance people of the country that State after State fell into line in the race for Prohibition, and the temperance representation at Washington, increased by the accession of members from these new States, gave Senator Sheppard hope when he brought his bill before the Senate. This is the text of the bill:

Section 1. The manufacture, sale or transportation of intoxicating liquors within, the importation thereof into, or the exportation thereof from the United States and all territories subject to the jurisdiction thereof for beverage purposes is hereby prohibited.

Section 2. This article shall be inoperative, unless it shall have been ratified as an amendment to the Constitution by the legislatures of the several States as provided in the Constitution within six years from the date of the submission hereof to the States by the Congress.

Section 3. The Congress shall have the power to enforce this article by appropriate legislation.

After a three days' consideration of the bill, it came to a vote on August 1, 1917. As the hand of the Senate clock moved from half past four to five it marked one of the most important moral events in the history of the world —the passage of the measure by 65 to 20, or more than three to one in favor of the resolution —eight more than the necessary two-thirds majority, if all the members were present and voting. As I listened to the roll-call and the answers and the result of the vote, I thought of the great leaders and members of the United States Senate since the foundation of this government, and of the momentous questions they debated and settled. And I said to myself, "No greater moral question was ever debated or settled than this one today, and the leaders and members who supported the resolution arose to the highest stature of mental and moral manhood, measuring up to the traditions and standards of the past in their guardianship of the interests of their fellow-men and the welfare and honor of their country." By this vote these giants seized King Alcohol, who had ruled the nation for fifty years, who had made his headquarters in that same Capitol building, and who had mastered and slain some of the ablest men who had ever graced its Senate halls, and hurled him headlong to earth, the weakest and most despised monarch ever dethroned.

On July 30, Senator Sheppard made a wonderful speech in support of his bill. It ought to be printed in booklet form and sent into every home in the land. I am sorry I can not make room for it in full here. But I asked Senator Sheppard to put his views on the subject in succinct form for insertion in this book, and in courtesy and hearty sympathy he gave me the following:

"This nation-wide Prohibition amendment proposes that the Federal Government shall coöperate with the States in the destruction of the liquor traffic. I can not see that it violates in any way the fundamental plan on which our Government was founded or contradicts in any sense the doctrine of State rights. As I understand our history, the Federal Government is the creature of the States and possesses only such powers as are expressedly or impliedly delegated by the States. I do not understand that the States are unable to delegate any further powers than those they conferred when the Constitution was originally framed. Whenever it appears to three-fourths of the States that the welfare of the country demands that additional functions should be delegated to the General Government, such States have the power and the right to delegate such functions through proper constitutional process on such conditions as they deem proper, and the whole performance is in consonance with the true theory of American Government. By this amendment the American people, speaking through the Federal Government, their only collective mouthpiece in a governmental sense, will declare that the liquor traffic is an outlaw in every part of the United States, that the Federal Government shall be empowered to enforce such declaration in concurrence, and only in concurrence, with the States, and that those States which have no laws against the traffic and desire no laws against it have not the right to harbor so frightful a menace to the happiness and prosperity of the Nation. Under this amendment no State will be deprived of the power to legislate against the traffic.

"We want the battle to continue in family, precinct, county, State and Nation. No unit of government or society is too small, no unit is too large, to have a place in the ranks now gathering for this conflict under the banners of Almighty God. The liquor traffic is so firmly intrenched in some sections of the country that national action will be necessary to exterminate it. We are not simply citizens of States. We are Americans above all things else. We can not wrap ourselves in the mantle of narrow localism.

HOUSE OF REPRESENTATIVES PASSES PROHIBITION RESOLUTION

On December 17, 1917, the National Prohibition Resolution, ably handled by Congressman Webb, passed the House of Representatives by a vote of 228 to 128. One of the most momentous and glorious experiences of my life was that of being present at the passage of this resolution which dealt Bacchus his death stab. The galleries cheered when the veteran Joe Cannon voted aye, and burst out into wild applause when Speaker Clark announced the result.

The next day the Senate promptly adopted the amended bill by a vote of 46 to 8 and the proposition was sent down to the State Legislatures, over three-fourths of which have ratified in the following order: Mississippi, Virginia, Kentucky, South Carolina, North Dakota, Maryland, Montana, Texas, Delaware, South Dakota, Massachusetts, Arizona, Georgia, Louisiana, Florida, Michigan, Ohio, Oklahoma, Idaho, Tennessee, Maine, West Virginia, California, Washington, Arkansas, Illinois, Indiana, Kansas, North Carolina, Alabama, Colorado, Iowa, Oregon, New Hampshire, Utah, Nebraska, Missouri, Wyoming, Minnesota, Wisconsin, and others.

WAR-TIME PROHIBITION

When war was declared it was confidently expected that war Prohibition would be one of the first measures adopted, for three reasons: because of efficiency to the military service, because more than half the States are dry and sixty per cent. of the population live in no-license territory, and because both Houses of Congress were dry by a two-thirds majority, while a bare majority only was necessary to pass the bill.

And so Congress promptly set itself to its task of passing Prohibition as a national emergency measure. Its committees in both Houses reported in favor of the Prohibition of all intoxicants, including beer and wine. Immediately an obstacle was struck; it was the whisky barrels and beer casks piled up as high as the dome of the Capitol. When the war broke out the brewers of the nation officially rushed to the front and offered their services to the President to aid in the war on Germany. The New York Methodist Conference was in session at that time, and as the chairman of its temperance committee, composed of Corneille, Tucker, Robbins and Robinson, I read the following resolutions on the subject, which were unanimously adopted by the more than 300 ministers present:

"Representing the opposite of what the brewers do, we suggest that they make good their offer of service to the country by closing their institutions at once, putting out the fires of the furnaces, stopping the vomit of the black smoke from their tall chimneys, or by turning them into mills where the grain may be ground into food instead of being rotted into poison. We suggest that the President and the members of Congress, to whom they have offered their patriotic service, will accept it by ordering them to close their concerns at once in the interest of the splendid men who are to fight for us on land and sea, close them (as the brewers say in their offer) 'for the honor of our flag, the integrity of our nation, and the spirit of our institutions.'"

The brewers were the obstacle Congress struck. What did these patriotic heroes, so greedily anxious to defend the "honor of the flag and the spirit of our institutions," do? Why, the very first thing they did was to rush down on Congress as a set of bullies and sandbag it. They compelled the Democratic caucus the very next day to rescind its action on Prohibition; they muddled up and paralyzed members of the committee and threatened that if beer were included in the prohibition they would hold up all war measures. A frightened Congress believed their threat and delayed summary action. The brewers never could have made good that threat. For a hundred years they made good that kind of a threat, but they can not do it now. Alcohol has been deposed. A long fight ensued in Congress over the question. When the final vote came John Barleycorn was thrown under the steam roller, and beer and wine escaped by the skin of their teeth. On September 9 the law went into effect that no food, fruits, food materials, nor feeds shall be used in the production of whisky and other distilled liquors intended for beverage purposes. Then whisky died during the war, pretty certainly forever.

The surrender of Congress to the demands of the powerful brewers' lobby so enraged the temperance conscience of the country that the people served an imperious demand on their representatives to pass the Sheppard National Constitutional Prohibition Bill. So the defeat in the beer war measure reacted in more overwhelming victory of the constitutional bill, which was of so much greater importance.

BEER

There was no good reason to divorce whisky from beer and wine in the war Prohibition. The States in their fights, without an exception, always couple them together as a common evil to be abolished together. Not one of the twenty-six dry States will listen for a moment to the plea that beer and wine are innocent, and promotive of temperance.

We deny that the beer and wine drinking countries are temperate, and claim that the facts show that they use the largest amount of alcohol, and are cursed with drunkenness and crime as the result. If beer is so innocent and commendable, and whisky is so devilish, why do the brewers, these promoters of temperance, own seventy per cent. of the places in the United States that sell whisky?

On September 23, 1918, the House of Representatives passed the war prohibition amendment to the agricultural bill by a vote of 171 to 24, which had already been acted upon favorably by the Senate, forbidding the importation of wine on signature of the bill, the manufacture of beer and wine on May 1st, 1919, and the traffic in all intoxicants on July 1st, 1919. The bill was passed and signed by the President, November, 1918.

President Wilson, after conferring with the food and fuel departments, issued an order closing the breweries on December 1st, 1918, as a necessary war measure. Many breweries are changing their properties into useful purposes in which their brains and enterprise will insure them success, and many of the employees are securing other positions at better wages.

The Federal Administration deserves great credit for the manner in which it has safeguarded our precious boys who have given themselves to their country's service in forbidding the dealers to stain their uniform with alcohol.

CHAPTER XVI

WORLD-WIDE WAR ON ALCOHOL

CONFERENCE ON WORLD-WIDE PROHIBITION

ONE of the most important moral conferences ever held in this country was the one which convened in the interest of world-wide prohibition in Columbus, Ohio, November 19-22, 1918. The Conference was called by the Board of Directors of the Anti-Saloon League of America.

The Conference began on Tuesday evening at the Deshler Hotel with a Thanksgiving and ratification service, participated in by stalwart workers from the field, and by distinguished delegates from our own and from foreign countries. Until Friday noon the day meetings were held in the Central Methodist Church, and those at night in the Chamber of Commerce Auditorium. Seldom has any convention been supplied with a better grade of talent, or higher order of speaking. On the program were:

Bishops James Cannon, Jr., W. F. Anderson, F. J. McConnell, T. Nicholson, G. M. Matthews, W. J. Bryan, Governor C. S. Whitman, Filmore Condit, F. Fosdick, S. E. Nicholson, P. A. Baker, H. H. Russell, E. Cherrington, E. J. Moore, W. B. Wheeler, E. C. Dinwiddee, J. G. Wolley, Sam Small, A. J. Scroggin, L. B. Musgrove, S. S. Kresge, J. S. Hoagland, Ex-Governors M. R. Patterson and F. B. Willis, G. B.

Safford, C. F. Swift, G. M. Hudson, R. P. Hutton, T. J. Bailey, J. Pope, D. M. Gandier, R. E. Farley, J. A. White, H. T. Laughbaum, G. D. Conger, C. P. Keen, R. A. Hutchinson, W. H. Anderson, Scott McBride, Ben. H. Spence, J. K. Shields, G. W. Crabbe, H. Tope, J. Wilbur Chapman, E. L. Bosworth, Father J. J. Curran, A. J. Davis, Brooks Lawrence, E. S. Shumaker, R. N. Holsapple, R. L. Davis, Miss Anna A. Gordon, Mrs. Richards, and others.

Dr. P. A. Baker the thinker, orator, organizer and fighter delivered an epoch making address in which among other things he said: "If weaker nations are to be protected from the brutally strong, weak men and women should be protected from those who would coin their weakness and wickedness into cash. The time is opportune for this great aggressive world-wide movement."

In the eloquent address of Dr. Howard H. Russell he said: "There is great danger the friends of sobriety will fold their hands and expect prohibition to enforce itself. Appetite and greed will still exist. 'Eternal vigilance is the price of liberty.' One of the best results of international organization for world-wide sobriety is this: We shall keep our army at home strong and alert to hold the fort which has been won. It will be the finest service ever rendered for the good of other lands, to give to them the truth which shall make them free. It will hasten all the work of missions and speed the savior's reign throughout the world."

Wayne B. Wheeler, National Attorney of the Anti-Saloon League in his strong, clean style told of the drastic enforcement laws that would be asked of Congress, to make the Federal Amendment practically effective, and said America's influence in drying up the world would be measured by her example of successful prohibition at home.

Rev. E. C. Dinwiddie, the National Anti-Saloon Legislative Supt., who has had such an important part in shaping prohibition in Washington, said that with his knowledge of the Parliaments of the world that he was certain that the Anti-Saloon Methods so successful in this country would work universally.

As the movement is to be world-wide a profound interest was manifested in the reports of the delegates from foreign countries as to the present condition of temperance sentiment, and organization in their respective fields, and as to their needs, and hopes for the success of the world organization. Prominent among the number were Canon S. A. Johnston of Birmingham, a prominent minister of the Church of England, Hon. W. Bingham J. P. of London, Robert A. Munro of Glasgow, Scotland and Cipriano A. Frausto of Saltello, Mexico and others, all of whom made able addresses full of seriousness spiced with humor and fired with patriotism and Christian hope.

Hon. Ben. H. Spence, Secretary of the Dominion Temperance Alliance of Canada, who has had such an important part in driving the liquor traffic out of Canada, in his interesting address was inclined to poke a little fun at the United States by saying that Canada had beaten her to national prohibition by both dominion and local option laws and war measures, and claimed that England so often criticized for its tardiness in this reform had made more progress in temperance since the war began than any other part of the world.

The most astounding information of the Conference

was contained in a communication from Mr. Lawrence Mott, the representative of the American Anti-Saloon League in Tokyo, which stated that there was a possibility of Japan adopting nation wide prohibition within a year by the action of the Japanese parliament and thus make a magnificent start to the plan of a world-wide prohibition.

The delegate from China said that though the brewers had established their death dealing institutions in that land that the people had not yet learned the drink habit, and that the world Anti-Alcohol League had made its appearance just in time, and should plant itself immediately in that territory.

Bishop James Cannon, Jr., who has had so much to do with making Virginia and the nation dry, read the report of the committee on Resolutions, which said: "Resolved, That the Executive Secretary of the Anti-Saloon League of America is hereby authorized to formulate and to carry into effect plans and methods for the efficient co-operation of the Anti-Saloon League with temperance and prohibition workers in the different countries of the world in the formation of such an International League. The Committee is further authorized to render such immediate assistance, financial and otherwise, as it may deem proper and advisable in promoting prohibition work in other countries.

Bishop Luther B. Wilson of New York one of the founders of the Anti-Saloon League, and its President, who receives the gratitude of the nation for his service in carrying cheer and Christ to our boys in France, superintending the Y. M. C. A. work there not being able to attend the Conference, sent a letter containing the following: "It is an auspicious day for such a conference. Victory on the field of battle and victories in the field of moral reform make the year forever memorable. We must conserve all the fruits of our victory upon the battlefield; likewise must we conserve the fruit of victory in moral reform."

During the session of the Conference the war prohibition bill was passed by the Senate and signed by President Wilson, the announcement of which caused the wildest enthusiasm and called for a resolution of congratulation and thanks.

It is not surprising that the leaders selected the man around whose business ability and personality one of the greatest printing plants of the world has been gathered to make the official declaration of the purpose of the Conference, and Mr. Ernest H. Cherrington, Manager of the American Issue Publishing Company, and of its literature, on Wednesday morning read a paper which was one of the ablest and most statesmanlike we ever remember to have heard, which we predict will have a permanent place in the best literature of the world, and become a potential factor in the world-wide war on moral evil. We read it over several times for the purpose of cutting it down into smaller space, but could not find anything that could be left out and so we make room for it in full.

MR. CHERRINGTON'S ADDRESS

I. INTRODUCTION

The world stands at the threshold of a new era. During the great world war, now happily drawing to its close, two forces have been contending for the control of the world's destiny. These forces represent two distinct types of civilization. One catches its inspiration from the past; the other faces the future. The essential quality in one is dictatorship; in the other it is leadership. One enacts law to be enforced because that law is the decree of the supreme power of the state; the other creates law to be obeyed because that law represents the highest expression of public opinion as to what is best for the individual and for society. The greatest issue in the world war has been whether the civilization of the future is to be interpreted in terms of license or in terms of liberty—in terms of reaction or progress. This issue has to do not only with government but with morality and religion, the impelling forces of all government.

Henceforth the acid test for Christian civilization and likewise for every institution that has to do with Christian civilization is therefore, not what it has done, nor yet where does it stand, but rather in what direction does it move?

II. WHY A WORLD-WIDE PROGRAM

The program proposed for adoption by the Anti-Saloon League of America is a world-wide program, because existing conditions compel the consideration henceforth of all human welfare problems in world terms.

The golden age of individualism closed when western civilization, moving westward, met eastern civilization moving eastward. The French Revolution and other European revolutions, together with the Civil War in America, set back upon the shelf of antiquity the principle of states' rights. The past fifty years has been especially marked as the era of nationalism. The new age is to be the age of internationalism. The wars, treaties of peace, and international relationships, from 1600 to 1775, concerned the rights of sovereigns and royal families. Those from 1775 to 1860 had especially to do with the rights of individual states. Those from 1860 to 1914 involved in a peculiar sense the rights of nationalities, while those from 1914 onward will center upon the rights of all the peoples of earth, regardless of race, language and geographical boundaries.

Already the trade of the world is international. The press spans the oceans and organizes the atmosphere for its service. Labor movements are being organized on the world basis. Education breaks the boundary lines of governments and the seclusion of races. Travel and modern invention have reduced the vast earth of a thousand years ago to a neighborhood; and the Christian religion holds the nations of the globe as its parish.

No great problem which has to do with human welfare can be solved fully and permanently, by a single nation regardless of the attitude of other nations. Consequently the law of self-preservation and self-defense compels one nation's effort for the solution of the same problem by neighbor nations. The revelations of this war are conclusive on this point. A democratic government in the United States was not safe so long as there existed anywhere upon the earth's surface a powerful autocracy.

Moreover, races and nations alike must be subject to the high law of international ethics which insists that the solution by any nation, of a problem which concerns the world, places upon that nation the duty and responsibility of passing on such solution to other nations. As "no man liveth unto himself," so it may well be said that in this new age no nation liveth unto itself.

III. THE EVOLUTION OF THE ANTI-SALOON LEAGUE
MOVEMENT

The rapid evolution of the Anti-Saloon League movement is one of the most significant facts in modern social history. A few years ago the principal objective of the temperance movement was to secure local Prohibition for townships and rural precincts. It was soon discovered, however, by those who were interested in the temperance reform, that the life of the rural communities was so closely interwoven with that of the neighboring towns and small villages that to insure Prohibition in rural townships Prohibition must also be secured in the incorporated villages surrounded or bordered by such townships. Thus the demand for township and municipal Prohibition evolved into the demand for county Prohibition. It was not long, however, until by reason of the rapid industrial progress of the western world, distances were conquered by automobiles and interurban lines and it became increasingly apparent that if Prohibition were to be effective in the counties the policy must be extended to the state as a unit. Moreover, as state after state fell into line in harmony with this demand, enacting state-wide prohibitory statutes and adopting prohibitory amendments to state constitutions, it became apparent by reason of the operation of the interstate commerce law and by reason of interstate traffic and travel that no single state as a unit could completely enforce state prohibitory laws. Gradually in these recent years, therefore, the sentiment for national Prohibition has grown until it has developed into an overwhelming demand upon the part of the people of the nation. But just as the hopes of the temperance forces are about to be realized in a national way we find ourselves face to face with the fact that in this day and age of international relationships, when the laws of commerce and trade so link together the nations of the world and when great principles of right must be defended and maintained only by the fullest and closest coöperation of many nations, the Prohibition of the liquor traffic in a single nation is practically impossible of complete enforcement without coöperation on the part of all nations having close relationships. The Robinson Crusoe stage of the Prohibition movement is past. The liquor problem is a world problem and the reform institution which would solve this problem must be world-wide in its scope.

The building of the Anti-Saloon League has required a quarter of a century of intensified effort. Its machinery and equipment have been moulded in the foundry of experience. It presents the unique character of an organized movement for moral welfare which has been able for the first time in human history to unite in common activity in a single progressive program the religious people of all creeds. The practical value of this institution as a successful fighting organization has been fully demonstrated. In truth, it is known by its fruits. To-day this League presents a thoroughly organized piece of machinery, the like of which for effectiveness in moral reform has never before been known. This organization in the United States employs a thousand people who give their entire time to its activities. In recent years it has been receiving and expending in the great fight for national Prohibition throughout the nation, more than one and one-half millions of dollars each year. A half million dollars has been invested in its extensive and modernly equipped publishing interests at Westerville, Ohio, and elsewhere. It publishes and distributes throughout the United States Prohibition periodicals to the amount of more than two million copies per month. More than a half million persons in all the several states are regular financial supporters and contributors to this League, while its active agents and coöperating friends in practically every city, village and county of every state, are numbered by the millions.

But more than all this, the Anti-Saloon League to-day holds the distinction (its enemies being judges) of being the most cordially hated and most greatly feared of all the organized Prohibition movements. Moreover, it holds the confidence of the moral and Christian forces of the nation. It has made good as an uncompromising foe of evil and an insistent advocate of righteousness. Hence it stands to-day in a position of greater strength than at any time since its inception. By virtue of the position of confidence and strength which it has won it is to-day in position to do more effective service than ever before in its history. To bring another institution into existence and to advance it to the position of efficiency and influence which to-day characterizes the Anti-Saloon League would require another quarter of a century, hence the utilization of this League in a larger sphere of world activity for universal Prohibition at once insures economy of time, money and effort which are of vital importance and concern at this stage in the world's history.

Shall this most efficient arm for righteousness, known as the Anti-Saloon League, be perfected and utilized in the larger sphere of action, or shall it be demobilized before the war against the liquor traffic is over?

Article two of the constitution of the Anti-Saloon League of America reads as follows: "The object of this League is the extermination of the beverage liquor traffic." That object will be accomplished only when in every nation of earth the liquor traffic shall live only in the archives and museums of civilization. The hands of the moral forces of America have been set to the plow, and there can be no turning back.

IV. CONDITIONS IN OTHER COUNTRIES

The conditions existing at the present time in the several nations and countries of the world, as those conditions are related to the liquor traffic and the Prohibition movement, present what in many respects is the greatest moral problem of the age. The Prohibition countries (assuming the ratification of the Prohibition Amendment to the United States Constitution) are: the United States of America, together with Alaska, Hawaii and Porto Rico; the Dominion of Canada and New-foundland; Iceland, Greenland and the Faroe Islands belonging to Denmark; Roumania and Russia as it was prior to the war of 1914, including Finland. This territory covers more than sixteen million square miles and includes a population of more than three hundred millions, or about one-sixth of the population of the earth.

The partially Prohibition countries are of two classes: first, those which have provided for Prohibition in local areas, and second, those which have prohibited the liquor traffic in part throughout the whole territory of the country. In the first class are to be found Denmark, Norway, Sweden, Australia, New Zealand and Scotland; while the second class includes those countries which have prohibited absinthe and other spirituous liquors such as France, Belgium, Switzerland and Italy.

The countries which are under the influence of the so-called Prohibition religions are China, Manchuria, Japan, India, Persia, Afghanistan, Turkey and Arabia, together with certain portions of Northern Africa and a few other sections of Asia. For the most part European and American intoxicants until recently have not been permitted in these countries. In all of them, however, the manufacture and consumption by the inhabitants of so-called native liquors which are distilled by simple processes and which in reality are as deadly as the beer and wine of western nations, have not been the subject of such intensive commercialization as in the countries of Europe and North America. The native liquor problem in these countries, however, as well as the more recent problem presented by the introduction and rapid development of western liquor industry and trade, are such as to insure the complete degradation of the natives unless the traffic is speedily arrested and suppressed.

Another class of countries are under nominal Prohibtion of the traffic in distilled spirits by international agreements of the great powers of Europe. These territories include practically all of the continent of Africa and a large portion of the islands of the sea. Unfortunately these international agreements for the suppression of the liquor traffic have not been generally enforced, and in most of Africa to-day the natives are being degraded and debauched by the deadly combination of their own native liquors and those thrust upon them by European and American liquor interests, with the consent of the responsible home governments.

The countries which have pursued the policy of regulation and taxation for purposes of revenue include the British Isles, France, Germany, Austria, Hungary, Italy, Switzerland, Belgium, Holland, Spain, Portugal and most of their colonial possessions.

The nations where the liquor traffic is practically unchallenged by the governments in any way and which are almost prostrate under the domination of alcohol, include the Balkan states, aside from Roumania, together with the republics of Mexico, Central America and South America. Practically all these countries are virgin soil for the Prohibition movement.

The proportions to which the liquor traffic in most of these foreign countries has already grown are such as to bring the moral forces of the civilized world to attention. Germany and Austria, before the war consumed more liquor per capita than any of the other nations of the earth. The pre-war consumption of beer in Munich alone was one and one-half pints per day for every man, woman and child. During the four years of the war Great Britain spent more than four billions of dollars for intoxicants. Four thousand breweries in the United Kingdom have been continuing to do their utmost to weaken the nation. Prior to the war there were more than a million small distilleries in France. There was one wine shop for every forty of the population. Paris had thirty thousand liquor shops. Belgium with seven and one-half million people, supported 220,000 liquor selling establishments. France, Italy, Spain and

Portugal enclosed most of the wineries of the world, one-half of the world's wine coming from France, one-third from Italy and one-seventh from Spain. Milan, Italy, had more than five thousand drinking places, or one for every forty-six residents, before the war.

The perplexing character and discouraging aspect of the problem in these countries, interwoven as the traffic is with other evils of the old world and with ignorance and superstition, present a mighty challenge to Christian statesmanship. The employment of barmaids is a most serious phase of the question. In the city of Berlin the barmaid establishments, called "animier kneipen," employ over 1700 "waitresses," while almost every London public house employs women as bartenders.

Drinking among women throughout Europe is also an alarming feature. In Germany and Austria this is almost universal, while in England, France and Spain the rapid increase of the habit by women is such as practically to constitute a rivalry of the sexes in beer and wine consumption.

Ignorance and superstition are mighty bulwarks of the liquor traffic especially in eastern Europe, Asia, Africa and the Americas south of the United States. An investigation in Moscow a few years ago revealed the fact that 90 per cent of the drinking population had acquired the habit while in school. Of 18,000 school boys in that city between the ages of eight and thirteen, 12,000 were drinkers, while 5000 out of 10,000 school girls were addicted to the use of liquor. Verily, the task which awaits Christian education in these countries is herculean.

The missionary work which needs to be done, however, is not confined altogether to the ignorant and superstitious.

Twelve hundred and fifty clergymen of the Church of England together with four hundred and seventy-two women in English rectories to-day own more than $8,000,000 worth of stock in English breweries. In the Pera quarter of Constantinople, on the same plot of ground with the Orthodox Greek Church, there are a dozen drinking places, owned by the church, which is kept up by the revenue from these drink shops.

That more home missionary work, moreover, is still necessary, is evidenced by significant recent events. With all the great work which foreign missionary representatives of the various churches have been doing throughout the missionary countries of the world, they have been tremendously handicapped by reason of the political standards of home governments and the greed of home liquor interests. In April, 1918, when neither flour nor sugar could be bought in Belgian Congo, Africa, and when freight, including a great many of the necessaries of life, was being held up in New York city for months, because of war needs, there sailed into Belgian Congo an American vessel discharging at the Congo ports its cargo, which was made up almost entirely of American beer. In August, 1918, when more than seventy missionaries of various boards, anxious to return to Africa and other foreign fields, were held up in New York city for several months because the government was in need of all the steamers for war work, a steamer left New York city for Liberia and Sierra Leone, West Africa. Only nine of the missionaries awaiting transportation to the Soudan were permitted to sail on this vessel because all the space was needed to accommodate the cargo, which consisted entirely of whisky for West Africa, including thirty thousand gallons of one prominent brand.

The money power of the French Bourse has been a most important factor in the propagation and protection of the wine industry and traffic. This Bourse, speaking through the government of France, ofttimes with the assistance of the governments of Spain and Portugal, has not only been responsible for holding back the Prohibition movement in Scandinavian countries and Russia, but has also repeatedly compelled the prompt repeal of temperance laws enacted by the countries of northern Europe on account of the demands of the wine traffic. Nor are the activities of France in this regard confined to northern Europe. When one of the leading brewing journals of the United States in a recent issue boasts that the government of France, in the interest of the wine traffic, by diplomatic representations has helped to hold up the war-time Prohibition measure recently passed in both houses of the American Congress and now in conference, is it not high time that the government of the United States proceed officially to represent the attitude of the people of this country on the liquor question by doing real missionary work with the governments of European nations, without violating diplomatic proprieties?

V. IMMEDIATE AND IMPERATIVE DEMANDS

The demoralized condition of temperance and Prohibition work in many warring countries and the depleted finances of even the strongest temperance organizations in Europe call for immediate assistance. The demands of the war have of necessity crippled every such move-

ment in Great Britain and on the Continent, while most
new temperance organizations which, prior to 1914, were
springing into existence in some of the more backward
countries, have been practically submerged. Many of
these organizations are already calling loudly for
assistance and the opportunity offered to them for effective
service at this crucial period is such as to make imperative
the demand upon the moral forces of America for
agitational and educational assistance. We must be
prepared, moreover, to serve these organizations with any
assistance which we may be able to render through wisely
directed counsel and conference, while, most of all, we
must put our shoulder to the wheel in a peculiar sense
in order to aid them with financial assistance commensurate with the gigantic task which is theirs.

The peace conference just now impending furnishes
another and most important demand. That conference
will deal with the control of native races. The Powers
represented in the original Brussels agreement for the
protection of these races from the curse of distilled
liquors, will all be parties to the coming peace treaty.
This phase of the liquor question will in all probability
be dealt with around the peace table, and it is highly
important that the original treaties on this point be
repeated and amplified together with reasonable provisions
for the full enforcement of the agreement throughout all
of the continent of Africa.

New international trade agreements should take into
account, hereafter, conditions in Prohibition countries,
thus protecting the numerous anti-liquor laws of the
several countries from infringement or encroachment by
foreign trade, regulations and treaties.

Imperative demands, moreover, are not limited to the peace conference. The important need for temperance reform must be recognized in the reconstruction program of the several nations of Europe; otherwise, because of depleted finances and because of financial arrangements which the liquor traffic will certainly atempt to make, the solution of the alcoholic problem in many of these countries may be indefinitely postponed. Already in Russia one government has announced its purpose of resuming the government monopoly of the vodka traffic in order to provide revenue. Quick work is essential if Prohibition is to continue in Russia.

VI. PRECEDENTS FOR INTERNATIONAL ACTION

If precedents for international action in the interest of the public health, the public morals and the public welfare were needed, such precedents are not wanting. Instances of international coöperation in warfare for these objects are to be found in the wars of the Crusades, the international action for the suppression of piracy on the high seas, the union against Napoleon, joint action for the protection of Christians in Turkey, the allied expedition in the Chinese Boxer uprising, the interference of the United States for the freedom of Cuba and other islands under Spanish rule, and, most important of all, the concert of nations comprising three-fourths of the population of the world in the present great war for democracy and righteousness.

Other peaceful treaties and agreements to this same end mark the pages of the history of international diplomacy during the past century, such, for instance, as the Monroe doctrine, the international agreement for the suppression of the slave-trade, resulting later in the simultaneous effort throughout the world for the abolition of human slavery, the Hague Conference provisions, international action for the suppression of opium in Oriental countries, the Brussels agreement provisions, looking toward the same protection of native races as has been given to American Indians and to Indian countries in both Canada and the United States, together with the co-operative world movement for the suppression of what is known as the white slave trade.

Numerous other instances of international action not subject to formal treaties or agreements may be found. The movement for the abolition of human slavery brought results in the freedom of the serfs in Russia in 1860, and the abolition of slavery in the United States in 1863, as well as similar successes in Great Britain and other countries about the same time. Numerous movements moreover in recent years have been directed toward the organization of the international sentiment against the liquor traffic. These include the international activities of the Good Templars, the Woman's Christian Temperance Union, the Sons of Temperance, the Rechabites, the International Congress Against Alcoholism, the International Prohibition Confederation and other educational movements along similar lines.

The necessity for precedent, however, in this day of the world's history, is not so essential as it has been in the past. The world is alive to progress and reform, while modern movements in the modern world look not so much to the past as to the future.

VII. THE PROPOSED PLAN FOR UNIVERSAL PROHIBITION

The proposed plan of organization for universal Prohibition involves: First, the enlargement of the scope and the extension of the activities of the Anti-Saloon League of America; second, the giving of substantial assistance to existing temperance organizations in other countries; third, the laying of the foundation for the creation of an international anti-alcohol league, formed after the plan of the Anti-Saloon League of America. The new situation, so far as Prohibition in America is concerned, together with the opportunity presented in the proposed world plan for universal Prohibition, demands not only the reorganization of the anti-liquor movement in the United States but a prompt extension of the activities of the Anti-Saloon League to a larger sphere of world influence. As there is a decided difference in many respects between these two spheres of action, there must be a difference to some extent in the methods employed. There are many things which the Anti-Saloon League has done and is doing in a national way which could not be properly done by the League in other nations. There is, however, much important work which can be conducted by the Anti-Saloon League of America in almost every foreign country, such, for instance, as personal and platform lecture work by field agents and missionaries of the Anti-Saloon League of America; the organization of an international Prohibition press association and the establishment of an international Prohibition periodical to be printed in different languages; the securing of coöperation in publicity work by interesting the daily and wekly newspapers in all countries, and the securing of valuable publicity through the literature of international travel companies and organizations. Great service also can be rendered to the missionary agencies in all mission fields for the building of and organizing of temperance sentiment.

Educational agencies, moreover, furnish an opportunity which should not be overlooked. Prohibition propaganda, if properly handled, can be conducted through exchange professorships in the universities, college lecture courses, general Chautauqua and lyceum bureaus, university extension work, as well as scientific temperance instruction in the public schools of all countries similar to that which has been so successful in the United States.

Industrial enterprises and trade organizations may also be used as agencies through which the industrial and trade organizations of other countries may be reached. The results of Prohibition in this country have converted to the program of total abstinence most of the heads of great manufacturing enterprises, and trade organizations generally throughout the country are undergoing a very decided change of sentiment both as to the practicability and the desirability of Prohibition from the standpoint of commerce and trade.

Another field which should by no means be neglected is that which is presented by labor organizations. The relation of the liquor traffic and the Prohibition movement to the welfare of the working man from every point of view must be brought home to the representatives of organized labor in America, and must through the labor organizations of this country eventually be brought to the attention of the labor interests in Europe and elsewhere.

In addition to all these other avenues of approach to the alcohol problem in other countries, special effort should be made to secure the right kind of diplomatic representations by the official agents of the United States government in all the United States consulates and legations. As the United States of America itself becomes a Prohibition country in accordance with the will of the people of this republic, the official agents of this nation abroad should actually represent the sentiment and attitude of the American people on this great question as that sentiment and attitude is expressed by the legislative bodies of the different states and by Congress. Moreover, since these agents of the government are the representatives of the President of the United States in his official capacity, the Prohibition forces of America should see to it that from the beginning of the Prohibition regime the occupant of the White House, who directs all the diplomatic agents of the United States in all the countries of the world, should himself represent the great body of the American people on this important question. The new position which the United States now occupies among the world powers gives to this government a peculiar opportunity for the investment of influence.

This proposed plan for the enlargement of the work of the Anti-Saloon League of America, moreover, involves special organized effort to assist existing temperance organizations abroad, not only by counsel and by full coöperation in movements toward the federation of these forces in other lands, but by appealing to the people of America for financial support commensurate with the demands of this world program, thus enabling the Anti-

Saloon League of America to render greatly needed assistance to temperance organizations abroad.

The proposed new plan, however, does not stop with the missionary enterprise contemplated by the Anti-Saloon League of America and the assistance which it is proposed to render to existing temperance organizations abroad. It involves finally the laying of the foundation for organization at the earliest practicable time of a new international league against alcohol, which shall bring together in one great international federation such organizations as the Anti-Saloon League of America, the Dominion Temperance Alliance of Canada, the United Kingdom Alliance in Great Britain, the Ligue Nationale contre l'Alcoolisme of France, and similar organizations in Australia, New Zealand, Holland, Denmark, Norway, Sweden, Italy, Germany, Austria, Japan and other countries.

VIII. THE PSYCHOLOGICAL TIME TO STRIKE

Nothing is clearer than that now is the psychological time to strike for world Prohibition. The remarkable success of the anti-liquor movement in America has encouraged the temperance forces of the world and has correspondingly weakened the defenses of the liquor traffic. The great whisky forces in America are already going out of the propaganda field. The breweries' international trade arrangements are more difficult at present than ever before. The invention of processes in Austria and Italy by which wine can be made free from alcohol, has had a tendency to lessen the inducements for alcohol propaganda work among the wine growers of Europe. This tendency has already been reflected in some slight degree in the attitude of the wine producers in the United States.

Moreover, the partial success of the Prohibition movements in certain countries of Europe have greatly helped as back fires against active propaganda of the liquor interests. The Prohibition of absinthe in France, Holland, Switzerland, Italy and Belgium, has greatly injured the spirits trade in Europe, while the increased strength of the social democratic parties not only in the Central Powers but throughout Europe makes Prohibition a burning question in the political arena, because of the anti-liquor pronouncements of these groups prior to the war, and because of the greater strength for political action which these groups are bound to have after the war is over.

The financial adjustment due to the war in practically every country of Europe has served to demonstrate that revenue for government purposes is not absolutely dependent upon the liquor traffic and that when a really great crisis arises the liquor traffic can be depended upon to furnish only a very small part of the revenue required. This fact strikes at the very heart of the strongest argument that has ever been advanced in defense of the liquor traffic.

The necessary war-time effort for conservation of food, fuel, transportation and man-power, has demonstrated in the most convincing manner the scientific fact that from every point of view, so far as any nation is concerned, the liquor traffic is a liability instead of an asset.

The present close international relationships of a majority of the world's great nations furnish opportune conditions for international representations on practically all questions of reform. The twenty-four nations that have declared war on Germany represent three-fourths of the population of the globe, and are not only united for harmonious military action but are enthusiastic for coöperation of every kind with other nations of the group. With such conditions existing, the part that the United States of America has played gives this country a greater opportunity to speak with force and influence on the liquor question, as well as on any other question, than America has ever had before. Moreover, the intensive world movement toward democracy which is radically affecting every country opens a clearer way for political action on moral reforms by the very fact that the reactionary political forces in all these countries have been greatly weakened, while the progressive forces in political life throughout the world have been proportionately greatly strengthened.

This is also the psychological time to strike because of the fact that the spirit of the world war in a peculiar sense has turned the world's attention to moral and spiritual realities. Business and politics, so far as their hold upon the people is concerned, have been temporarily relegated to the rear, while the tragedies of war have softened the hearts of the people and made them receptive to moral and religious considerations. The great forward movement of all church organizations and denominations in the intensive missionary campaigns now being emphasized, opens wide the gate for an additional phase of missionary programs which must include temperance and Prohibition work.

In short, the general psychology of world conditions presents an unparalleled opportunity for the prompt organization and speedy success of such a movement for moral betterment as that represented by the anti-liquor crusade. Verily, for a world movement such as the one proposed, the hour has already struck.

IX. CONCLUSION

The remarkable temperance progress of recent years in North America is prophetic of permanent victory for the Prohibition movement throughout the world. The great advance of science, in revealing to the medical world the true nature of alcohol, has sealed the doom of the liquor traffic and points the way to abstinence and Prohibition wherever the voice of science is heard. The active propaganda against the liquor habit and the liquor traffic as well, which in recent years has been conducted by great industrial enterprises and transportation companies, insures the coöperation of the world of industry in the effort for international Prohibition. The attitude of political parties in America, as well as that among the social democratic parties of almost every country in Europe, insures the joining of the forces of Prohibition and the forces of political democracy in a way that eventually will bring results. The leaven influence of the Anti-Saloon League movement has been one that reaches even far beyond the solution of the liquor problem. It has been a great factor in the movement for church unification, a purifying factor in politics, and has given to the word federation, a new and significant meaning. Just as the political influence of the Anti-Saloon League through moral legislation has exalted national political standards in America, so the proposed international movement of the League may well prove to be a helpful factor in international political relationships. Just as the Anti-Saloon League of America has made for closer relationship between the churches and has given to the so-called moral forces outside of the churches in America a better insight into the value and necessity of Christian work and church organization, so this proposed international movement of the League may well make for world federation of church and religious forces in which those points on which all religions are agreed may be emphasized to the end that a real world kingdom of righteousness may be established.

The possibilities of such a movement as that which is proposed challenge the imagination. The unparalleled opportunity presented by existing world conditions is such as has never before been presented in the Christian era. For the moral forces to fail to grasp the significance of the opportunity thus presented would be a political, social, economic, moral and religious crime. The organized temperance forces of America cannot avoid responsibility. They dare not fail.

> "On before us gleam the camp fires—
> We ourselves must pilgrims be;
> Launch our Mayflower and steer boldly,
> For the desperate winter sea;
> Nor attempt the Future's portals
> With the Past's blood-rusted key."

On Friday afternoon the delegates went in a body to Westerville, 15 miles from Columbus, to visit the American Issue Publishing Company's printing plant. I felt amidst the rattle of the presses that they furnished much of the ammunition for the guns that shot to death

John Barleycorn in this country, and will help to supply the guns for the battle on the other side of the water.

The delegates then walked from the printing plant to the Methodist Church in the village, where the closing service was held, presided over by Dr. Howard H. Russell, the founder of the whole Anti-Saloon League movement in America. And the same man who in his early ministry carried the Anti-Saloon League as a babe to the church in Oberlin, Ohio, to be christened, led the same League grown to be a strong man, a giant, honored by the moral conquest of a nation into a church for its ordination to the larger ministry of a world-wide mission for prohibition. After appropriate scripture lesson and song Dr. Russell preached a short sermon, all looking toward the world conquest, and then called the delegates to come forward and kneel at the altar and consecrate themselves to the new task. The whole audience came forward and many volunteered to lead in prayer. We felt the Holy Spirit descending upon us and filling our hearts and arose with a new spiritual anointing to follow Christ our captain out into the world conflict for the destruction of King Alcohol. To men and women with such a just cause, with unfaltering faith in a righteous God, inspired with the infinite love of a living Christ with a deep determination to destroy the demon which most hinders the establishment of His kingdom, there can be no such thing as failure.

CHAPTER XVII

FIGHTING ORGANIZATIONS

BACK of all organizations hostile to the liquor traffic is the home. It is the assault of King Alcohol on the home, on husband, father, sons and daughters, on wife and mother, more than anything else, that has stirred the American conscience to anger and has prompted the people at the polls to dethrone and banish him from the several States and from our Federal Nation.

Woman's love for home and the dear ones in it, whom God has given her to guard, and her fierce warfare on King Alcohol, their worst enemy, to avenge his cruelties and crimes, more than any other one thing, has made the public sentiment which has crystallized into ballots, which are the bullets that are being shot into the body of the demon king.

There can be no created life without organization. This fact is not more manifest in the vegetable and animal world than in the mental and moral realm. Woman's love for home and hatred of alcohol, its enemy, has been splendidly organized, and on that account has been so powerful. Without the public sentiment that it has aroused by its messages, its example and its militancy, there would have never been any Anti-Saloon League, the voting agency in the destruction of the saloon. I requested Miss Anna A. Gordon to give me some facts connected with the Woman's Christian Temperance Union, of which she is the national president, and received from her the following, which in spirit and literary style is not unlike that of the great founder, Frances Willard, and which will be read with deep interest.

WOMAN'S CHRISTIAN TEMPERANCE UNION

The National Woman's Christian Temperance Union is an organization of Christian women banded together for the protection of the home, the abolition of the liquor traffic and the triumph of Christ's Golden Rule in custom and in law. It is the lineal descendant of the great Woman's Temperance Crusade of 1873-74, and accepted from the early crusaders a legacy of faith and faithfulness. From the day the first praying band knelt on the sanded floor of an old-time saloon, an extraordinary task has challenged the home-loving, home-protecting women of this nation.

For over four decades this God-given task has been ours. We have been true to its sacred obligations, patient under its daily discipline, happy in its heavy hardships, undismayed in its severest storms. Its hope, its happiness, its bigness and its blessedness have led to a consecration commensurate with its challenge. Today half a million women gratefully recognize the extraordinary progress made toward the fulfilment of the vision of Frances E. Willard, founder of the World's W. C. T. U., for our white ribbon emblem, typifying organization and membership and the adoption of our principles of total abstinence and Prohibition, is now worn in every section of the world.

The principles of the Woman's Christian Temperance Union are significantly embodied in Miss Willard's famous epigrammatic saying: "Only the Golden Rule of Christ can bring the Golden Age of Man." "We are organized to make the world wider for women and more home-like for humanity." "Agitate, educate, organize, are our gleaming watchwords of success." "Womanliness first, afterward what you will." "Be steadfast as gravitation, good-natured as sunshine, and as persistent as a Christian's faith." "The joy of life is doing good according to a plan."

The total abstinence pledge is the foundation of our platform, for we believe in the gospel of the Golden Rule and that each man's habits of life should be an example safe and beneficent for every other man to follow. When humanity's chorus catches the keynote of total abstinence now vibrating the world around we shall hear in the psalm of each life the glad harmonies of hope and happiness.

The National Woman's Christian Temperance Union had its birth in Cleveland, Ohio, in November, 1874. It is organized in every State, Territory and dependency of the United States, and locally in more than 20,000 towns and cities. Young people and children are enlisted in the Young People's Branch and the Loyal Temperance Legion. In addition to the paid membership of 400,000, there are hosts of philanthropic women affiliated with the W. C. T. U. Almost every institution or philanthropy has its temperance aspect, and with that the W. C. T. U. is in close touch. Our national society owns its headquarters in Evanston, Illinois, and maintains headquarters in Washington, D. C., for its legislative work. Its publishing house and its Publicity Bureau are located at Evanston. The "Union Signal," its well edited weekly organ, makes temperance and Prohibition sentiment the world around. Its monthly paper for children, "The Young Crusader," is an attractive illustrated publication. Its Frances E. Willard Memorial Organizing Fund sustains our great work in new territory and among foreign-speaking people and negroes. Its Lillian Stevens Campaign Fund is used in campaigns for State and National Prohibition.

The W. C. T. U. is essentially a home protection society. It is the greatest anti-liquor, anti-vice, anti-everything-that-strikes-at-the-home organization in existence, and numerous are its activities for social betterment. Our thirty departments of work are classified under these six general heads, preventive, educational, evangelistic, social, legal, and the department of organization. It is this "Do Everything" policy that makes our organization unique and powerful.

We have a vast and ever-extending network of telegraph lines along which fly swift, blessed and constructive messages. Building these lines, establishing the stations and enlisting State, country and local workers is the difficult and adventurous task of our ninety-five National

W. C. T. U. superintendents, organizers, lecturers and evangelists.

These indefatigable and devoted W. C. T. U. specialists are guardian angels for the little ones; they educate for a life of total abstinence the child in public school and Sunday school; they help mold the young for purity, for health, for total abstinence from alcohol and tobacco, for thrift, for mercy, for industrial training and for all temperance activities. They teach our great principles through literature, the press, the pulpit, the medical world; through coöperation with missionary societies; through the betterment of labor interests; through the awful struggle with vice conditions; through W. C. T. U. institutes, medal contests, prison reform; through our Gospel carried to railway men, to lumbermen and miners, to soldiers and sailors; through social meetings, flower mission and relief work, fairs and open-air gatherings; through many forms of legislative effort for Prohibition, woman suffrage and Christian citizenship. The achievements of these mighty sentiment-makers read like a thrilling romance, or would make picture film of surpassing interest.

It was the W. C. T. U. that originated the idea of scientific temperance instruction in the public schools, and it was chiefly through its influence that mandatory laws were secured in every State; also a Federal law governing the District of Columbia, the territories, and all Indian and military schools supported by the government. Many States have provided by law for the observance of Temperance Day in the schools. In most of them it is designated as "Frances E. Willard Day." Temperance teaching and training of the children make deep and lasting sentiment for Prohibition and its enforcement. Another great educative agency, the public press, is being utilized by the W. C. T. U. In addition to work done in this direction by State and local organizations the National W. C. T. U., through its Bureau of Publicity, supplies material which is used by papers all over the country in the form of ready-prints and plates.

The extraordinary influence of the petition work of the W. C. T. U. has been felt by the Legislatures of every State and by the United States Congress. During the debate in the Senate, July 30 and 31 and August 1, 1917, on the Sheppard resolution for a referendum to the States on national constitutional Prohibition, there stood in front of the Senate platform a huge roll of petitions collected by the W. C. T. U., representing twelve million endorsers of the bill. It is generally conceded that to the W. C. T. U. belongs much of the credit for the anti-liquor sentiment which has given this country so much Prohibition territory and which is soon to give it national constitutional Prohibition. It has borne a leading part in State Prohibition campaigns and has secured many reform laws, particularly those for the protection of women and children. It has been a prize-winner at all the great expositions of recent years, notably in the recognition of its Anti-Alcohol Exhibit at the Panama-Pacific Exposition in San Francisco, California, in 1915.

In coöperation with the Department of Labor, the Bureaus of Immigration and Naturalization and the Americanization Committee of the National Chamber, the National W. C. T. U. is promoting varied and beneficient plants for Americanizing immigrant women, and for securing them as allies in our great battle for righteuosness.

For more than thirty years the W. C. T. U. has actively conducted a patriotic welfare service for soldiers and sailors. Every encampment, fort and battleship has been reached. In the present national crisis this work has been greatly enlarged. In cities and localities near the camps the boys in uniform are made welcome in rooms conducted by "White Ribboners," who give them the home atmosphere and wholesome entertainment and treats. One young recruit gratefully exclaimed: "The Y. M. C. A. fathers us, but we also need mothering, and the W. C. T. U. is our mother." A supreme effort is being made by our organization to bring about the abolition of saloons and dens of vice near training camps and mobilization centers. Large numbers of our local auxiliaries are making hospital supplies. The department of Flower Mission and Relief Work reaches with its beautiful benefactions even the little French orphans made fatherless by the European War.

Over forty countries are federated in the World's W. C. T. U. Its motto, "For God and Home and Every Land," suggests the breadth of its work and the depth of its patriotism. The W. C. T. U. coöperates with missionary societies and works for the passage of bills prohibiting the transportation of alcoholic liquors to native races. The famous Polyglot Petition originated with Miss Willard and was written by her. It is addressed to the governments of the world asking them to do away with the manufacture of and traffic in alcoholic liquors and opium, and the legalization of impurity. It has 7,000,000 signatures and attestations, and already has been publicly presented to representatives of the governments of the United States, Great Britain and Canada.

WOMEN COLLEGE LIBRARY

The National W. C. T. U. early advocated an International court and arbitration for the settlement of differences between nations. World-wide Prohibition and woman's ballot will help bring permanent peace. A clear-brained generation of men who have not inherited the alcohol taint will maintain peace, for they will ever exercise good-will and sane self-control.

Extensive plans are being made for a nation-wide celebration in 1924 of the fiftieth birthday of the National W. C. T. U. Exultant praise fills our hearts as we dare to prophesy that this jubilee convention will be signalized by the triumph of national constitutional Prohibition and of international and lasting peace.

WOMAN SUFFRAGE

Women have done their marvelous work in this temperance revolution in making public sentiment and affecting legislation without the ballot. No Southern State has adopted woman suffrage, and the South has become solid for Prohibition without a woman's vote. Only in three or four of the Western States has woman suffrage cut any figure in the Prohibition contest; in these few instances woman has opposed the saloon.

The defeat of woman suffrage in Maine, the pioneer no-license State, by a majority of two to one at the same special election at which the people put into the constitution a provision removing sheriffs for not enforcing the liquor law, and the opposition of the saloonless South to woman's vote, have raised the interrogation mark in the minds of its friends, as well as opponents, as to the relation that woman suffrage sustains to Prohibition.   It is pretty clear, however, that, as would be naturally expected, women have it in for the saloon and will with the men knife it at the polls when they have an opportunity.

I spoke at the Methodist church at Oyster Bay, New York, one Sunday morning, and after the service a young woman who said she was from Kentucky, snapped her black eyes and said, "What you said about woman's influence in driving out the saloon is true.   But when you pictured woman on her knees praying God to wipe out this curse, why did you not suggest that men help God to answer that prayer by giving her the right to vote?"   Colonel Roosevelt, who attended service at that church that morning, standing near, heard her question and said, "She is correct in her belief that women would vote against the saloon. I have just returned from a tour of Michigan in behalf of woman suffrage, and in the windows of the saloons I saw large placards 'Vote against Woman Suffrage,' and on the streets I saw advertisements of the saloon in living forms muttering out in their intoxication 'Vote against the women.'   Of one thing I am convinced, and that is that the liquor people fear woman's vote as a deadly enemy."

When woman suffrage had been so badly beaten in New Jersey, the day after the election the cartoonist of one of the New York City papers pictured a banquet in a bar-room with bloated guzzlers around the table as guests celebrating the victory. Their hands were waving and their mouths were open wide in shouts, and underneath the picture it said, "Hurrah, Hurrah, we have saved our homes." A saloon bum was quite active on election day against woman suffrage, and he said, "Let the women stay at home where they belong." Some one knowing the facts asked him where his wife was, and he said, "She is out washing." Yes, she was out washing because her husband would not support her and the family, but made her support him.

MORAL SUASION MOVEMENT

The moral suasion movements of Father Mathew and others led to the ballot. In 1840 the public sentiment against the liquor traffic was so strong that the people felt that they should make an attempt to vote it out, and they secured local option laws in a number of States and eliminated the saloon from many districts. Ten or twelve years after, the Prohibition votes got so numerous that they secured State Prohibition in Maine and a number of other States. Then the Civil War came on and the American conscience turned itself to the destruction of slavery. After the war, the fight on the saloon was renewed. In 1865 the National Temperance Society and Publication House was organized at Saratoga, New York, by 325 delegates from twenty-five States and about every temperance society and religious denomination, including the Catholic. Its great service in making public sentiment would be worthy of a volume by itself. About the time this society was started the conviction was deep in the minds of the temperance people that they should organize to vote the saloon out. But there was a split in the camp as to the method to be used. One group thought that a temporary political party should be organized, with local, State and national ticket; the other group seriously objected to the proposition, and insisted on a non-partisan war on the saloon, using both of the old parties against it.

THIRD PARTY PROHIBITIONISTS

The faction favoring a new party was the more enthusiastic and persistent, and on September 1, 1869, in Farwell Hall, Chicago, 500 delegates organized a political party which was named the Anti-Dramshop Party, but which before the adjournment of the Convention was changed to the National Prohibition Party. Three years later they ran a Presidential ticket, and have had one in the field every presidential election since, including that of 1916. They are the most interesting group of moral reformers this country has ever had. Possessed of one idea, the badness of the saloon and the collusion of both political parties with it, they started out to hammer that thought into the mind of the nation, and they did. They were fighters from way back. They fought the saloons, fought the old parties, and sometimes their friends, if they did not agree with them. But they were fighters, and nothing so stirs public sentiment as a fight. A dog fight will stir a neighborhood; a man fight will start a town.

These moral militants, well organized, with a bravery unsurpassed, went through all parts of this country and banged away at the saloon and all whom they thought had any responsibility for it, until they stirred the whole nation to arms against the public evil. They never found the practical path of political success in the elimination of the saloon, but they found the path of moral success. They were never large in numbers, but in the battle of the centuries it is not numbers but principles that count. With supreme optimism they expected that the growth of the Republican Party, from a small beginning in its revolt against slavery, would be repeated in their little band becoming the dominant political force of the nation. For forty-five years they have fought and been beaten every time, but not de-

feated morally.   And now after forty-five years
of defeats they find the whole nation has come
to adopt their idea, and they find themselves on
the platform with the allied temperance forces
for national Prohibition.   Any just estimate of
the modern temperance revolution must give these
party Prohibitionists, with their bravery, con-
stancy, and conscientious conviction, their share
of credit for its success.   At my request Mr. Virgil G. Hinshaw, the able chairman of the Prohibition National Committee, gave me the following:

The Prohibition Party has been the John the Baptist of
the Prohibition reform.   For forty-eight years it has gone
by its present name and has held to the one purpose, the
prohibition of the sale, manufacture, transportation, importation, and exportation of alcoholic liquors for beverage
purposes.   It took upon itself that name when the mention of the word Prohibition invited to obloquy and scorn.
It conceived its one great purpose when, among all the
organizations striving toward truth and morality and industrial economy, it walked alone.

It has been more than a John the Baptsit.   It has
helped to bear the cause of National Prohibition on tri-
umphal entry into popular public consciousness.   Its representatives, along with the representatives of 113 other
national organizations, marched down Pennsylvania Avenue, Washington, D. C., in December, 1913, and sounded
together its oft-repeated slogan "National Prohibition of
the Liquor Traffic."

It has done more than merely stand for the principles

it enunciates. It has borne its banner into the halls of State Legislatures, and finally into the halls of Congress, carried by men elected on the Prohibition Party ticket, and in every presidential campaign since 1872 it has disputed the right of any man to be President of these United States who owed his election to the quadrennial slaughter of a half million of the American populace.

The achievements of Congress the past two years, among the most notable in American history, are most vitally and necessarily interwoven with the career of Charles H. Randall, Party Prohibitionist, elected from the Ninth District of California.

Those who have honored the Prohibition Party as candidates for President since its organization are the following: James Black in 1872, Green Clay Smith in 1876, Neal Dow in 1880, John P. St. John in 1884, Clinton B. Fisk in 1888, John Bidwell in 1892, Joshua Levering in 1896, John G. Woolley in 1900, Silas C. Swallow in 1904, Eugene W. Chafin in 1908, Eugene W. Chafin in 1912, J. Frank Hanly in 1916. Those who still survive are Joshua Levering, John G. Woolley, Silas C. Swallow, Eugene W. Chafin and J. Frank Hanly.

The story of each of its campaigns is a story of heroism and sacrifice, of the launching of great movements with only the eye of faith witnessing from day to day the manna of support provided as by a miracle hand—a story too lengthy to be recounted in this brief sketch, but which will live and burn brighter with the roll of years.

THE ANTI-SALOON LEAGUE

The other faction of the early prohibitionists held that the way to vote the saloon out was not to

start a new party, but to use the old ones as the
instrument for the purpose, and in 1885 they organized the National League for the Suppression
of the Liquor Traffic, non-partisan and non-
sectarian, with Rev. Doctor Daniel Dorchester as
President, and headquarters in Boston.

Eight years later, Rev. Doctor Howard H.
Russell, at Oberlin, Ohio, organized the Anti-
Saloon League as the omnipartisan inter-denominational agency of killing the saloon with the ballot. Rev. Doctor Alpha G. Kynett of Philadelphia caught the idea at about the same time, and
was putting it into execution but was not able
to give his whole time to putting the movement
into shape. Russell felt called to give his life to
the task, and did. Russell is an intellectual genius,
and out of his fertile brain there sprang the well-
defined plan of the great movement that was to
destroy the rum traffic at the polls. At first he
started out himself alone to speak, raise money
and fight the saloon at every step. Then he got
money enough to hire other helpers, and then
others. He manifested almost superhuman sagacity in the men he gathered about him at the
start, men of the highest intellectual ability, sterling character and indomitable industry. And one
of the most significant facts is that these really
great men whom he selected as founders of the
League have stayed with him ever since and are
now just as vigorous and efficient, or more so,

as when they began the fight. It seems most incredible that a great moral movement should lead in the final destruction of so great an evil, in the lifetime of the man that founded it, and of those he first gathered about him in doing so. Russell went from city to city and from State to State planting his idea in organization, until every State and Territory in the United States and the Federal Government at Washington had its Anti-Saloon League. There has scarcely been a session of any State Legislature that there has not been some bill unfriendly to the saloon introduced by the League, and most of the measures of Prohibition in the States and at Washington have been handled by its representatives. The State and district superintendents are splendid men.

I heard forty State superintendents make three minute speeches at a convention on one day. They were superb men, most of them young. I was profoundly impressed. I do not remember ever to have heard such an array of talent, moral courage and real enthusiasm at one time. Having been for nearly ten years New York City superintendent of the Anti-Saloon League, I knew nearly all of these men personally, and I said, "No wonder the liquor traffic is being so rapidly destroyed with such giant generals to lead the fighting forces in the States. The national officers, including the Headquarters Committee, are men of the same splendid type. Rev. E. C. Dinwiddie, a Lutheran minister, whom Russell selected as one of the founders, possesses political sagacity and knowledge of parliamentary law equal to the members in either House, and his influence as national legislation superintendent can not be calculated. Together with Dinwiddie, Wayne B. Wheeler, National Attorney of the League, James Cannon, Jr., and Doctor Barton, make a powerful lobby at Washington respected and coöperated with by the Prohibition Congressmen and Senators, and by the representatives of the other temperance societies coöperating with them at the capital.

Doctor Russell was the first who acted as the National Superintendent of the Anti-Saloon League, and then Rev. Doctor P. A. Baker became his successor, and to his generalship, statesmanship, forensic ability, character, his incessant labors, and to the executive ability, literary talent and efficient management of the great publishing department of the institution by Mr. Ernest Cherrington can be attributed much of the success of the movement. I asked Doctor Baker to give me a short account of the League and he gave me the following:

The Anti-Saloon League was born not only at an opportune but providential time in the history of the Temperance reform. Strictly speaking, the League is just what its name indicates—a League—a League of all churches and societies that hate the liquor traffic and are willing to coöperate for its overthrow. A prominent gentleman said recently, "I did not at first like the League, and refused to coöperate with it; but I discovered we got along better whenever the League was in the fight, so I swallowed my prejudice and became a Leaguer."

It has three distinct departments of activity to which it has strictly adhered, viz., Agitation, Legislation and Law Enforcement. These are logical steps. Agitate, which means to educate, that we may wisely legislate. This is the political department of the League. It looks carefully to the nomination of candidates on the major party tickets for all officers that have to do with the enactment and enforcement of laws touching the liquor traffic, friendly to such legislation and law enforcement. Failing to secure such nomination on one party ticket and succeeding with another, we appeal to our constituency to be big enough to vote for a good candidate on the opposite ticket rather than a bad one on their own. After a law is enacted it must be placed in the hands of its friends for enforcement, if it is to be a success. The League does not transform its agents into policemen to enforce law. It proceeds on the assumption that most men in public life would rather be right than wrong, if you make it as politically safe for them to do right as it is to do wrong, and the business of the League is to make good at the ballot-box by making it safe for public officials to do right.

It has been rightly called "The Church in Action Against the Saloon." Hundreds of thousands in the churches find it a desirable agency through which to coöperate, and the churches contribute above a million dollars annually to its support. The League is directed and governed everywhere locally by members of the churches. The policy of the League is to push the reform just as fast and just as far as the average sentiment of the church will permit. It chooses the church as the basis for organized effort rather than a political party, first because the working church is the natural foe of the drink traffic, and second because the church is dogmatic in policy while political parties are timid. The church can meet defeat as often as is necessary to settle any question according to the Ten Commandments and the Sermon on the Mount. Political parties abandon issues when in the judgment of their leaders to do so means more votes for the party. Besides, it is expensive in both money and energy to keep up a political organization. The sixty per cent. of the population and the more than eighty per cent. of the territorial area of the republic now under Prohibition, if not made so under the leadership of the League was made so by the methods which the League has always employed: the omnipartisan and inter-denominational method. It has taught the Christian voter independence in politics as no other agency ever has. It has been opportune in method but dogmatic in principles. It has striven to do the thing that could be done while pushing forward toward the thing that ought to be done. It has never been averse to taking the half loaf when it could not get the whole. It has believed that small victories were more inspiring to its forces than big defeats. It has placed greater emphasis on the direction in which we were going than in the rapidity of the movement. It has always preferred to wait and win rather than to fight and fail. In other words, it has distinguished between a fighting chance and a chance to

fight. It marshals the sentiment that exists and brings it
to bear at a given point for immediate results. It seeks
municipal option where it cannot get county option, and
county where it cannot get State-wide Prohibition. As
the engine on the track makes steam faster when in mo-
tion than when standing still, so sentiment on this question grows by exercising the franchise even in the smaller
political units. By being political and not partisan it
has an appeal that does not run counter to that strongest
of all prejudices—party prejudice.

The wisdom of the League's policy has been amply
justified by results. A dozen years ago the most sanguine
did not dream the present advance would be made in a
generation. Two or three things have greatly contributed
to these results.

First. When the natural friends of the League criticized its methods and scolded and denounced its policies
it did not reply in kind. It very seldom replied at all.

Second. While the leaders of the movement have differed sharply at times, those differences have been fought
out in Conference Councils and never carried to the public. There has never been a split in the ranks of the
leaders.

Third. It has always had a continued sustained money support. It is no sooner through with one fight than
it is ready to enter another with equal or greater vigor.
Hitherto the traffic has been able to wear out the opposition and to recuperate and repair any damage that may
have been inflicted. A great advance was made when the
liquor business was driven from the association of things
that were decent and made to stand alone before the
world, exposing its hypocrisy and its hideous deformities.

It was then that it became the best asset for the Prohibition forces.   There is a rapidly growing sentiment that the traffic in intoxicating liquors has no rightful place in our modern civilization.   An institution of such a character that war must first make war upon it before it can conduct war scientifically and successfully, certainly has no claims for protection at the hands of a civilized people. Everything in the world that is of good repute is against it, and it must go.   It is going.   Already it has no advocates and few partisans.   It must depend for the continuation of its worthless life upon appetite which it has created, and greed for gain, both of which appeals to the weakness and wickedness of humankind.

In the past it has made and unmade public officials at will, but that is of the past.   Public officials no longer bow the "pregnant hinge" before it.   Its threat of political extinction and boycott has no terrors for men in office or business.   It is a liability and not an asset.   Its known support of a candidate for any office in almost any State or community means the undoing of that candidate.   Its foul breath spreads miasma and death wherever it touches. More laws, State and national, are passed against it and over its protest than are passed on any other subject. The final drive for the speedy and complete overthrow of the traffic is now on.   The Senate by a vote of three and one-half to one voted to submit the question to the States for ratification or rejection, which means ratification.   The Lower House will follow its example.

To attempt to stop National Constitutional Prohibition is as futile as to attempt to stop the mouth of Vesuvius with a bundle of straw, or to turn back Niagara with a child's hand.   The accumulated Christian con-

360 KING ALCOHOL DETHRONED

science and Christian forces of a century are pouring an irresistible flood of wrath against this monster of horrors. Commerce, business, science, industries of all kinds have joined hands with religion to make common cause against this decivilizer of the race. Not only must the world be made safe for democracy, but it must be made safe for childhood and womanhood as well. We are soon to see the fulfillment of the vision of Abraham Lincoln when he saw the day when there should be neither a slave nor a drunkard under the ample folds of the Stars and Stripes, and when childhood throughout the Republic shall have a fair chance for citizenship in the Coming Kingdom.

THE ORDER OF GOOD TEMPLARS

The Good Templars are a world-wide organization composed of more than half a million total abstainers. In 1851 it was organized in this country and has been one of the most efficient agents in the destruction of the saloon.

The Sons of Temperance, which sprang out of the old Washington Maine movement, has been efficient in saving men from drink and fighting the saloon in America.

While the Anti-Saloon League has taken the lead at the voting end of the destruction of the liquor traffic, it has not done all the work. Most of the temperance and church forces of the nation have coöperated with it in the war on the saloon; among these organizations, besides those mentioned, are the National Temperance Council, the

Scientific Temperance Federation, the International Reform Bureau, the Inter-collegiate Association, the National Inter-Church Federation, the Templars of Honor and Temperance, the Independent Order of Rechabites, and the temperance societies of the various churches. Representatives of most of these organizations have visibly and vigorously promoted the cause of State and Federal legislation.

CHAPTER XVIII

ALCOHOL AND THEOLOGY

THE liquor problem is a psychological one, having as its basis a soul thirst of drink and a soul hunger for gold. It is a theological one, because God is the drink and food of the soul, because He is the medicine that cures the perverted appetites and the physician that keeps the sin-sick soul alive.

The problem is elementally a theological one, involving the relationship of the human soul to its Creator. God has no earthly enemy so inveterate as King Alcohol. No such assaults have been made on the Church as those waged by the saloon. There never was a more clearly defined issue between right and wrong than in the conflict between the Church and the saloon during this modern temperance revolution. They represent ideas exactly opposite. One stands for everything that is bad, the other for everything that is good. The saloon breeds disease, disorder, misery, crime; the Church brings order, health, wealth, happiness and virtue. The Church represents the idea of God the best, the saloon the idea of the devil the worst in the world. The saloons are the breeding place of all kinds of vice and crime. In them the thieves, the gamblers, the murderers, the gunmen, the ballot-box stuffers, grafters, purchasers of law, the debauched and the ruined find their education and protection, and from them go out to prey upon society. How could the Church with the spirit and mission of her Master do other than fight such an institution and fight it to the death? Precisely this thing it is doing. Science, Big Business, law, the ballot, have been powerful factors in the destruction of the saloon, and those who do not look back far enough to find the origins think that these have done it all. But the fact is that back of all and more powerful than all is Religion, which is destroying the saloon. It is right beating down the wrong, love conquering hate; it is righteousness overcoming iniquity; it is happiness putting an end to misery; it is heaven banishing hell. It is God through His Church who is dethroning and killing the Devil King Alcohol. God made the world, He made the people in it, and He is in it Himself, a real factor, the most real factor in human life. He is in this world not to witness events, but to shape them; not to see man toil, but to help him in it; not to watch the battle, but to marshal His soldiers and to lead them in the fight against moral evil. The leading figures who have appeared in the temperance movement in this country from the beginning until now have not stood out in bold relief more plainly than has the form of the Son of Man as He has marched down the years and taken an active part in the battle against King Alcohol.

Father Mathew, an Irish Catholic priest, in organizing a total abstinence society in 1838, said: "If through any humble instrumentality of mine I can do good to my fellow creatures, and give glory to God, I feel I am bound as a minister of the Gospel to throw all my personal considerations aside and give a helping hand. Indeed, if only one poor soul could be rescued from destruction by what we are now attempting, it would be giving glory to God, and worth all the trouble we could take." And when he took the pen and signed the pledge at the head of sixty other names he said, "Here goes, in the Name of God." And God was so sensibly with him that under his divine spell 150,000 men signed the pledge in four days. Rev. Doctor Theodore Cuyler, one of the greatest apostles of temperance in America, said that when he was a young minister he attended a Father Mathew meeting in Edinburgh, Scotland, at which 50,000 men were gathered on the lawn, and multitudes kneeled down on the grass to take the pledge from the priest, who had them ask God to help them keep it. In describing this meeting Doctor Cuyler said: "Father Mathew spoke with modest simplicity and deep emotion, attributing all his wonderful success to the direct blessings of God upon his efforts to persuade his fellowmen to throw off the despotism of the bottle."

John B. Gough, the most eloquent temperance orator of the nineteenth century, was as devout a Christian as he was eloquent as a speaker, and much of his magnetism was due to the ethical and spiritual element.

The work of Francis Murphy, one of the greatest temperance reformers the country ever had, was not more manifest than was God's call to him to enter it, and the divine presence in it. He was a saloon-keeper in Portland, Maine, sent to prison for illegal selling in 1873. God's Spirit sent a little band to the jail one Sunday, who came in singing, "All Hail the power of Jesus Name," to hold a Gospel service. Murphy, seated on his iron bed in the cell, was coaxed out into the meeting and was so deeply convicted that he became converted. He asked the sheriff to let him hold a prayer meeting, at which fifty prisoners professed conversion. When his time was out, he determined to devote his whole time to the rescue of men from drink by the pledge and by the conversion of the soul by the Gospel. God sent him with this Gospel temperance message through this country and to other nations of the earth.

The idea of God is the central thought of the Prohibition Party. It was organized to fight a wrong which God hates and which they claimed good people ought to hate. It was a religious idea pure and simple, and that is why the institution has lived so long and fought so hard. That is why nearly all of the five hundred men who organized the party were ministers, or members of the Christian Church, and that is why to this day nearly all who vote that ticket are ministers or devout Christians.

The Woman's Crusade, the mother of the Woman's Christian Temperance Union, was a religious movement entirely, born in the agonizing prayers of women imploring the Heavenly Father to come down and save their families and remove the saloon curse from their community. The women wrestled with God in prayer in that church in Ohio. They prayed and cried, and cried and prayed, until they received the full assurance of faith, and then they marched out of the church brave as lions and said with the strength of Israel's God that they would fight the saloon till it was destroyed, and went out on the streets and in front of the saloons to pray to God and plead with men. Some of the saloon-keepers got mad, others took it good-humoredly. Some of the saloon-keepers laughed at the performance as a huge joke. They were mistaken, as they have since learned; for nothing with God in it is a joke.

When the Woman's Christian Temperance Union succeeded the Woman's Crusade, it inherited the same prayer and faith in divine guidance and victory. And it was this intense

spiritual element in the movement which attracted
to it one of the most brilliant young women this
country ever had, Miss Frances Willard, who
felt a special call of God so to organize the
women of America that their influence might be
focalized in its opposition to the saloon.   When
she and Miss Anna Gordon, her secretary, went
through every state in the Union, planting the
societies, she put the name "Christian" in the new
organization, calling it the Woman's Christian
Temperance Union.   She did so because she
claimed that Christ had put the thought of the
new organization in her mind, and because it was
on Him that she relied for success in the warfare
on the liquor traffic.   During her long service as
head of the society, and since to this day, the
Christ element has been magnified, and that is
why it has had such influence in this nation and
throughout the wide world.   It is the Christ who
has sanctified woman's love for home and family
and made it more than mortal in its energy in
fighting its worst foe.

The religious ingredient in the Order of Good
Templars and some other temperance organizations is marked.

Religion is the element that dominates the Anti-
Saloon League.   This organization, raised up by
Providence to take so important a part in teaching
the people how to vote to kill the saloon, and to
impel them to do so, is a strange combination of

the most human political machine with the strongest faith in divine guidance and help. From the human side there has scarcely been anything like it in the history of American politics in the last two decades—nothing like its political sagacity, its persistency, its desperate hand-to-hand fights in the campaigns, and in its continued and startling success at the polls and in legislative halls. But the human faith in the divine energy is the paramount element in the League. It was so in the foundation and has been so till the passage of the National Prohibitory Resolution by the Senate and House. The League was born in the heart of a preacher, and that heart was filled with love for the Christ. Doctor Russell is a Congregational minister, and the son of an Episcopal rector, and the new movement was the child of agonizing prayer and faith in Almighty God. Impelled with this religious impulse, he naturally went to the church for the material of his new organization. The morning after he held the funeral service of a mother whom drink had killed, he said to himself, "I will go out to my brethren of the churches and demand that they become responsible for an organized activity that shall hasten the day when such a tragedy will be done away." So Russell took his religious thought to a church for organization, the old First Church in Oberlin, Ohio, at a union meeting of the pastors and members of all the churches of the place, and on June 4, 1893, was

born the Ohio Anti-Saloon, which soon grew into
the National Anti-Saloon League. All of the
leaders the founder called about him at the start
came into the movement after earnest prayer impelled by deep religious conviction. About all of
the workers in the twenty-six years following
have entered and pursued their tasks under the
divine impulse and blessing. About two-thirds
of all the State superintendents of the League are
ministers of the Gospel, representing most of the
denominations, and the other third are laymen
who are just as consecrated to the task of destroying the greatest enemy of the Church and
establishing the Kingdom of Christ as any minister could be.

Bishop Wilson, the able and honored resident
Methodist Bishop of New York City, one of the
founders of the League, has for many years been
president of the National Anti-Saloon League.
In one of the most eloquent addresses in the temperance literature of any land Bishop Wilson thus
expresses his faith in the divine guidance to ultimate victory: "Facing now our opportunity, re-
solving that for the welfare of the Republic, for
the good of all, rich and poor, high and low,
wise or unlettered, Prohibition should be written
in the Constitution, and declaring ourselves for
the accomplishment of this most worthy end, let
us this hour send up to the God of nations our
solemn pledge that, whatever happens, there shall

be no turning back. It may be—it must be—that as we join in such a pledge our Divine Leader shall give to us His token of approval."

At first the churches were slow and timid in accepting Russell's idea, or coöperating with him in it. But he and his enthusiastic band of religious reformers hammered and hammered on the church doors till one after another opened to them, and to-day on every Sabbath, in every State in the Union, there are hundreds, perhaps a half thousand official representatives, who occupy the pulpits delivering a religious message at a religious service, and at its close taking up an offering for a religious purpose which in the aggregate amounts to over $1,000,000 a year. Pretty close relation this between religion and the destruction of the liquor traffic; between the Church and the death of the saloon.

And yet there are those who say that the Church has lost its power, and waste their time in dissertations on why it is so. It is not so at all. The Church was never so strong since Christ founded it as it is to-day. The triumph of the Church over the saloon in our time is one of the most gigantic religious victories in the history of the world for a thousand years. God's Nature, Word and Kingdom are not more pledged to defend and maintain the right than they are pledged to fight against and overthrow the wrong. It is as religious a thing to fight and

abolish a saloon as it is to say prayers or take the communion. To say the prayers and take the communion and have no hand in destroying the moral evil about us is the faith without works which is dead. If the Church had done nothing else in the last hundred years than drive the liquor evil out of the land, it would have justified its existence and its divine mission. For it involves the salvation of the precious bodies and souls of hundreds of thousands of the people, the checking of suffering, vice and crime, and the promotion of health, happiness and prosperity to millions of citizens such as no language can describe and no arithmetic can compute. Next to the great modern missionary movement, which is to possess the world, is this Christian temperance revolution of to-day, which is defeating and destroying the drink traffic, the most powerful incarnation of moral evil in this world. This victory should awaken profound gratitude in the hearts of Christians and prompt renewed courage and action against all human wrongs.

Dulled by materialism, it is considered quite the thing by some people to leave out sentiment and God in human calculations. They claim that the cold scientific fact that alcohol is a poison, with no sentiment or morals in it, is abolishing the saloon; and they make the more metallic statement that Big Business on the ground of efficiency, cold dollars with no sentiment or duty about

is alone responsible for making the nation dry. These materialists are right in the contention that science and business have been strong factors against the saloon; but they are mistaken in over-looking the moral and spiritual forces that have been more powerful than they. If they will wipe the scales from their eyes they will see that the drink problem is a religious one, a question of right and wrong; a theological problem that the Almighty is solving; they will see that it is God the Omniscient One who is the source of all science, and God the Omnipotent One, who has conducted a big business in manufacturing worlds and intelligences, is here in this world, which belongs to Him, to take charge of it and save it, and in so doing He is using science, business, law, the ballot and other agencies as weapons with which to destroy the saloon. If they will look with the eye of Faith they will see it is Jesus Christ, the Captain, with the soldiers of the Cross, who have marched under his banner, that have put the vile hordes of King Alcohol to ignomini-ous flight and have dragged him from his throne.

Alcohol is a psychological and a theological question, because it involves the soul and God's relation to it. He is not only the food of the soul but is also its medicine to cure the appetite for strong drink, and every other spiritual malady. The liquor problem is a psychological and theo-logical one because it involves human conduct,

character and immortal destiny. Alcohol does not unfit the individual for the duties of this earthly existence more than it disqualifies him for the endless life which is to follow. The diabolical tragedy is that alcohol, besides breaking down the body and blighting the mind, burns and blasts the soul with its limitless capabilities, unfitting it for the scenes, the employments, the enjoyments of immortality. King Alcohol takes man made in God's image, with wings to fly to Him and with Him through eternity, and breaks those wings and sinks him, a leaden force in the universe, away from beauty, from truth, from love, from life— a lost soul. In the discussion of this question, we must take account of things that neither the dissecting knife, nor microscope, nor test tube, nor scales can apprehend; that drink spoils a man for this life and for the heaven which is to come. Word has just been flashed over the wires that more than three-fourths of the State Legislatures necessary have ratified the Amendment. Let all the people of the nation arise and sing the Long Meter Doxology, "Praise God, from whom all blessings flow," and let them hold up their right hands and pledge each other and God to carry this war to other lands, for universal democracy, universal prohibition, and universal Christianity.

THE END

INDEX

A

Abbott, Dr. Lyman, 120
Abstinence in mill by C. L. Huston, 89; Jas. Brown, 91; G. D. Selby, 93; Ex. Gov. Foss, 94; in big business by J. O. Armour, 95
Absinthe abolished in Europe, 334
Alabama, 225
Alaska, 288
Alcohol and psychology, 1; injury of to brain, 5; and insanity, 21; and physiology, 33; a poison; slays Paraclesus, 33; causes diseases, 33; condemned by physicians, poisons life's organs, 41; Dr. Stockard's experiments with, 41; blights the cradle, 46; and athletics 48; and literature, 55; curses Burns, 61; kills Poe, 77; and capital, 82; and labor, 97; and theology, 362; destroys soul, 373
Alexander, Gov., 272
America sends beer to Africa, 325
America Issue Pub. Co., 320, 337
American poets temperate, 73
Anheuser Busch Co., 252
Anti-Saloon League, 348, 352
Arizona, 259
Arkansas, 248

B

Baker, P. A., 312, 355
Bamberger, Gov., 283
Barmaids, 324

Base ball and abstinence, 49
Bilbo, Gov., 231
Bingham, Wm., 313
Bok, Edward, 103
Boran, Senator, 273
Breckenridge, C., signed pledge with Lincoln, 158
Brooks, Noah, on Lincoln's Abstinence, 149
Bryan, W. J., 289; Wineless dinner, 289; addresses, 12,000, 290; banquet to, 290; President Wilson congratulated, 290
Burns cursed by drink, 61
Burrell, Dr. David J., 291

C

Campbell, Gov. T. E., 260
Cannon, Bishop, Jas., Jr., 247, 314
Capper, Gov. on " dry," Kansas, 179
Carmack, Senator, murdered, 235
Carnegie, Andrew, opposed drink, 104
Chamberlain, Senator, 264
Cherrington, Ernest H., address of, 315
Children hurt by drink, 46
China and prohibition, 314
Choate, Joseph, on saloon and crime, 120
Church fights saloon, 363
Clergymen and liquor problems, 325
Colorado, 261
Cobb, Ty., abstainer, 49

375

Condit, Filmore on insanity, 24–27

Crook, Col., declares Lincoln abstainer, 156

Cummins, Senator, 274

Curtis, Senator on dry Kansas 183

D

Daniels, Secretary, abolishes wine mess, 115

Dinwiddie, E. C., 313

District of Columbia dry, 220, 281, 298

Dow, General, Neal, 173

Dow, Col. Fred, 173

Drink and accidents, 96

Drink and school children, 324

Dry nation, world obligation, 332

E

Eliot, C. W., President Emeritus, favors abstinence, 116; on drink danger at Harvard, 119; on drink and social evil, 118; favors war prohibition, 119; becomes abstainer and prohibitionist after eighty years of age, 119

Emerson, Dr. H., against alcohol, 33

F

Farmers favor prohibition; foreign countries and liquor problems, 321

Federal legislation, 293, 310

Fernald, Senator, 177

Ferris, Ex. Gov., 280

Florida, 253

Foreign temperance society, riot by war, 326; aid given to, 330; and anti-saloon legislation, 330

Frausto, C. A., 313

Frazier, Gov. on N. Dakota, 190

French money opposing prohibition, 326

G

Gallinger, Senator, 285

Galloway, Bishop, C. B., 229

Georgia, 214

God is killing saloon, 363; employing science, big business law, ballot and church, 363–372

Goldsmith injured by drink, 55

Good templars, 360

Goodrich, Gov., 282

Gordon, Miss Anna A., 340

Gronna, Senator, 191

Gunter, Gov. J. C., 261

H

Hanly, Gov., 282

Harris, Gov. N. E., 222

Hatfield, Ex. Gov., 246

Hawaii, 288

Hinshaw, Virgil, 351

Hobson, R. P., 301

Home against saloon, 339

Hooper, Gov., 236

I

Idaho, 272

Indiana, 282

Insanity from drink, 24

Iowa, 274

J

Japan and prohibition, 314

Johnston, Canon, S. A., 313

Jones, Sam, 215

Jones, Senator, Wesley L., 267

K

Kansas, prohibition in, 179

Kentucky, 251

Kenyon, Senator, 275; Kenyon Webb bill, 294; declared constitutional, 296

King Alcohol, God's Greatest enemy, 362

Kirby, Senator, 249

L

Labor and drink by T. Powderly, 97; John Mitchell, 98; Senator Borah, 98; Chas. Stelzle, 101
Lea, Senator Luke, 242
Lee, Robt. E., abstainer, 161
Lester, Gov., 266
Lincoln falsely claimed by liquor men, 121; was life long abstainer, 123; worked for Ills. State prohibition, 126, 131; favored abstinence in Civil War, 131; intended to take up national prohibition, 135; gave notification Com. only cold water, 151, 154; banished nine from White House, 143; speech of at South Fork School Home, 143–158; wrote and signed pledge, 158; address at Springfield against drink, 162; his prophecy of world wide democracy and prohibition, 167, 168
Lincoln-Lee Legion founded by Howard N. Russell, 157–161
Liquor revenue not necessary, 334; a liability not asset, 334; Civil War tax on, a crime, 136
Longbillow, abstainer, 75
Louisiana, 254

M

Maine, first prohibition state, 173
Manning, Gov., 250
Maryland, 251
Mathew, Father, 348
Maus, Col., on abstinence for Soldiers, 111
Merwin, Major, worked with Lincoln for prohibition, 124–137
Michigan, 280
Milliken, Gov., 178
Munro, R. A., 313
Mississippi, 228
Missouri, 252

Montana, 276
Mott, L., 314
Murder from drink, 226, 232

N

National Constitutional prohibition passed by Senate, 303; Senator Sheppard on, 304; passed by House, 306; and ratified by forty states, 306; favored by Roosevelt, 213
Nat. Temp. and Publication Society, 349
Nat. Safety Council, 92
Navy wine mess abolished, 115
Nebraska, 277
Neville, Gov., 277
New Hampshire, 284
Norbeck, Gov., 278
North Carolina, 232
North Dakota, 187
Nov. 5th, 1918, four new dry states, 288

O

Oklahoma, 223
Oregon, 264

P

Paraclesus, drink killed, 33
Parents drinking injures children, 46
Party prohibitionists, 349
Patterson, Gov., his conversion, 237
Poe, Edgar Allen, drink ruins, 77
Poindexter, Senator, 270
Pollock, Judge C. A., 187
Porto Rico, 288
Prize ring and abstinence, 51–53
Proprietors, abstainers, 103
Prohibition wave sixty years ago, 172
Prohibition War, 307–309
Prohibition National Constitutional passed by Senate, 303; by the House, 303

HV5089 .I3   c.1
Iglehart, Ferdinand   100106 000
King alcohol dethroned, by Fer

3 9310 00067987 6
GOSHEN COLLEGE-GOOD LIBRAR

Date D

178
159